Sisterhood *of* Faith

365 Life-Changing Stories about Women Who Made a Difference

Sisterhood of Faith

To Al J.,
May Sisterhood inspire your love for God & others!
Shirley Brosius
Proverbs 3:5-6

Liz Curtis Higgs
Angela Hunt
Thelma Wells
Gloria Gaither
Patsy Clairmont
Martha Bolton
Lisa Whelchel
Catherine Marshall

HOWARD BOOKS
A DIVISION OF SIMON & SCHUSTER
NEW YORK LONDON TORONTO SYDNEY

Shirley Brosius

Our purpose at Howard Books is to:

- *Increase faith* in the hearts of growing Christians
- *Inspire holiness* in the lives of believers
- *Instill hope* in the hearts of struggling people everywhere

Because He's coming again!

HOWARD BOOKS

Published by Howard Books, a division of Simon & Schuster
1230 Avenue of the Americas, New York, NY 10020

ISBN 13: 978-1-4516-6816-2

10 9 8 7 6 5 4 3 2 1

HOWARD is a registered trademark of Simon & Schuster, Inc.

Printed in China

Edited by Between the Lines
Cover design by John Lucas
Interior design by John Mark Luke Designs

Library of Congress Cataloging-in-Publication Data
Brosius, Shirley, 1940–
Sisterhood of faith : 365 life-changing stories about women who made a difference / Shirley Brosius.
p. cm.
Includes bibliographical references (p.).

1. Christian women—Biography. 2. Christian women—Prayer books and devotions—English. 3. Devotional calendars. I. Title.

BR1713.B76 2006
277.30092'2—dc22
[B]

2006043738

To the glory of God,
in memory of my infant daughter

Christy Marie

who returned all too soon to the Lord she loved

and

in honor of my grandchildren,

Rachel, Daniel, Grace, Scott, and Elizabeth,

with prayers that the women they meet on these
pages will inspire them to love and serve God.

Preface

As I researched this book, I was inspired, intrigued, and humbled by the stories of women who have served God in spite of limitations, obstacles, and sometimes rejection. Although I had earned a master of arts in religion and had served as a director of Christian education for ten years, my background had not informed me of all that the gentle sex had accomplished in the name of Christ.

The idea for this book began germinating in the mid-1990s when I was invited to instruct a seminary course on women in ministry. As my students and I reflected on the challenges we had faced firsthand as women in ministry, the stories of other women who had done great things, often with little support, made our experiences seem less remarkable.

This book, the result of those discoveries, is meant to be read as a daily devotional, with time spent pondering the messages and responses drawn from the lives of those women.

I think of the women on these pages as big sisters and little sisters—famous and ordinary women—who have joined forces to build the kingdom of God. They represent all eras since the birth of the church and have served as bridge builders between generations as they passed on their legacy of faith to natural and spiritual sons and daughters.

My main objective has been to let women know that opportunities for effective Christian service are limitless. By reading of how others have used their spiritual gifts—in the church, in the home, in the workplace, on the mission field, on the airwaves, on the firing line—women may discover options they never dreamed of. The women on these pages have been unstoppable. If they ran into roadblocks, they simply waved a hand and kept going—either straight ahead or by embracing the detour.

I also wanted to encourage women, and men too, who have grown weary in ministry. Many on these pages have labored for decades with little reward. Some have faced resistance to their roles as women in leadership. Some faced danger as they took the message of freedom in Christ to women in countries where they were (or are) considered inferior to men. Many of the women in this book have faced seemingly insurmountable odds. They gave birth to and buried babies, often far from home. Some buried husbands and remained on the field to finish the work they had begun together. Some have done great things; others, small things that bring little recognition. Our personal burdens seem lighter when we read of sisters who have endured.

Finally, I wanted to shine the spotlight on women who have been hidden behind the scenes, many times behind their husbands. What do we know of Emma Moody or Idelette Calvin? What do we know of missionary wives raising families in jungle settings—who also teach, nurse, and confront the forces of evil? Many women have devoted their lives to Christian service yet have been overlooked by Christian biographers.

My criteria for including the women in this book was that, like Mary, who poured her precious perfume on the feet of Jesus, these women have poured out their lives in utter devotion to their Savior. They come from various theological backgrounds and cultures. Their interpretations of women's roles differ. But Protestant or Catholic, teachers or preachers, single or married, traditionalists or trendsetters, Victorian or postmodern—they stand as role models of grace and dignity for us all. May their stories inspire us to serve God.

SHIRLEY BROSIUS
Millersburg, Pennsylvania
October 2006

Acknowledgments

Heartfelt appreciation for support of my effort to publish this book goes out to many people:

The women whose life stories appear on these pages and the writers who recorded their stories for my reference. Special thanks to those women who personally shared their stories with me so I could share them with others.

My husband, Bill, for never complaining during the twenty months I spent in my "Upper Room" office.

My agent, Mary Busha, for taking a chance on a brand-new author.

My mentor, Georg Sheets, for his professional guidance.

My friends Janine Boyer and Kim Messinger for inspiring me during our small-group meetings. They brainstormed subjects, cheered me on when the task seemed impossible, and read the finished product with "fresh eyes," pointing out missing information and weak links.

My proofreading friends, Linda Baer, Carol Kehler, Shelby Schultz, Kathleen Weaver, and Dolores Wiest.

My sons and daughters-in-love, Ted and Deb and Terry and Caren, for their understanding during the weeks Nana didn't have time to babysit because of a looming deadline.

Dawn and Tammy at Between the Lines for making my writing look good.

And last but certainly not least, the Howard Books family for offering me a venue to connect with readers.

January

The authorities are God's servants,
who give their full time to governing.
Romans 13:6

HER SERVICE: Served her country as a patriot and homemaker

HER MESSAGE: The moral and ethical direction of a country—and a congregation—is shaped in the homes of its leaders.

HER STORY: The only woman besides Barbara Bush to both marry and give birth to presidents of the United States, Abigail Adams viewed caring for her family as a simple act of patriotism.

Born to a Congregational minister and his wife in Weymouth, Massachusetts, young Abigail read the classics and learned French. She and John Adams, nine years her senior, married in 1764. For some of their fifty-four years of marriage, they spent longer periods apart than together. John worked as an itinerant lawyer, served as a representative to the First and Second Continental Congresses, and represented the country abroad on his road to the presidency. During his absences Abigail ran their farm, raised four children, and cared for extended family members.

Abigail taught her children to live virtuous lives and to remain committed to God. While she advocated the education and legal autonomy of women, she felt they could best serve their country by being good wives and mothers in the home.

MY RESPONSE: If everyone lived by the values modeled in my home, would I feel proud?

No one who puts his hand to the plow and looks back is fit for service in the kingdom of God.
Luke 9:62

HER SERVICE: Education and evangelism

HER MESSAGE: A lifetime spent sowing seeds of faith yields a bumper crop of souls.

HER STORY: After reporting to the Presbyterian-operated girls' boarding school in Uduville, Ceylon, in 1839, Eliza Agnew never returned home to New York. She served as principal of the facility for forty years, and as a result of her effective administration and skillful teaching, the school earned a good reputation.

Eliza was devoted to the girls of Ceylon. She visited regional church centers annually, and rather than taking furloughs, she spent her school vacations visiting in the homes of former students.

Those who taught at boys' schools in the region struggled to win converts. But not Eliza. She led more than six hundred girls to Christ and became known as the (spiritual) mother of a thousand daughters. After retirement, Eliza remained in Ceylon until her death four years later.

MY RESPONSE: Is my service to God based on convenience or commitment?

Sharon Linn Hoffman Ambler, 1962–

I have become [the church's] servant by the commission God gave me to present to you the word of God in its fullness.
Colossians 1:25

HER SERVICE: Mission work

HER MESSAGE: The effective Christian models a lifestyle of obedience to God both at home and in the world.

HER STORY: Since 1998 Sharon Ambler has served in the Strategic Frontiers Department of Youth With a Mission (YWAM). She spent ten years pioneering the mission's work in the Philippines and Haiti.

Sharon Hoffman grew up in rural Pennsylvania. A baby sister died when Sharon was five years old, and Sharon learned that if Jesus was her Lord, she would see her sister again in heaven. This gave the young girl a burden to lead other people to Christ. At fifteen, Sharon heard a preacher speak of visiting Haiti and felt a calling to mission work. After college Sharon worked as a respiratory therapist, then joined YWAM in 1984. Five years later she married John-Mark Ambler, who also serves with YWAM. The couple considers parenting their five adopted sons—two from Haiti and three from China—part of their ministry.

On mission trips Sharon offers medical relief, distributes Bibles, and evangelizes. Some people criticize her for leaving John-Mark at home with the children. But the Amblers release each other to follow God's directives, and their efforts bear fruit both at home and abroad. All five sons have accepted Christ, and two have gone on mission trips to Mexico.

MY RESPONSE: How can I fulfill my calling to minister both to my family and to others?

The Lord will fulfill his purpose for me; your love, O Lord, endures forever—do not abandon the works of your hands.
Psalm 138:8

HER SERVICE: Worked for women's suffrage and anti-lynching laws

HER MESSAGE: Good women, banded together, can accomplish great work.

HER STORY: Involvement with Methodist women's groups led Jessie Daniel Ames to participate in the women's suffrage movement. In 1919 she served as founding president of the Texas League of Women Voters. In 1930 she rallied other white women and founded the Association of Southern Women for the Prevention of Lynching (ASWPL).

Born and raised in Texas, Jessie Daniel graduated from the Ladies Annex of Southwestern University and married Roger Post Ames. Roger's work as an army surgeon took him to Central America, leaving Jessie in Texas. Roger died of blackwater fever in 1914, the year the last of the couple's three children was born.

In 1916 Jessie organized the Georgetown Equal Suffrage League. She also wrote a newspaper column on voting rights, and her efforts contributed to Texas's becoming the first Southern state to ratify the Nineteenth Amendment, giving women the right to vote.

Jessie became director of the Texas Council of the Commission on Interracial Cooperation in 1924 and later moved to Atlanta to be the national director of that commission's Women's Committee, which financially backed her ASWPL work. Southwestern University recognized her contribution to social justice by establishing the Jessie Daniel Ames Lecture Series.

MY RESPONSE: Who might join me to address needs in my church or community?

And the God of all grace . . . after you have suffered a little while, will himself restore you and make you strong, firm and steadfast.
1 Peter 5:10

Her Service: Singing

Her Message: God uses ordinary women to do extraordinary things for His glory—in spite of others' rejection.

Her Story: Fondly remembered for the popular tune "He's Got the Whole World in His Hands," Marian Anderson's career spanned decades and continents.

The director of Marian's church choir was the first to spotlight her rich contralto voice. A singing contest won her a performance with the New York Philharmonic Orchestra. Other contests and fellowships followed, funding her study of music and voice at home and in Europe. Yet her path wasn't always easy.

In 1939 the Daughters of the American Revolution refused to let her perform as scheduled in Constitution Hall in Washington DC because she was African American. But that wasn't the end of the matter. First Lady Eleanor Roosevelt resigned from the group in protest and helped arrange an alternate concert site—at the Lincoln Memorial. The concert drew seventy-five thousand people, and millions more listened by radio, making it a banner event for civil rights.

Although Marian repeatedly dealt with racial prejudice, she credited God's directing hand for sustaining her as she worked hard to succeed in her career.

My Response: Has anyone ever rejected my ministry? Have I placed the outcome in God's hands?

Go out quickly into the streets . . . and bring in the poor, the crippled, the blind and the lame.
Luke 14:21

HER SERVICE: Serving as an adoption advocate, writing, and speaking

HER MESSAGE: We offer the highest service as we stoop to embrace the lowly.

HER STORY: Already parents to a blended family of seven children, Patty Anglin and her husband, Harold, have also adopted nine special-needs children of various nationalities. One was rescued from a trash can, another from an attempted abortion. Several have multiple disabilities. The book *Acres of Hope*, coauthored by Patty, tells of their ministry by the same name.

Patty grew up in Africa, where her parents served as medical missionaries. She accepted Christ at age nine and dreamed of running an orphanage for African babies. The family returned to Michigan when Patty was in high school. She later married but divorced after nine years.

After Patty married Harold, they took in foster children in response to a social worker's plea. Attachments led to adoptions. In the early 1990s the family moved to a Wisconsin farm. They later built a new home, added a cottage to house women who'd just given birth, and turned the original farmhouse into a maternity home. When their new home burned to the ground in 2003, the family moved back into the farmhouse and used the insurance settlement to open Acres of Hope, Liberia, the orphanage that had always been Patty's dream.

MY RESPONSE: How might I offer my time and skills to embrace a needy child?

Sons are a heritage from the Lord, children a reward from him.
Psalm 127:3

HER SERVICE: Mission work, founded orphanage

HER MESSAGE: People don't care about our religion until they know we care about their welfare.

HER STORY: During a three-year famine, Louisa H. Anstey began caring for starving children in India. Within a few years she was looking after six hundred boys and girls. Her home became an orphanage, and a Christian community sprang up around it.

Louisa originally went to India under assignment for the London Missionary Society, but poor health forced her return to England. In the 1860s she traveled to southern India as an independent missionary and began visiting native women. Few residents of the high-caste Brahman village showed interest—until famine struck. Louisa took food to as many people as she could and took in emaciated children whom desperate parents abandoned in her path. Cholera claimed the lives of many of the children she took in, but more came. Villagers began to ask why a well-educated, cultured woman would care about children. Such conversations opened hearts to the gospel.

Funds to support Louisa's ministry came from India, Europe, and America. In 1890, after twenty years of caring for children, Louisa turned her work over to the Methodist Episcopal Church. Her orphanage grew into a great mission center.

MY RESPONSE: How might I show a nonbeliever that I care?

Let justice roll on like a river, righteousness like a never-failing stream!
Amos 5:24

HER SERVICE: Worked for civil rights

HER MESSAGE: Speak up about social injustice.

HER STORY: Although Susan B. Anthony died before women were granted the right to vote, her tireless campaign for women's suffrage led to the passage of the Nineteenth Amendment.

Growing up in a Quaker community, Susan developed a keen sense of justice. Men and women were treated equitably, and Quakers did not own slaves. Her father had always encouraged her to speak out against evil and injustice, and Susan first raised her voice against the use of alcoholic beverages. When she was denied the platform to address the New York State Sons of Temperance, she organized the Woman's New York State Temperance Society. She also spoke out against slavery.

Susan traveled extensively to promote her causes, in spite of being treated disrespectfully. She was even, as an agent for the American Anti-Slavery Society, hung in effigy.

But Susan pressed on. In her push for women's rights, she made speeches, wrote letters, and testified before congressional committees. Along with Elizabeth Cady Stanton, she published a newspaper about women's rights and organized the National Woman Suffrage Association. She also helped to organize international suffrage associations and contributed to writing the four-volume *The History of Woman Suffrage*.

MY RESPONSE: What inequalities do I observe? How might I address them?

The fear of the Lord is the beginning of knowledge,
but fools despise wisdom and discipline.
Proverbs 1:7

HER SERVICE: Mission work

HER MESSAGE: Investing in education pays dividends in changed lives.

HER STORY: The first Korean-born American missionary, Alice Rebecca Appenzeller served as president of Ewha College in Seoul, Korea, from 1922 to 1939. Supported by Alice's fund-raising, a new campus was opened in 1935 with 450 students. Fifty years later Ewha had grown to be the largest university for women in the world. Many Ewha graduates have become prominent women in South Korea.

Alice was born during her parents' missionary service in Korea. Back in the United States, she attended college and taught. Then, in 1914, she returned to Korea as a missionary. Alice earned a master's degree and encouraged other missionaries to use their furloughs for education.

Until Alice's tenure, Korean music had been used only in secular entertainment and shamanistic worship. She offered native Korean music lessons, and her influence added a spiritual dimension to that means of expression.

Alice also considered liberty essential to education. At Ewha she lifted restrictions on social interaction with men and ended the censorship of letters so that women learned to accept responsibility for themselves.

In 1939 the Korean government banned foreigners from leading educational institutions, so Alice ministered to the Korean Methodist community in Hawaii for a few years before returning to Korea in 1946. There she continued to serve as Ewha's honorary president.

MY RESPONSE: How might I invest in education, my own or others', in a way that will change lives?

Do not be afraid.
Revelation 1:17

HER SERVICE: Directing missions program

HER MESSAGE: We can't freely serve God until we're free from fear.

HER STORY: As director of missions at Irving Bible Church in Irving, Texas, Kathy Appleton coordinates ten short-term mission trips each year. She oversees fifty missionaries, administers a budget of more than $500,000, and offers resources and training to churches in various countries.

Kathy grew up in Toledo, Ohio, and accepted Christ at age eleven. She earned a degree in elementary education and married Greg Appleton in 1980. After her daughter, Kallie, and son, Scott, were born, Kathy quit her teaching job.

Having grown up in the shadow of her mother's mental illness, Kathy struggled with insecurity and found it difficult to release her family into God's hands. She even feared being away from home for any length of time. But a description of Christ as King in Revelation 1 made Kathy aware that her fearfulness was insulting to God. After confessing her sin, Kathy experienced peace.

Her fear of leaving home evaporated, and Kathy hungered to learn more about mission work. When her church called for volunteers to minister in Russia, Kathy went willingly. She returned burdened by the number of people there living and dying without Christ, and in 1995 Kathy began her new career as missions director.

MY RESPONSE: What fears or worries are keeping me from serving God as fully as I might?

Annie Walker Armstrong, 1850–1938

They urgently pleaded with us for the privilege of sharing in this service to the saints.

2 Corinthians 8:4

HER SERVICE: Supporting mission work

HER MESSAGE: Supporting others and rejoicing in their work is a privilege and a calling.

HER STORY: In 1887 Annie Walker Armstrong cofounded the Woman's Missionary Union, an auxiliary to the Southern Baptist Convention, and served as the group's first corresponding secretary. During her second year of office, she wrote letters to Baptist mission societies to request a Christmas offering for Lottie Moon, a missionary to China. That first fund-raiser drew contributions of $2,833.49, and annual Lottie Moon Christmas Offerings continue today.

Annie grew up in Baltimore, Maryland, the daughter of wealthy parents. She worked for the Woman's Mission Union for eighteen years out of her Baltimore office without drawing a salary, and she paid for her own travel until 1901. Annie once covered thirty-three hundred miles and spoke twenty-six times in just twenty-one days. She ardently solicited funding for home missions and spearheaded missions among Native Americans, African Americans, and people with disabilities.

Annie kept in touch with missionaries at home and abroad and wrote for various mission publications. Her legacy of support for missions within the United States continues through what has become the Annie Armstrong Easter offering.

MY RESPONSE: What might I do to support someone on the mission field?

Make me to understand the way of thy precepts:
so shall I talk of thy wondrous works.
Psalm 119:27 KJV

Her Service: Writing and teaching

Her Message: To turn your life around, let it revolve around God's Word.

Her Story: Kay Arthur traded immorality for Christianity, and God's Word became her pathway to wholeness. Today she helps others walk the same path through Precept Upon Precept inductive Bible studies. Kay has written more than thirty-six books and edited *The International Inductive Study Bible* and *The New Inductive Study Bible.*

As a young woman Kay sought the love she needed from men. Yet she was miserable. After one man suggested she quit telling God what she wanted and tell Him Jesus was all she needed, she cried out to God. After praying, she felt deep peace—and a hunger to learn God's Word. She began diligently reading and studying the Bible.

In 1965 she married Jack Arthur, and the couple went as missionaries to Guadalajara, Mexico. But three years later, after Kay contracted pericarditis, they had to give up the work. The Arthurs returned to Chattanooga, Tennessee, and bought a thirty-two-acre ranch where they could hold Bible classes and minister to teens. Their initial disappointment turned out to be God's appointment to start Precept Ministries International, which ministers in 114 countries. Kay's fervent pursuit of Scripture study has led her to develop guides that help people of all ages study God's Word.

My Response: How might I deepen my Bible study so that God's Word becomes a guiding force in my life?

Do to others as you would have them do to you.
Luke 6:31

HER SERVICE: Entrepreneur and mentor

HER MESSAGE: God's principles and business principles are not incompatible.

HER STORY: In 1963 Mary Kay founded a direct-sales cosmetics company. She asked that everyone associated with her company—from employees to the independent sales force—strive to live by the Golden Rule and to put God first, family second, and career third. As an entrepreneur her idea of awarding pink Cadillacs and other "Cinderella gifts" to successful sales consultants has become legendary. Mary Kay, Inc., has grown into one of the largest direct-selling skin-care and color cosmetics companies in America, and it does business in more than thirty international markets. Mary Kay is widely esteemed as America's foremost woman entrepreneur. Her seminar draws more than fifty thousand independent beauty consultants to Dallas, Texas, each summer, and Mary Kay's worldwide sales force numbers more than 1.6 million on five continents.

As a girl Mary Kay had to pitch in at home when her father became terminally ill and her mother was forced to work long hours to support the family. Later, as a single mom, Mary Kay attended college and entered the direct-sales workforce. In 1963, after twenty-five years of working for others, she quit her job and wrote a book, based on her work experience, to help women succeed in a male-dominated world. Using her savings of five thousand dollars, she founded Mary Kay, Inc., and determined that her management style would be fashioned around the Golden Rule. In 1996 she established the Mary Kay Ash Charitable Foundation, which today funds research on cancers affecting women, as well as programs to end domestic violence.

MY RESPONSE: How can I implement godly principles in the way I do business?

Always be prepared to give an answer to everyone who asks you to give the reason for the hope that you have. But do this with gentleness and respect.
1 Peter 3:15

HER SERVICE: Martyrdom

HER MESSAGE: Stand firm for what you believe, even if it means falling from favor.

HER STORY: Anne was born in England at a time when the church was under pressure to reform. Her Bible study and personal devotion did not please her husband, and he threw her out of their home, even taking their two children from her, when she refused to embrace all Roman Catholic doctrines.

Civil and religious leaders condemned Anne to death for refuting the belief that the sacraments of bread and wine become literally the body and blood of Christ. After imprisonments and torture on the rack in the Tower of London, Anne's body was so crippled that she had to be carried on a chair to the stake to be burned. She and three others were given one last opportunity to recant. They refused.

Anne Askew's break with religious tradition came at the cost of her home, her family, and finally her life—but she held fast to her beliefs.

MY RESPONSE: How important to me is the approval of others when weighed against God's approval? At what point do I need to stand up for my faith regardless of the cost?

Let us not become weary in doing good, for at the proper time we will reap a harvest if we do not give up.
Galatians 6:9

HER SERVICE: Mission work

HER MESSAGE: Ministry may be messy and unpredictable, yet greatly used by God.

HER STORY: Born in London, Gladys Aylward ministered in China for seventeen years. Her story was dramatized in the movie *The Inn of the Sixth Happiness.*

Gladys's application to China Inland Mission was rejected, so she saved her earnings as a maid and set out on her own at age twenty-six. She joined elderly missionary Jeannie Lawson in Yangchen, China, but residents called them foreign devils and hurled mud at them. Undeterred, the two opened an inn. As mule trains drove by, Gladys grabbed the reins of the lead mules and dragged them into the courtyard, forcing the muleteers to follow. The women provided meals and entertained their guests with Bible stories.

In addition to her duties at the inn, Gladys was appointed as a government foot inspector and assigned to travel around making sure women unbound their feet (as was the recently reversed custom). As Gladys roamed the country, she shared the gospel.

Gladys also took in orphans and, as the conflict leading to World War II heightened, led one hundred children on a twelve-day march over the mountains to an orphanage in Sian.

Throughout her life, Gladys used every opportunity she had to minister to others.

MY RESPONSE: How might I more zealously devote myself to ministry?

We spend our years as a tale that is told.
Psalm 90:9 KJV

HER SERVICE: Storytelling and presenting living lectures

HER MESSAGE: Live your life as an example and inspiration for those who follow.

HER STORY: Through "Living History Heroines" Bonnie L. Bachman inspires women today to greatness through the examples of great women from history.

Few people have heard of Hannah Penn. Hannah was a remarkable woman who administered the province of Pennsylvania after her husband, William Penn, was incapacitated by and later died of a stroke. Although Hannah died in 1727, her legacy lives on—thanks to Bonnie L. Bachman and "Living History Heroines."

Through Bonnie's presentations, Hannah and more than fifty other historical women come to life in churches, conventions, colleges, and women's gatherings. Dressing in historically accurate costumes, Bonnie gives voice to each woman's story, drawing listeners back to another time and helping them know and love a heroine of history.

These historical women have an important message for people today, Bonnie believes. Their struggles and triumphs resonate with modern women, and each story testifies to God's faithfulness. No matter how much history and women's situations change, God remains the same.

Bonnie sums up her unique ministry this way: "It is time to inspire and challenge a new generation with the example of women who were so in tune with God and loved the Savior in such a way as to accomplish great things."

MY RESPONSE: If someone were to tell my story fifty years from now, what would my life demonstrate about the faithfulness of God?

Offer the parts of your body to him as instruments of righteousness.
Romans 6:13

Her Service: Mission work

Her Message: Our part is to surrender to God; His part is to schedule our ministry.

Her Story: Linda Smallback Baer has happily donned many ministry hats during her years as a missionary, wife, and mother. She has offered hospitality, volunteered in shantytown ministries, taught English as a second language (ESL), and served on a Christian youth-camp board.

While attending Wheaton College, Linda Smallback surrendered her life to God for Christian service. But her applications for short-term mission projects were rejected. Then she met Dave Baer. He told her that his future spouse would have to be missionary minded, and that suited Linda just fine.

After marrying, the couple led Bible studies and served as youth pastors. The Baers joined Latin America Mission (LAM) in 1988, just after the birth of their second son. For sixteen years the Baers lived in Costa Rica, where Dave served as president of ESEPA Seminary and Linda ministered in the community and offered LAM member care to new missionaries. During a study leave to the United Kingdom, Linda taught ESL and trained missionaries. In 2004 the family moved to Indianapolis, where Linda teaches ESL while Dave serves as president of Overseas Council International.

Throughout the years Linda has maintained an attitude of openness and flexibility in order to serve God through whatever opportunities He presents.

My Response: Have I told God what I want to do for Him or, better yet, asked God what He wants to do through me?

The Lord said to me, "Write my answer in large, clear letters on a tablet."
Habakkuk 2:2 NLT

HER SERVICE: Writing and ministering to writers through conferences

HER MESSAGE: Christians need a platform to impact the world for Christ.

HER STORY: Marlene Bagnull's passion is to encourage and equip Christians to write for God through Write His Answer Ministries. She directs Christian writers' conferences, publishes books, and writes articles for Christian magazines.

Marlene felt called to full-time Christian service as a teenager. Though she had never enjoyed English or public speaking in school, in 1967 Marlene began work at her denomination's editorial office. That experience laid the groundwork for her ministry. In 1983 she founded the Greater Philadelphia Christian Writers Fellowship and continues to direct its annual conference, which now includes a faculty of more than fifty agents, publicists, authors, and editors. She also directs the Colorado Christian Writers Conference.

Offering practical tips and spiritual motivation, Marlene has taught at more than seventy-five Christian writers' conferences and led dozens of writers' seminars around the nation. Dedicated to impacting our culture, she has published more than a thousand articles in Christian magazines. Her five books include *Write His Answer—A Bible Study for Christian Writers,* which inspires many people to walk in her footsteps.

MY RESPONSE: What God-given insight might I share with my family, my community, or the wider world?

If anyone gives even a cup of cold water to one of these little ones because he is my disciple, I tell you the truth, he will certainly not lose his reward.

Matthew 10:42

HER SERVICE: Mission work and teaching

HER MESSAGE: Effective teaching ministries are driven by faith in God, a love of learning, and the life needs of students.

HER STORY: For a total of forty-two years, Mary Baldwin invested her time and money in serving God, leaving in her wake a legacy of education and caring. She was one of the first unmarried missionaries to go out from the United States.

Mary Baldwin simply wanted to serve God. A grandniece of President James Madison, she reflected on the lifestyle of Virginia aristocracy and hungered for something more. When American missionaries in Athens pleaded for help in their school, Mary saw an opportunity to give back to society. Finding an impoverished population, she took charge of the school's sewing department and taught students a craft along with their lessons. Mary groomed some girls to serve as teachers, and through them her influence spread. In time Mary used her private wealth to open a boarding school for girls.

In 1866 Athens was flooded with Cretan refugees, so Mary devised a program to feed, educate, and prepare the refugee women to survive economically by teaching them to sew, knit, and market their work.

MY RESPONSE: What skills might I share at a shelter or a neighborhood center for children?

Warn those who are idle, encourage the timid, help the weak, be patient with everyone.
1 Thessalonians 5:14

HER SERVICE: Writing and speaking

HER MESSAGE: We can use what we learn through everyday life to help others.

HER STORY: Emilie Barnes helps women get organized. Through her writing and speaking ministries, she offers timesaving tips on everyday tasks. She also encourages women's creativity by showing them how to host tea parties and entertain with simplicity and elegance.

Emilie speaks from experience. By the time she was twenty-five, she and her husband, Bob, were raising five children under the age of five—two of their own and three of Emilie's brother's children. As she struggled to get all of her work done, Emilie developed techniques of time management, and eventually she and Bob developed "More Hours in My Day" seminars to help others meet the daily demands of life.

Those time-management skills also serve Emilie well outside the home. She has written sixty-five books, including The Emilie Marie Series for young readers, and she sparks the faith and creativity of her audience through radio and television appearances.

MY RESPONSE: What have my experiences taught me that I can use to help or encourage others?

I consider everything a loss compared to the surpassing greatness of knowing Christ Jesus my Lord.
Philippians 3:8

HER SERVICE: Ruled as a godly monarch

HER MESSAGE: No earthly treasure compares to the riches we have in Christ.

HER STORY: Bathildis reigned over the Frankish kingdom, using her influence and riches to fight abuses in the church and in the country.

Born in England, Bathildis was taken as a slave to the Frankish kingdom. She served in the court of King Clovis II, and the two married in 649. When Bathildis ascended the throne after her husband's death in 657, she bought and freed large numbers of slaves and permitted former slaves to own property as citizens. Always mindful of her impoverished past, she paid debts for the poor and eliminated a burdensome tax. Queen Bathildis also used her influence to correct abuses in the church, where at that time offices were bought and sold.

Bathildis founded St. Denis Monastery and a Benedictine convent. She restored the Abbey of St. George, near Paris. Although in later years she suffered with a painful illness, she spent her last fifteen years living and working at the convent instead of enjoying the comfort of a palace court. Her subjects admired her generosity and faithfulness to God's work.

MY RESPONSE: How might I better focus on the riches in Christ and use my material resources to help others?

Where two or three come together in my name, there am I with them.
Matthew 18:20

HER SERVICE: Founded international women's ministries

HER MESSAGE: Women need each other for support, encouragement, and fellowship in Christ.

HER STORY: Helen Duff Baugh and her husband organized the first Christian Business and Professional Women's Council in San Jose, California. Since then, Stonecroft Ministries, Friendship Bible Coffees, and other interdenominational outreaches built on that foundation have extended to six continents.

Helen and her two sisters started in ministry by offering gospel concerts along the West Coast of the United States. Helen also preached in her father's evangelistic meetings. After she married, Helen read Matthew 18:20 during a daily devotional time and called another woman to join her for prayer. Soon she had established twenty-four prayer groups, and one of those women's prayers was for a ministry to reach out to women.

Helen accepted invitations to speak in neighboring areas and soon was traveling throughout the country, leaving in her path professional women's groups. She also recruited missionaries to reach regions of America that lacked churches. In 1948 she teamed with Mary Clark to launch Christian Women's Clubs for homemakers.

MY RESPONSE: Is there a forum in my region where women of all backgrounds can stand on common ground in Christ?

"I know the plans I have for you," declares the Lord, "plans to prosper you and not to harm you, plans to give you hope and a future."
Jeremiah 29:11

HER SERVICE: Speaking and writing

HER MESSAGE: God receives the glory when faithful servants accept losses in His strength.

HER STORY: With "Let's roll!" Lisa Beamer's husband, Todd, mobilized passengers to overpower hijackers on an airliner that crashed in a Pennsylvania field on September 11, 2001, killing all on board. His pregnant widow emerged as a quiet, smiling symbol of faith and hope in the midst of tragedy.

Tragedy first touched Lisa's life when she was fifteen. Her father, whom she adored, died suddenly. Grieving and angry with God, Lisa questioned her faith. Then she discovered God's promise in Jeremiah 29:11, and her faith was rekindled. She realized that instead of expecting God to "fix" problems, she could trust God to be with her through them.

When Lisa suffered her second devastating loss, the loss of her husband, she faced an uncertain future with courage and faith. Their daughter, Morgan, was born in 2002, and Lisa established the Todd M. Beamer Foundation to help young people, especially those orphaned by the events of 9/11.

Her book *Let's Roll!* offers a testimony of God's grace and has inspired millions of people to find hope in the midst of life's losses.

MY RESPONSE: Whom might I tell of God's faithfulness during a loss I've suffered?

These commandments that I give you today are to be upon your hearts. Impress them on your children. Talk about them when you sit at home and when you walk along the road, when you lie down and when you get up.
Deuteronomy 6:6–7

HER SERVICE: Providing support and resources for homeschoolers

HER MESSAGE: God holds parents responsible for transmitting godly values to their children.

HER STORY: Convinced that parents of the emerging homeschooling movement needed better resources, Ruth Beechick not only developed materials to help instill godly values in children but also published books herself. The contributions of this pacesetting Christian educator stimulated the independent publishing industry.

Ruth took seriously the biblical mandate that parents teach their children. Two of her books became classics: *Three R's* offered instruction for teaching kindergarten through third grade, and *You Can Teach Your Child Successfully* for fourth through eighth grade. The latter won a 1982 "Best of the Year" award.

Rather than focusing on the abstract theories of traditional textbooks, Ruth's resources offered parents practical, down-to-earth teaching. Her approach to learning developed during her work as a schoolteacher, a professor of education, and a children's editor of Sunday-school curriculum. She has written extensively and spoken at many homeschooling conventions. Ruth offers parents confidence that they can handle the task of educating their children.

MY RESPONSE: How am I passing on godly values to the next generation?

January 25

Christine VanderLaan Beezhold, 1920–
Henrietta VanderLaan Mollahan, 1925–

He sent them out to preach the kingdom of God and to heal the sick.
Luke 9:2

THEIR SERVICE: Founded school for special-needs children

THEIR MESSAGE: God calls us to show His grace to families with special-needs individuals.

THEIR STORY: In an era when some people thought a mental handicap in children was God's punishment, sisters Christine and Henrietta VanderLaan stepped out in faith and opened a Christian school for children with disabilities.

A pastor with a mentally challenged son first suggested the women establish a school for special-needs children. Henrietta had always enjoyed visiting the sick, and Christine had volunteered at a skid-row mission, so their pastor's request appealed to their concern for those who needed special support.

The sisters' venture into the world of special education required much patience. To prepare, they studied disabilities at the University of Chicago. The college agreed to supply curriculum and to evaluate children who enrolled at the church school for a six-week trial term. Christine drove her father's car up to seventy-five miles per day to pick up the school's first seven pupils.

Two years later, when more specialized teachers were needed, the women resigned, satisfied that their dedication had established a ministry to some of God's most precious children. Today Elim Christian School draws children with physical and mental handicaps from across the nation.

MY RESPONSE: How might I support individuals and families with special needs who attend my church?

In all your ways acknowledge him, and
he will make your paths straight.
Proverbs 3:6

HER SERVICE: Writing and speaking

HER MESSAGE: We need to recognize our limitations and reorder our priorities according to God's.

HER STORY: Lisa Tawn Bergren devoted her life to Christian writing. Before long she was working full time and writing books on weekends. Lisa found balance by prioritizing her schedule.

Lisa married Tim Bergren in 1992, and as their children were born, she relished motherhood. Lisa had felt confident that she could juggle homemaking, writing, and working, but she found herself frazzled and exhausted. Stepping back, she determined that serving God personally would be her top priority, followed by caring for her family, then serving God through her work. She reluctantly resigned from her position as head of a publisher's fiction division.

But as one door closed, another opened. Lisa has written ten novels, three novellas, and two children's books and receives many invitations to speak. Her first romantic novel, *Refuge,* became a bestseller and led to her Palisades line of romance books. Lisa inspires others through her books and through her determination to put God and family ahead of work.

MY RESPONSE: How might I better prioritize the responsibilities I juggle?

For to me, to live is Christ and to die is gain.
Philippians 1:21

HER SERVICE: Showed the importance of being ready to meet Christ

HER MESSAGE: Be ready! Death may snatch you at any moment.

HER STORY: Teenager Cassie Bernall was shot at close range and killed when two classmates went on a shooting spree at Columbine High School in Littleton, Colorado.

The daughter of Brad and Misty Bernall, Cassie enjoyed swimming, fishing, and rock climbing. She dreamed of becoming an obstetrician. But there were dark years too. When she was a freshman, her parents found notes to her from a friend, containing drawings of weapons and musings of murder. Cassie's parents went to the police. It turned out Cassie had written similar notes. She had smoked, drunk alcohol, and practiced self-mutilation.

Cassie's parents insisted that she attend a Christian school and youth group and give up her unhealthy friendships. In the spring of 1997, Cassie returned from a youth retreat a changed young woman. A friend later told how she had heard Cassie crying out to God for forgiveness. The Bernalls let Cassie transfer to Columbine. As Cassie searched for her identity as a Christian, she read Christian books and contemplated God's plan for her life. At times she told of her inward struggle, but she also told her mother she was not afraid of dying—because she would be in heaven. No one could have known how soon that day would arrive.

MY RESPONSE: What steps have I taken to prepare to meet God?

Train a child in the way he should go, and
when he is old he will not turn from it.
Proverbs 22:6

HER SERVICE: Promoting Sunday school

HER MESSAGE: Sunday school offers valuable Christian teaching and a venue for serving God.

HER STORY: Joanna Graham Bethune recognized the potential for Christian education through Sunday school. She organized and served as the first director of an interdenominational effort to provide educational and religious instruction.

A Scottish immigrant who settled in New York City, Joanna shared her mother's passion to teach poor adults to read. Joanna converted to Christianity in 1794, and a few years later she and her mother opened a Sabbath school to educate children who worked in factories and could not otherwise attend school.

After hearing of Robert Raikes's Sunday-school movement in England, Joanna called a meeting to discuss organizing such a ministry in America. The several hundred women who attended were moved by her plea. The Female Union for the Promotion of Sunday Schools grew out of that meeting, and soon 136 students enrolled in Sunday schools.

In spite of opposition to what some called Sabbath-breaking, within six years the program had six hundred teachers and about seven thousand students. Joanna continued teaching until she was more than eighty years old. The group later came under the umbrella of the American Sunday School Union, an organization Joanna and her husband, Divie, also helped establish.

MY RESPONSE: How might I support or start a Sunday school in my church?

Mary McLeod Bethune, 1875–1955

There is neither Jew nor Greek, slave nor free, male nor female, for you are all one in Christ Jesus.
Galatians 3:28

HER SERVICE: Education

HER MESSAGE: Altering the status quo requires determination, dedication, and decisive action.

HER STORY: Mary McLeod Bethune's tireless work for equality and education of blacks drew national attention. She founded a school for girls, which grew into a leading black college, and became the first black woman to lead a federal agency.

Born the daughter of former slaves in South Carolina, Mary was the only one of seventeen siblings to attend school. As a teacher in Chicago, Mary visited prisoners, ministered to homeless people, and counseled slum residents. In 1904 she opened the Daytona Normal and Industrial School for Girls in Daytona Beach, Florida, with five students. In 1923 this school merged with Cookman Institute, and Mary served as president of Bethune-Cookman College until 1942.

In 1927 Mary was elected president of the National Association for Colored Women, a platform she used to fight discrimination and segregation. She later founded the National Council of Negro Women, which championed the equality of black women. From 1935 to 1943 Mary served as Director for Negro Affairs and supported the creation of the Fair Employment Practices Commission. In recognition of her commitment to the advancement of blacks, her statue stands in Lincoln Park, Washington, DC.

MY RESPONSE: What action might I take to assure that everyone in my church is treated equally, regardless of race, social standing, or education?

Is not wisdom found among the aged? Does not long life bring understanding?
Job 12:12

HER SERVICE: Writing

HER MESSAGE: Nourish your dreams—your golden years may offer golden opportunities to serve God.

HER STORY: At age forty Lawana Blackwell enrolled in a novel-writing course, and her instructor affirmed Lawana's way with words. Since then Lawana has written three popular series of Christian fiction books: Victorian Serenade, The Gresham Chronicles, and Tales of London.

Growing up in Louisiana, Lawana enjoyed writing. But she thought her dream of becoming a writer was too lofty and kept it to herself. Lawana tried to write a novel at age twenty-three but grew discouraged and gave up her dream. Her creative urge, however, would not be squelched: it found expression in skits Lawana wrote for her church. People told her she had talent, and her confidence grew. Lawana became a protégé of author Gilbert Morris and was encouraged to discover that he had not begun writing seriously until his midfifties.

Lawana strives to show the impact of the gospel message through the lives of her characters.

MY RESPONSE: What is keeping me from fulfilling a dream?

Janet Chester Bly, 1945–

If you do the will of God, you will live forever.
1 John 2:17 NLT

HER SERVICE: Writing, speaking, ministering as a pastor's wife

HER MESSAGE: The abundant life requires balancing work, service, and relationships.

HER STORY: A prolific writer, a speaker, and a pastor's wife, Janet Chester Bly has coordinated the ebb and flow of her career with the needs of her family. She has authored eleven books on wonder, God's goodness, and lifetime relationships and has coauthored eighteen others with her husband, Stephen.

Born and raised in California, Janet Chester attended church at times with godly grandparents. In 1963 she married Stephen Bly, a high-school classmate. The assassinations of prominent political figures in the 1960s set Janet thinking about life's uncertainties. On the sly, she began reading a Bible. Stephen discovered her secret and joined her. They committed their lives to Christ, and Stephen became a pastor.

In 1974 Janet quit her office job to focus on her role as pastor's wife—and began a search to discover her own spiritual gifts. Her explorations led to writing. She submitted adaptations of her husband's sermons to magazines, and in 1976 two of her manuscripts were accepted. In 1991 Janet earned a degree in literature and in fine and performing arts. She now speaks to women's groups and teaches at writers' conferences, and the couple ministers together on family themes.

MY RESPONSE: What is my first priority at this stage of life?

February

The Lord said to him, "What is that in your hand?"
Exodus 4:2

HER SERVICE: Launched Internet-based ministry

HER MESSAGE: Each era offers fresh opportunities to use our abilities to serve God.

HER STORY: Peggie Bohanon's family Web page, www.peggiesplace .com, escalated into one of the largest Christian ministry home pages in the world. Enhanced with music, animation, and lots of humor, Peggie's Place offers extensive links to multilingual, Christian, and family resources.

A stay-at-home mom, Peggie enrolled in two computer-related courses at a local college. God miraculously provided funds for a computer, and she began to surf the Web. When she launched a family Web page, she incorporated Christian resources. Peggie's School Room now offers resources for students, educators, and homeschooling parents, and her weekly newsletter goes out to fifty-five hundred subscribers.

Peggie's Place draws three thousand to four thousand hits a day, with more than twelve million page views since 1995. It has attracted viewers from 185 countries and won numerous awards, including the Award for Ministry Excellence from the Pastor's Helper and the 1997 Best of the Christian Web Award.

Peggie has appeared on *Focus on the Family* and other broadcasts. She calls herself the "walk-on-water woman" because, like Peter, she stepped out of the boat when Jesus called her to serve as executive editor of Gospelcom.net's *Internet for Christians Digest*.

MY RESPONSE: How might I use my talents to "step out of the boat" in the twenty-first century?

A cheerful heart is good medicine.
Proverbs 17:22

HER SERVICE: Writing humor and music

HER MESSAGE: God created us with a funny bone and sends humorists to tickle it.

HER STORY: Martha Bolton credits her mother for passing on her faith—and a funny bone. While working as a church secretary, Martha began writing skits that poked fun at church personalities. People laughed. She has now published seventeen books of comedy sketches and monologues.

"Life's tough. God's good. And laughter's calorie free." That's the mission statement of the woman who has written for Bob Hope, Mark Lowry, Phyllis Diller, and other comedians. Three Angel Awards pay homage to Martha's contributions of moral and ethical content in the media. She was nominated for an Emmy Award for outstanding achievement in music and lyrics, and her children's musical *A Lamb's Tale* was nominated for a Dove Award. Many of her fifty books were written for youth and children. Martha is also known as the Cafeteria Lady of *Brio* magazine.

MY RESPONSE: How might I bring a smile to someone's face?

You know when I sit and when I rise;
you perceive my thoughts from afar.
Psalm 139:2

HER SERVICE: Singing, speaking, and writing

HER MESSAGE: God's grasp holds us and God's grace molds us—in good times and in bad.

HER STORY: Renee Bondi inspires people with her story, her music, and her courage as a quadriplegic.

Renee sang professionally, led music in her church, and taught music. But her life took an abrupt turn in 1988. In a deep sleep, Renee dove from her bed one night and awoke hearing bones crunch in her neck. The nightmarish diagnosis: She would never walk again. In fact, she could barely speak above a whisper. Doctors told her she would never sing again.

But Renee worked to strengthen her diaphragm and miraculously regained her voice. She even survived a high-risk pregnancy to give birth to a beautiful son. No matter how impossible her circumstances, Renee surrenders them to God. Secure in His hands, she knows He's molding her into someone He can use for His glory. Instead of becoming frustrated, she has learned to accept God's peace as she struggles with tasks others take for granted.

Renee was United Catholic Music and Video Association's 2000 Inspirational Artist and the California State Senate's Woman of the Year in 2000. The title of her book testifies to her attitude: *The Last Dance but Not the Last Song: My Story.*

MY RESPONSE: How can I trust God in circumstances beyond my control?

One of those listening was a woman named Lydia. . . . The Lord opened her heart to respond to Paul's message.
Acts 16:14

HER SERVICE: Social work

HER MESSAGE: The best vacation may be working to help others.

HER STORY: Allyson Hodgins-Bonkowski sees vacations as times for giving back. She helped found a nonprofit organization and serves as financial manager of a Romanian orphanage.

A seventh-grade trip to Russia gave Allyson a new appreciation for all she had. After college she accepted a job with a corporation and later earned a master's degree in business administration. In 1995 Allyson went to Romania and saw the terrible plight of the country's many abandoned children—on the streets and in orphanages. God touched her heart.

Allyson scaled back her work at a San Francisco consulting firm so she could devote more time to helping these needy children. For several years, she took four months of unpaid leave each year to work with the nonprofit organization she helped found: Children's Aid International Relief and Development (CAIRD) of Edmonton, Alberta. Allyson is financial manager for Father's House, a group of small Romanian orphanages operated by CAIRD.

Allyson's future plans include passing on what she has learned to other nonprofit organizations and churches through consulting. By using her business skills and dedicating her time away from work to sharing God's love with orphans half a world away, Allyson works to change the world—one child at a time.

MY RESPONSE: How might I use my leisure time to change the world?

February 5

Marguerite Bonneman, 1913–
Mary DeBoer VandenBosch, 1916–

May he give you the desire of your heart
and make all your plans succeed.
Psalm 20:4

THEIR SERVICE: Founded orphanage

THEIR MESSAGE: A dream turns into reality as we share it with God and others.

THEIR STORY: Marguerite Bonneman and Mary DeBoer turned their dream of founding an orphanage into reality. They borrowed money to buy real estate and, at first, worked without a salary.

As a girl in Cleveland, Ohio, Marguerite Bonneman passed a Catholic orphanage every day on her way to school and decided that she would open one herself someday. After becoming a nurse, she enrolled at the Reformed Bible Institute in Michigan, where she roomed with Mary DeBoer. As they got to know each other, the roommates discovered they both dreamed of founding an orphanage. After graduating, they worked together at a local mission. When a Native American family sought their help, Marguerite and Mary agreed to take in the baby girl. Before long Marguerite was caring for five children while Mary worked to support them.

In 1945 Marguerite and Mary's dream became a reality when they founded Bethany Home in Grand Rapids, Michigan. Today Bethany Christian Services continues to provide homes for children while also ministering to pregnant women and offering family-related services. Marriage didn't stop Mary's mission to help orphaned or adrift children. In addition to parenting their own two children, Mary and her husband cared for twenty-nine foster children.

MY RESPONSE: Who might share my dream to touch the future?

What does it matter? The important thing is that in every way . . . Christ is preached.
Philippians 1:18

HER SERVICE: Preaching, cofounding the Salvation Army

HER MESSAGE: God gives the same spiritual gifts to men and women.

HER STORY: Catherine Mumford Booth served alongside her husband, preaching, teaching, and ministering on the streets. Through the Salvation Army, an international ministry to the downtrodden that she and her husband founded, she supported women's rights to use their talents and spiritual gifts to serve God.

The daughter of a Methodist pastor, Catherine was disciplined in Bible reading and prayer. A religious experience at age sixteen gave her a boldness that later equipped her to minister with her husband, William, also a Methodist minister. Once, as her husband closed a service, Catherine stood to add a word, which was unusual for women in her day. So impassioned were her words that she soon received invitations to preach. Fifty thousand people gathered to hear her final message on the Salvation Army's twenty-fifth anniversary.

Catherine and William founded the Christian Mission at London's East End. From a small beginning the Salvation Army grew. The organization encouraged women, including Catherine's daughters and daughters-in-law, to serve in leadership positions alongside men. In the Salvation Army to this day, men and women use their spiritual gifts of teaching, preaching, and administrating what the Booths called their militant and triumphant Christian force.

MY RESPONSE: Am I fully using all of my spiritual gifts?

Live in a right way in undivided devotion to the Lord.
1 Corinthians 7:35

HER SERVICE: Evangelism and leadership in the Salvation Army

HER MESSAGE: A single woman can devote all of her time and energy to serving God, and God will provide for her needs.

HER STORY: Within the international ministry founded by her parents, the Salvation Army, Evangeline Cory Booth served in the highest positions of leadership in various countries. At her father's request, she never married so that she might devote her life to Christian service.

As Evangeline tagged along with her family into the slums of London for ministry, she learned firsthand of poverty and human depravity. At age thirty-one Evangeline succeeded her brother as the Salvation Army's territorial commissioner of Canada. There, on rough frontiers, she commanded respect as she confronted miners with their need for salvation. Eight years later she was named commander of the Salvation Army in the United States. Evangeline served in that capacity for thirty years before returning to London for a five-year term as general of the entire worldwide organization.

Although Evangeline honored her father's request to remain single, she adopted four children and raised them on her own. She found the Lord more than adequate to provide for her every need, whether for protection while ministering in dangerous places or for food to feed her family.

MY RESPONSE: What needs do I have that I must rely upon God to meet instead of relying on others?

Let him who boasts boast in the Lord.

1 Corinthians 1:31

HER SERVICE: Writing, speaking, and teaching

HER MESSAGE: God remains faithful even when others let us down.

HER STORY: Veda Boyd and friend Laurette Connelly minister through a speaking ministry called Odds & Ends, presenting biblical messages with doses of humor. Veda's book, *One Came to Stay*, tells of her life in a foster home.

At age twelve, Veda was stunned to learn that she was a foster child. Feeling rejected and unloved, she rebelled against her parents' strict rules. Her life changed, however, when a neighbor invited her to an evangelistic service. Veda gave her life to God at age sixteen.

She married a World War II paratrooper just three months after meeting him. But after twenty-three years of domestic abuse that endangered Veda's life and the lives of their four children, the couple divorced in 1977.

Veda realized that although others had let her down, God had remained faithful. As it seemed everything was slipping away from her, God became everything to her. Veda stepped out in faith and joined her friend Laurette in ministry. She now serves her church as a youth team leader and teacher.

Through her ministry, Veda directs women to God, rather than others, as their source of happiness and satisfaction. God's faithfulness inspired Veda and Laurette to write *Catch the Fun, Catch the Laughter, Catch the Joy*, a book on joyful living.

MY RESPONSE: How is God filling the holes left by relationships missing from my life?

The Lord is with me; I will not be afraid.
Psalm 118:6

HER SERVICE: Mission work and prison ministry

HER MESSAGE: As we step out in faith, we overcome fear.

HER STORY: During Jeannine Brabon's decades of missionary service, she has developed a highly successful prison ministry.

Jeannine was born to missionary parents Harold and Margaret Brabon, serving in Colombia during a period of political upheaval when believers were sometimes beaten with the flat sides of machetes. Jeannine understood the dangers of missionary work, but at age eleven she prayed for courage to follow in her parents' footsteps.

God answered her prayer. Jeannine graduated from Asbury Seminary in Kentucky and served in Spain before she returned to teach at Medellin's Biblical Seminary of Colombia. Then Jeannine's ministry took her into the "Jaws of Hell," Columbia's violent Bellevista Prison, which averaged two murders a day within its walls. After Jeannine preached at a worship service, twenty-three men accepted Christ. Since then more than two hundred inmates have graduated from a Bible Institute course of study she developed. Thousands have come to Christ through her ministry, and the prison's violence and murder rate dropped dramatically. In spite of personal danger, including death threats, Jeannine has persevered. She ministers in faith, overcoming her fears and pointing out, "Security is not the absence of danger; it's the presence of Jesus."

MY RESPONSE: What fear do I need God's help to conquer so I can step out in faithful service to Him?

We loved you so much that we were delighted to share with you not only the gospel of God but our lives as well.
1 Thessalonians 2:8

HER SERVICE: Mission work

HER MESSAGE: A transformed heart and obedient spirit leave a legacy of faith for those who follow.

HER STORY: Dr. Margaret Brabon, with her husband, Harold, and others, pioneered the Oriental Missionary Society (now OMS International) in Colombia.

While in college, Margaret accepted Christ. Later, after Harold's plant closed and he lost his job as a research chemist, the couple prepared for missionary service. They went to Colombia in 1946 and settled in Medellin. Margaret taught, preached, and raised their four children. Obeying the direction of God's Spirit, she led locals to Christ and reached out in motherly love to others. Once, when paying a protocol visit to the wife of the U.S. consul, she courageously witnessed to the woman, who was touched spiritually and healed physically. In turn, this woman testified of Christ to visiting dignitaries and later started a Christian university for girls in Taiwan.

From 1952 to 1955 the Brabons ministered in Ecuador. Margaret tells their story in her book *What Now, Lord?* Still an articulate advocate for missions, she resides in Kentucky. And her legacy of service lives on. Her daughter Jeannine Brabon teaches at a Colombian seminary and ministers to prisoners and their families. The other Brabon children have also been active in missionary work.

MY RESPONSE: To whom might I pass on a legacy of faith?

I will praise you, O Lord, with all my heart;
I will tell of all your wonders.
Psalm 9:1

HER SERVICE: Writing poetry

HER MESSAGE: We can commune with God—and invite others to the meeting.

HER STORY: Anne Dudley Bradstreet was the first American to publish a book of poetry.

Anne Dudley grew up in an English castle where her father served as business manager. She married Simon Bradstreet, her father's protégé, when she was sixteen and he was twenty-five. Later Anne's Puritan family, under persecution from the Anglican Church, sailed for America.

On the crude frontier of the Massachusetts Bay Colony, life was hard—especially for a woman with eight children whose husband was often away on political business. Anne was sickly and grappled with her faith as she struggled to survive. Reading and writing poetry helped her cope by centering her thoughts on God. Anne wrote about family life, nature, and earthly and divine love. Little did she know that her words would someday encourage others and point them toward God.

Finding Anne's poems worthy of a wider audience, her brother-in-law John Woodbridge secretly copied them and had them published in England in 1650. An American edition published posthumously in 1678 included some of her later work. Anne's poetry offered a glimpse of a pioneer woman's spiritual struggles in a way that encouraged the hearts of others on the frontiers of America.

MY RESPONSE: How might sharing my struggles—in writing or in conversation—encourage others?

A friend loves at all times.
Proverbs 17:17

HER SERVICE: Writing, teaching the Bible, and speaking

HER MESSAGE: Women need to nurture relationships with other women.

HER STORY: Dee Brestin has written several books and Bible study guides, many on the power of the relationships of women, sisters, and friends. In demand as a retreat speaker, Dee offers women scriptural models of friendship on which to pattern their lives.

During her early years of marriage, Dee and her husband, Steve, moved frequently; maintaining friendships was challenging. Through the years, though, Dee corresponded with friends, and when Steve died in 2004, Dee received notes from across the country. Many friends traveled hundreds of miles to attend his funeral.

An editor first suggested that Dee write a book on friendship, and the result, *The Friendships of Women*, published in 1987, became a bestseller. Rereleased in 2005, the book now includes stories of how women from her church showered her with caring e-mails, casseroles, and lots of hugs during her bereavement. She had established close friendships with them through the years.

Through her teaching and her personal experiences, Dee Brestin shows us the power and beauty of women's friendships—and the value in nurturing those relationships.

MY RESPONSE: Whom might I call today to meet me for lunch?

My son, do not forget my teaching, but keep my commands in your heart.
Proverbs 3:1

HER SERVICE: Writing and advocating prayer

HER MESSAGE: To change the world, reach young adults who will share their faith in their various professions. And pray!

HER STORY: Vonette Bright founded the Great Commission Prayer Crusade and the National Prayer Committee. She and her husband founded Campus Crusade for Christ (CCC) in 1951, which has grown into CCC International, a vibrant movement on more than a thousand college campuses across the United States and beyond.

While in college, Vonette Zachary received a letter from a hometown acquaintance. Bill Bright's note started a long-distance romance that led to their engagement. Vonette, however, did not share Bill's deep faith. He invited her to California to meet his mentor, Henrietta Mears, who led Vonette to Christ. The couple married in 1948.

One night Bill woke Vonette to share his vision for a campus ministry. She embraced his dream that college students won for Christ would become young professionals who could wield influence for Christ wherever their work took them. The young couple moved near a college, organized a twenty-four-hour prayer chain, and opened their doors to students.

In 1988 Vonette was successful in requesting legislation that made the first Thursday of May an annual National Day of Prayer. Now nearly fifty thousand prayer events are held on that day. Vonette also founded Women Today International to disciple new believers.

MY RESPONSE: What ministry might I start or join to minister to young adults?

My heart is steadfast, O God; I will sing and make music with all my soul.
Psalm 108:1

HER SERVICE: Music ministry and editing hymnbook

HER MESSAGE: If properly understood, the words of hymns pave the way for private reflection and personal connection with God.

HER STORY: Dr. Emily Ruth Brink is the first woman ever to serve on a steering committee of her denomination, the Christian Reformed Church. She received accolades for her editorial work in revising a denominational hymnal to reflect cultural diversity and gender sensitivity. In 1990 she accepted the presidency of the Hymn Society in the United States and Canada.

Emily's parents frequently entertained church visitors, and Emily came to enjoy theological discussions. But while taking a college course, she found the love of her life—music theory. She was ecstatic when her professor suggested she major in music and take organ lessons from him.

Teaching at universities in New York and Illinois, Emily passed along her knowledge and her love of music to students. Soon after she completed her doctoral dissertation, she accepted an appointment to the Psalter Hymnal Revision Committee. As editor, she faced the challenge of updating the thirty-year-old songbook's language so today's worshipers would be better able to connect with God. The hymnal was published in 1988 with revisions that accommodated cultural traditions, included updated language, and offered expression to both genders. When the work was completed, the denomination's all-male synod gave Emily a standing ovation.

MY RESPONSE: What hymn might I meditate on today?

The Lord God said, "It is not good for the man to be alone. I will make a helper suitable for him."
Genesis 2:18

HER SERVICE: Pastor's wife and minister at large

HER MESSAGE: Our greatest fulfillment may come in a partnering role.

HER STORY: Jill Briscoe affirms pastors' wives and women in ministry and has written or coauthored more than fifty books plus many articles.

Converted at age eighteen, Jill, a native of Liverpool, England, thought she had found her life's calling—youth evangelism. On a youth retreat she met Stuart Briscoe, and they later married. Eventually Stuart turned from a banking career to ministry, and the two produced a radio-and-television media ministry, *Telling the Truth*. Sought-after conference speakers, the Briscoes moved to America, and Stuart took the reins as senior pastor at Elmbrook Church, Brookfield, Wisconsin.

Jill expected to continue in youth work. But to her surprise, Jill found fulfillment ministering to youth and women, and her expertise in teaching and evangelizing complemented her husband's preaching ministry. As executive editor of *Just between Us*, a publication for ministry wives and women in leadership, Jill offers a forum for concerns close to her heart. The Briscoes have three children and thirteen grandchildren.

MY RESPONSE: How might I partner with someone who serves Christ and His kingdom?

We have this treasure in jars of clay to show that this all-surpassing power is from God and not from us.
2 Corinthians 4:7

HER SERVICE: Mission work

HER MESSAGE: A true disciple remains true to Christ's calling despite obstacles, physical limitations, and setbacks.

HER STORY: Harriet Brittan overcame great personal challenges to serve as a foreign missionary for fifty years.

Injured in a fall as a girl, she spent her youth in bed and experienced lifelong difficulty walking. In spite of her disability, Harriet served as a missionary to Africa, where she was repeatedly afflicted with fevers and forced to return home. Rather than have her fiancé, a fellow missionary, leave the field with her, she broke her engagement and returned home alone. Once she recovered, Harriet served in Calcutta, India, where she got to know the local women by teaching them needlework. She wrote several books exposing the deplorable treatment of women of India.

During a year of work at a New York hospital, Harriet organized concerts that raised thousands of dollars for missions. She spent her last seventeen years in Japan, where she directed a mission school for poor Eurasian children and later ran a home for missionaries.

By the time Harriet retired, her personal fortune had dwindled because of her generosity and business losses. Yet despite her physical limitations, the challenges of ministry, and her financial losses, she had remained true to her calling and led many into the Kingdom.

MY RESPONSE: What obstacles must I overcome to fulfill God's calling?

Give us property among our father's relatives.
Numbers 27:4

HER SERVICE: Preaching, writing, and advocating women's rights

HER MESSAGE: Women may share in church leadership.

HER STORY: An outspoken advocate of women's equality, Antoinette Brown was the first woman ordained in the United States by a recognized denomination, the Congregational church. She believed God called women as well as men to be church leaders.

While studying theology at Oberlin College in 1850, Antoinette wrote a paper refuting Scripture interpretations that prohibited women from preaching. She viewed verses such as 1 Corinthians 14:34 as warnings against excesses in public worship. Because of her gender, the school would not award her a degree or ordain her to preach. Officials relented in 1878 and gave her an MA degree. The college also awarded her an honorary doctorate in 1908.

At the first National Woman's Rights Convention in Massachusetts, Antoinette refuted arguments against women preaching. Because of that, she lost a promised job at a New York City mission and so turned to lecturing. For a few years she pastored a Congregational church.

When Antoinette served as a delegate to the World's Temperance Convention in New York City, she was shouted down and not allowed to speak because she was a woman. After marrying Samuel Blackwell in 1856, Antoinette spent eighteen years out of the public eye, raising five daughters. During that time she wrote articles and books, then resumed her active public life as a reformer for another forty years.

MY RESPONSE: What is my place of leadership in the church?

When we are slandered, we answer kindly.
1 Corinthians 4:13

HER SERVICE: Singing, political activism

HER MESSAGE: Convictions may be costly.

HER STORY: Anita Bryant gained fame as a singer and entertainer. She was the youngest person ever to receive the USO's Silver Medallion Award for entertaining military personnel on Bob Hope Holiday Tours.

The doctor who delivered Anita thought she was dead, but at a grandfather's urging, tended to her, and she soon demonstrated a healthy pair of lungs. When she was a high-school junior, Arthur Godfrey's television show *Talent Scouts* shone the spotlight on Anita's singing. After being named second runner-up in the 1957 Miss America pageant, Anita regularly performed on Don McNeill's *Breakfast Club*. Her rendition of "Battle Hymn of the Republic" became an American favorite, and her face became familiar as the spokesperson for Florida orange juice.

But as her career flourished, detractors denounced her outspoken stance against homosexuals teaching in public schools. By standing up for her convictions, she lost her product endorsement deals as controversy swirled and gay supporters boycotted those products. Protesters and comedians made her the butt of jokes. Her family endured prank calls and death threats.

MY RESPONSE: How would I respond if I were criticized for speaking out about my beliefs?

You prepare a table before me in the presence of my enemies.
Psalm 23:5

HER SERVICE: Mission work

HER MESSAGE: God is with us—even when we face our worst fears.

HER STORY: Gracia Burnham became internationally known when she and her husband, missionaries with New Tribes Mission, were abducted by terrorists from a resort in the Philippines while celebrating their eighteenth wedding anniversary.

Born in Illinois, Gracia met Martin Burnham, a "missionary kid" trained as a pilot, while attending college in Kansas City. They married in 1983 and had three children while serving in the Philippines.

The Burnhams embraced missionary life—Martin flew a plane while Gracia manned the radio—until that fateful day when they were yanked from their beds, along with eighteen others. In the months that followed, some hostages were released while others were added to the group. The kidnappers beheaded one man to show the world they meant business. The hostages sometimes survived in the jungle by chewing raw rice or leaves. For more than a year they feared for their lives and yet demonstrated the joy, peace, and love of God to their captors, a Muslim terrorist group.

During a rescue attempt by Philippine soldiers in June of 2002, Gracia was wounded, and Martin and another hostage were shot and killed. Gracia's book, *In the Presence of My Enemies*, tells her story about the God who never left her, even in her darkest days.

MY RESPONSE: How might I cultivate a sense of God's presence even when I'm afraid?

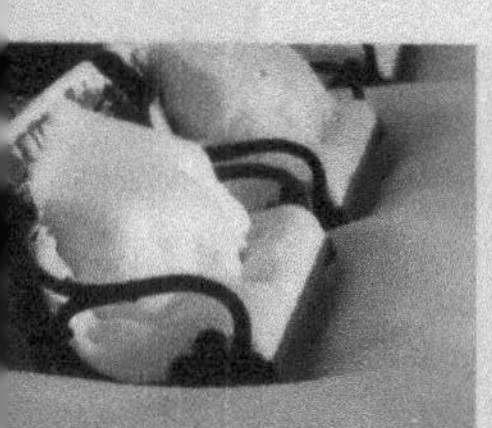

Buy the truth and do not sell it; get wisdom, discipline and understanding.

Proverbs 23:23

HER SERVICE: Being First Lady, teaching, promoting books and learning

HER MESSAGE: If you learn to read, you're ready to learn.

HER STORY: Laura Welch Bush became First Lady in 2001 when her husband, George W. Bush, became the forty-third president of the United States. She has championed a national reading initiative.

From childhood Laura loved books and reading. She earned a master's degree in library science at the University of Texas at Austin. Before her marriage in 1977, Laura worked as a schoolteacher and a librarian. Once twin daughters, Barbara and Jenna, joined the family, Laura enjoyed reading to them.

Through her national initiative, Ready to Read, Ready to Learn, Laura strives to prepare young children for school through early childhood programs that offer language play, sound games, and other prereading and vocabulary activities. Her program recruits and trains teachers with a goal of providing qualified teachers in impoverished neighborhoods.

The National Book Festivals, introduced by Laura in 2001, have turned into events that draw thousands of authors and book lovers from across the nation. Mrs. Bush is often shown in newspaper photographs reading to young students. She challenges parents to read to their children long before they enter school so that their education will be built on a firm foundation.

MY RESPONSE: To whom might I read a book?

Receive her in the Lord, as one who is worthy of high honor. Help her in every way you can, for she has helped many in their needs, including me.

Romans 16:2 NLT

HER SERVICE: Social reform, evangelism, education, and healing

HER MESSAGE: Women should not be limited by the expectations of others.

HER STORY: Dr. Katharine Bushnell denounced the subjugation of women and believed male domination was unscriptural.

While serving as a medical missionary in China, Katharine discovered that a Chinese translation of Scripture had been slanted to fit cultural traditions that kept women in subordination. This made her wonder if similar bias might be present in English translations, and she began a lifelong study of the Scriptures in their original languages. Katharine became convinced that mistranslations were responsible for the social and spiritual suppression of women.

In 1885 she gave up medicine for the task of righting social injustices and human degradation through work as an evangelist with the Women's Christian Temperance Union (WCTU). After investigating rumors of women being enslaved in lumber camps, she wrote a report that resulted in the Kate Bushnell Bill, which corrected such abuses.

She devoted the last fifty years of her life to writing and teaching what she believed the Bible truly said about the full equality of women and men. Her book *God's Word to Women* continues to be an important resource.

MY RESPONSE: What preconceived notion of my own or of society's may be hindering me from being all I can be for God?

All my fellow townsmen know that you are a woman of noble character.
Ruth 3:11

HER SERVICE: Founded hospitals, orphanages, convents, and schools

HER MESSAGE: To get things done, trust in God's power rather than in your own effort.

HER STORY: Frances Xavier Cabrini was canonized by Pope Pius XII in 1946, the first American citizen to achieve that honor. The untiring nun founded institutions throughout Latin America, Europe, and the United States.

Born Maria Francesca, she grew up on a farm in Italy, the youngest of thirteen children. After her parents died in 1870, Maria applied to join a religious order. She was refused admittance because of her frail build. So Maria went to work at an orphanage, took religious vows three years later, and when the orphanage closed in 1880, established the Missionaries of the Sacred Heart. Seeking approval for her order, Maria visited Pope Leo XIII, who suggested she go to America to minister to Italian immigrants.

In spite of initial resistance by the archbishop, Mother Cabrini organized a convent, an orphanage, and a hospital in "Little Italy" on New York City's East Side. Regardless of the attitudes of others, Mother Cabrini resolutely carried on her work and urged the nuns of her order to rely on God's power rather than their own.

MY RESPONSE: How might I show faith in God instead of in my own efforts?

Before I formed you in the womb I knew you,
before you were born I set you apart.
Jeremiah 1:5

HER SERVICE: Singing, pastoring, and evangelism

HER MESSAGE: Don't let temptation lure you from your calling.

HER STORY: Dr. Shirley Caesar has received nine Grammy Awards and several Dove Awards. She pastors a church and ministers to the wider body of Christ as an evangelist.

Shirley grew up in Durham, North Carolina, among twelve siblings. Her father, who led a gospel quartet, died when Shirley was a child. To help support her family, she sang with a traveling group from her church. At the age of seventeen, Shirley felt called to be a singing evangelist.

When finances prevented Shirley from returning to college after her freshman year, she toured with a black female gospel group. Eight years later she set out on her own and, in time, developed the Shirley Caesar Singers. The "Queen of Gospel Music" married Bishop Harold Ivory Williams in 1983. Shirley completed college and has received honorary doctoral degrees. She has sung before three presidents, and since 1990 has served as pastor of Mount Calvary Word of Faith Holy Church in Raleigh, North Carolina. An NAACP Image Award and an *Essence* magazine award honored her for staying true to her calling rather than veering into a secular music career. Her autobiography, *Shirley Caesar: The Lady, the Melody, and the Word*, tells her story.

MY RESPONSE: In what ways am I holding to or drifting from my calling?

Her husband has full confidence in her and lacks nothing of value.
Proverbs 31:11

Her Service: Supporting reform

Her Message: We can serve as full-time Christian workers in our own homes.

Her Story: Idelette de Bures Stordeur Calvin devoted herself to caring for her Reformer husband, John Calvin. She graciously entertained those who visited him from near or far—and they were many.

Idelette's first husband, John Stordeur, died of the plague, leaving her with three children. Although the Calvins had children of their own, none of them lived beyond infancy. Idelette ran a busy household as she dealt with grief and chronic ill health. She visited the sick and the poor. She softened Calvin's posture as an authoritarian Reformer. And she tended a vegetable garden to help put food on the table.

John Calvin was long plagued by headaches, and he found Idelette to be the wife he needed to care for him. She handled practical matters while he devoted himself to studying, writing, and preaching. When her health permitted it, she accompanied Calvin on his visits to the sick and imprisoned. He called her "the faithful helper of my ministry" and "the best companion of my life." After her death, just nine years after their marriage, Calvin kept his vow to raise her preadolescent children, and he never remarried. Idelette served the Lord as she served those of her own household and offered hospitality to others.

My Response: How might I bless those in my household?

Be strong and do not give up, for your work will be rewarded.
2 Chronicles 15:7

HER SERVICE: Writing

HER MESSAGE: What we love to do may be what God asks us to do for Him.

HER STORY: Melody Carlson has published more than one hundred books for women, teens, and children.

As she was growing up in Oregon, Melody's teachers encouraged her to become a writer. After a dramatic conversion at age fifteen, she embraced missions and became the youngest short-term assistant ever to serve with Wycliffe Bible Translators in Papua, New Guinea.

After college, Melody married Chris Carlson. While raising two sons and working, she dabbled in writing. After Melody published several books, a conference speaker told her she was gifted. Stepping out in faith, she quit her job to do what she felt God calling her to do. Since then she has followed her heart and devoted her time to writing. Some of Melody's books address tough issues, such as addiction and mental illness. Melody assures young people that God is faithful, even when life is less than perfect.

Melody and her family live in Oregon, where she enjoys camping, biking, skiing—and answering messages left for "Caitlin," the protagonist of her series Diary of a Teenage Girl. Several of her children's book titles have been Evangelical Christian Publishers Association bestsellers. *King of the Stable* won a 1999 Gold Medallion award.

MY RESPONSE: What do I love to do that God might love for me to do for Him?

Never be lacking in zeal, but keep your spiritual fervor, serving the Lord.
Romans 12:11

HER SERVICE: Mission work

HER MESSAGE: Do what you can—here or there, for rich or poor, in health or sickness—as long as you can.

HER STORY: Amy Carmichael founded Dohnavur Fellowship to raise and educate the children she rescued from Hindu temple prostitution in India. She wrote numerous letters, songs, poems, and books.

Amy grew up in a Christian home in England and, from the age of fifteen, took her faith seriously. As a young woman she held prayer meetings for girls and Bible classes for "Shawlies," factory-working women who wore scarves. Through talking with preachers and missionaries, Amy felt God telling her to "go" and witness for Him.

Although her health was poor, Amy sailed for Japan. But her experience was a disappointment, and a year later she returned home. The following year, 1895, she accepted an assignment in South India. Although afflicted with a tropical disease upon arriving, she never again returned home. Amy never married, but more than a thousand children called her Amma, *mother* in the Tamil language. After a fall, Amy was confined to bed for the last twenty years of her life. She devoted her time to writing. Her book, *If*, a compilation of inspirational thoughts, earned recognition in *100 Christian Books That Changed the Century*. By serving God in various ways through every stage of life, Amy faithfully served God.

MY RESPONSE: What might I do for the Lord in my current life situation?

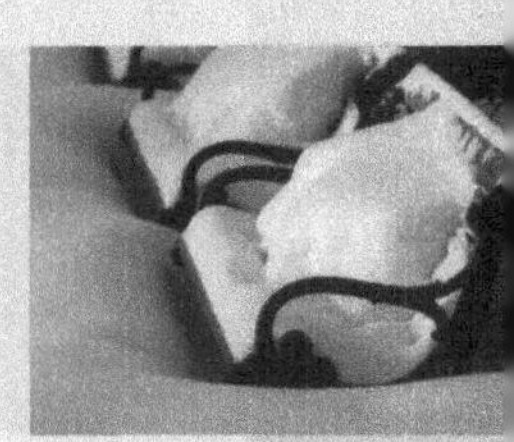

Let us, therefore, make every effort to enter that rest, so that no one will fall.
Hebrews 4:11

HER SERVICE: Writing, publishing, and speaking

HER MESSAGE: Good works must be balanced with rest and renewal.

HER STORY: Dr. Nancie Carmichael has written seven books and co-authored five books on marriage and family with her husband, Bill Carmichael.

Nancie was raised on a Montana wheat ranch, and she, her parents, and seven siblings were faithful church attenders. She recommitted her life to Christ as a college freshman. In 1966 she married, and as a pastor's wife, her goals of writing and ministry merged.

When Nancie was in her late thirties, she struggled to manage both a demanding career and a busy household. She and Bill had started their own magazine company in Oregon, their daughter had complex learning disorders, and Nancie was grieving the loss of her father. The added stress of publishing deadlines and an overly busy life pushed her into depression and illness. It was during this period of forced rest that she learned to stop and enjoy God's grace. Nancie now writes and speaks from experience, encouraging women not to feel they have to do it all.

Nancie received an honorary doctorate from Western Baptist College in Oregon and was recognized by the Evangelical Press Association for her column in *Woman's Touch* magazine.

MY RESPONSE: What boundaries should I establish to protect my personal and spiritual well-being?

Freely you have received, freely give.
Matthew 10:8

HER SERVICE: Volunteer work

HER MESSAGE: One size does not fit all; God uses women in the home, the workplace, and the community.

HER STORY: A stock analyst turned stay-at-home mom, Susie Case teaches Bible studies and volunteers in her neighborhood.

When Susie became pregnant with her first child, she was traveling for business two hundred days of the year. God spoke to her heart, and others confirmed her decision to stay home. As a professional go-getter, it was difficult to step out of the limelight. For a while Susie taught a course at Columbia Business School, but then she decided to stick with volunteer work so that others might step in and cover her work if her husband or two children needed her at home.

Freed from work responsibilities, Susie for a time taught Bible Study Fellowship classes, which drew as many as two hundred women to sessions. Now she teaches a Bible study for twenty parents at her son's school and offers biblical insight to problem solving in volunteer positions such as the tenant board of her apartment building. Eventually Susie plans to hang out her shingle as a counselor to women on issues of career, relationships, and faith. She encourages all women to find the place to which God calls them—in the home, in the workplace, or in the community—as she has done, through the various stages of life.

MY RESPONSE: What avenue of service is most appropriate for my stage of life and faith?

March

I delight greatly in the Lord; my soul rejoices in my God.
Isaiah 61:10

HER SERVICE: Nursing, advocating prayer

HER MESSAGE: Prayer prompts rather than precludes work.

HER STORY: Catherine of Genoa became known for her contemplative life, even in the midst of a busy lifestyle.

The daughter of the viceroy of Naples, Catherine Fieschi Adorno wanted to enter a convent at thirteen. Because of her age, the chaplain refused her request—for three successive years. Upon her father's death when she was fifteen, Catherine's brother arranged a marriage for her that he felt was politically advantageous. Her new husband, Guiliano, was cruel, unfaithful, and rarely home. Suffering from depression, Catherine lived in seclusion for five years, then tried to find happiness in an active social life. Neither approach made her feel better.

In December 1472 Catherine begged God to help her. The following year, as she knelt in confession, she experienced an overwhelming sense of God's love. With that, she entered a prayerful life—but also felt called to work as a nurse. After her husband went bankrupt, he turned to Christ and joined the Franciscans. Until his death twenty years later, he and Catherine chose to live together chastely as they ministered to the poor. For six years she administered a 130-bed hospital, organizing open-air wards during the plague of 1493, at which time she caught, yet survived, the plague. Her love for God inspired others as she served Him with all her strength.

MY RESPONSE: How do my prayers and my actions work together for God's kingdom?

You yourself must be an example to them
by doing good deeds of every kind.
Titus 2:7 NLT

HER SERVICE: Prayer, social work, and activism

HER MESSAGE: Strive to improve the good and eradicate the bad.

HER STORY: Although she lived only thirty-three years, Catherine of Siena demonstrated a balanced life of devotion and service. She was influential in restoring the papacy to Rome from France.

Catherine Benincasa was greatly influenced by a Dominican monastery near her home, and when she was twelve she dedicated herself to celibacy. From fourteen to seventeen Catherine lived in solitude, offering unceasing prayer from a small basement room in her home. She then joined the Dominican Tertiaries so she might do for others the deeds she longed to do for Christ in the flesh. Wearing a veil of white and a cape of black, she served the sick and imprisoned. When an outbreak of plague struck, Catherine ministered, unafraid.

Learning to write only shortly before her death, Catherine still authored important theological works through dictation, including *The Book of Divine Doctrine.* Her prayers and nearly four hundred letters to secular and religious rulers, political groups, and individuals were also compiled into books. Catherine advised popes, attacked corruption, and modeled a life of love for God and others.

MY RESPONSE: What good works might I do in the name of Christ?

Jane Chalmers, birth date unknown–1879

Be strong and courageous. Do not be afraid or terrified because of them, for the Lord your God goes with you.
Deuteronomy 31:6

HER SERVICE: Mission work

HER MESSAGE: Conquer fear with courage.

HER STORY: Jane Chalmers and her husband, James, served as missionaries with the London Missionary Society at Rarotonga and New Guinea.

The Chalmers faced going to the mission field with courage and determination, and they would need both. Their ship struck a reef and then, after it was repaired, they were shipwrecked. Lifeboats saved the Chalmers' lives, but their supplies (along with supplies for other missionaries) were lost. The couple arrived at Rarotonga in May 1867, a year and a half after leaving England. James opened a Training Institution for tribesmen, and Jane taught the students' wives to read, sew, and understand Scripture.

In 1877 the Chalmers were assigned to New Guinea, an island of savage tribesmen bent on revenge for mistreatment suffered at the hands of trading vessel crewmen. Jane and James visited two hundred villages, where many had never seen a white person. Some nights hostile tribesmen shouted for the Chalmers to leave the mission station they had established. But Jane and James conquered their fear with prayer and courage. To signal good will, Jane stayed alone at the station while James left for supplies. Her bold gesture earned the respect of tribespeople.

MY RESPONSE: What fear do I need to face with courage?

Whatever you do, do it all for the glory of God.
1 Corinthians 10:31

HER SERVICE: Stenography and publishing

HER MESSAGE: No skill is too "secular" to be used for God's glory.

HER STORY: Gertrude "Biddy" Hobbs Chambers compiled fifty books containing the sermons and teachings of her husband, Oswald Chambers, including *My Utmost for His Highest,* a Christian classic.

To free money for her siblings' education, Gertrude, a native of England, quit school, taught herself shorthand, and learned to take dictation at the phenomenal rate of 250 words per minute. When Gertrude went to visit a friend in America, her mother asked Oswald, who was going to America on a preaching tour, to watch over her. He and Gertrude, whom he nicknamed Biddy, married in 1910.

Biddy took notes of Oswald's sermons and his lectures at the Bible Training College, a London school he opened in 1911. During World War I, when Oswald volunteered as a chaplain in Egypt, Biddy took their young daughter, Kathleen, and went along. Biddy offered hospitality to scores of soldiers.

Oswald died after an appendectomy in 1917, and Biddy returned to England after the 1918 armistice. There, pen and notepad in hand, she found her calling. Without Biddy's careful note taking, transcription, and publishing, the life-changing words of Oswald Chambers might not have survived.

MY RESPONSE: What skill might I use for God?

He called ten of his servants and gave them ten minas.
"Put this money to work," he said, "until I come back."
Luke 19:13

HER SERVICE: Banking

HER MESSAGE: Christians bloom as beautifully behind plate glass as behind stained glass.

HER STORY: As a corporate executive, Pin Pin Chau is driven by faith. Set in the midst of corporate America, she demonstrates a life set apart for God.

Pin Pin came to America from Hong Kong to attend college. Her husband, Raymond, was a believer, but Pin Pin questioned why Jesus is the only way to heaven. Finally she accepted salvation by faith, and by the time she entered banking, Pin Pin was a Christian.

After almost completing a doctoral degree in literature at Yale University, Pin Pin Chau took a job as a customer-service representative at a bank. From that small beginning, she advanced to become president and CEO of Summit National Bank in Atlanta. Pin Pin's faith has governed her work. In handling employee relationships, she relies on Scripture for guidance, confronting and apologizing as God directs. She uses opportunities for public speaking to share her faith, carefully noting that her views are not sanctioned by her company or her host. She hosts and encourages Bible studies, insisting they be held on personal time so it does not appear that Christians are being given special favors. In the professional world, Pin Pin offers a solid testimony for Christ.

MY RESPONSE: How can I let my faith bloom in my workplace?

Praise him with the sounding of the trumpet,
praise him with the harp and lyre.
Psalm 150:3

HER SERVICE: Music performance and study, linguistics, and teaching

HER MESSAGE: God strengthens and directs us to move forward after life sets us back.

HER STORY: A college professor emeritus, Vida Chenoweth has overcome disabling injuries to enjoy careers as a classical marimba artist, a missionary linguist, and an ethnomusicologist, one who studies music of various cultures.

Vida was considered the world's leading marimba artist, but her interest in that instrument had developed only because a childhood injury to a finger made it impossible to play most other instruments. Additionally, a car accident left her with a fractured skull and a thumb injury. When she was burned in a fire and gangrene set in, it seemed likely her hand would be permanently disabled. As Vida lay hospitalized, she learned of Wycliffe Bible Translators and determined to devote her life to reaching people with no Scripture in their own language.

When God had strengthened her enough that she could return to work, she accepted an assignment to the highlands of Papua, New Guinea. There Vida combined ethnomusicology with linguistics and translated the New Testament into the Usarufa language. Since then Vida has taught others what she learned and has written books and articles on music traditions. Through life's setbacks, God developed and used Vida's varied interests to reach others with the gospel.

MY RESPONSE: How may God be redirecting my life through my experiences?

You are the salt of the earth.
Matthew 5:13

HER SERVICE: Leading others

HER MESSAGE: Use your influence for good.

HER STORY: As the wife of China's Generalissimo Chiang Kai-shek, leader of the Nationalist Party, Madame Chiang Kai-shek played a key role as an anti-Communist spokeswoman during the 1950s. She started the country's New Life Movement in 1934, a campaign designed to call the nation back to traditional Chinese values. Known for her political genius and Christian testimony, she was recognized as one of America's ten most admired women during the late 1960s.

Madame Chiang Kai-shek was born Soong Mei-ling. Her father, a Methodist minister and Shanghai businessman, had spent fifteen years in America. In 1917 Mei-ling graduated from Wellesley College in Georgia.

Madame Chiang Kai-shek came to be her husband's valued confidante and, at times, his skilled negotiator. In 1943 she was the first Chinese national and only the second woman ever to address a joint session of the U.S. House and Senate, at which she requested American support against Japan. She also pleaded for missionaries to come to Taiwan, where her husband served as president after fleeing the Communists on mainland China. After her husband's death in 1975, Madame Chiang Kai-shek lived in New York.

MY RESPONSE: How might I promote Christian values in my area of influence?

Ask and you will receive, and your joy will be complete.
John 16:24

HER SERVICE: Founding a ministry, advocating prayer, writing

HER MESSAGE: Prayer is the key that opens the door so unbelievers may step into God's kingdom.

HER STORY: Through books and seminars, Evelyn Christenson has challenged Christians around the world to pray.

While attending a Baptist convention with her husband, Chris, a pastor, Evelyn was asked to conduct a six-month experiment to see what happens when women pray. What happened opened Evelyn's eyes: lives were transformed as people came to Christ. Evelyn wrote *What Happens When Women Pray*, which became a bestseller, and found her life's calling. Eventually she founded the United Prayer Ministry, a nonprofit corporation based in St. Paul, Minnesota.

Evelyn advocates "triplet praying": three Christians meet weekly to pray for unsaved people. She has traveled the world and served on international committees to raise up prayer warriors. Evelyn's books have garnered awards from the Evangelical Christian Publishers Association. Her *Study Guide for Evangelism Praying* has been translated into fifty languages. Even in retirement, Evelyn continues speaking and, of course, praying.

MY RESPONSE: With whom might I form a prayer triplet to pray for unsaved friends?

She is clothed with strength and dignity;
she can laugh at the days to come.
Proverbs 31:25

HER SERVICE: Humor, writing, and speaking

HER MESSAGE: Instead of hiding at home, you can hide in God—and feel comfortable anywhere.

HER STORY: As a member of the Women of Faith Conference team, Patsy Clairmont speaks to thousands of women each month. She has written and coauthored several books.

Young Patsy grew up scared—scared of being seen in public, scared of people, and scared of pressures—so scared that she dropped out of high school and ran away from home. But after picking potatoes for pocket money, she returned to her family. Patsy dropped out of high school a second time to marry Les Clairmont, but marriage introduced new problems. Finally, Patsy sought help from an anxiety self-help group. She conquered agoraphobia and developed a thirst for educational and spiritual growth. Her marriage was mended, and now the little woman, barely five feet tall, draws big laughs from audiences of thousands.

Patsy helps women accept themselves as "cracked pots" living in imperfect families. Her books include *Sportin' a 'Tude*, *Normal Is Just a Setting on Your Dryer*, and *God Uses Cracked Pots*. Patsy points to herself as evidence that instead of hiding out, you can learn to laugh at yourself and go anywhere—even on center stage.

MY RESPONSE: What fear is keeping me from functioning for God?

Blessed are those who help the poor.
Proverbs 14:21 NLT

HER SERVICE: Founded a religious order

HER MESSAGE: Giving up earthly treasures brings heavenly pleasures.

HER STORY: Along with Francis of Assisi, Clare of Assisi founded the Franciscan Order of Poor Clares. By the time of her death, Clare had founded branches in at least six Italian locations as well as in France and Germany.

Clare, the daughter of an Italian count, grew up in a castle with the privileges of nobility. At age sixteen she dedicated herself to a religious life, and Francis of Assisi became her mentor. In 1211 Clare took a vow of perpetual virginity and exchanged her fashionable clothes for an ash-colored, black-hooded robe belted with a rope. Later she and her sister lived in a small house, the first nuns of the Second Order of Franciscans. Donating her inheritance to hospitals and the needy, Clare began the work of the Poor Clares after her mother and wealthy friends joined her. They took literally Jesus's command to sell what they had to give to the poor, expecting to receive rewards of spiritual joy then and more fully in heaven.

Clare taught the Sisters to sew and spent much time in prayer. She lived such an austere life that she was later unable to walk. Clare was canonized just two years after her death.

MY RESPONSE: How might I lay up treasures in heaven?

Praise be to the Lord, to God our Savior,
who daily bears our burdens.
Psalm 68:19

HER SERVICE: Mission work

HER MESSAGE: Life may be more utilitarian than utopian, but all activities can glorify God.

HER STORY: Known as Madame Coillard, Christina Mackintosh Coillard served for thirty years beside her husband, François, as a missionary to South Africa. The couple planted churches for the Paris Evangelical Missionary Society as they ministered to tribal kings and families.

Christina grew up in a parsonage in Scotland. As a girl she subscribed to a missionary paper for children, which piqued her interest in missions. When she married François Coillard, he was already serving as a missionary in Africa. Christina became his able helpmate while they served first in Basuto Land, where French Protestants ran a mission, then in Zambezi.

Life was difficult in the land of virgin forests and white plains. Christina taught children by writing in the sand beneath the trees. She baked her own bread and made her own soap and candles. But perhaps her most important task was telling Bible stories to African women as she showed them how to cut out material for dresses. While teaching the tribal women to live more enlightened lives under the most primitive circumstances, Christina grasped every opportunity she was given to witness of Christ's great love.

MY RESPONSE: How might I weave an outreach into tasks I perform with others on a daily basis?

Two are better than one, because they have
a good return for their work.
Ecclesiastes 4:9

HER SERVICE: Encouraging others, writing

HER MESSAGE: Faith shared through words of encouragement inspires others to heights they might not reach without us.

HER STORY: Known as the first woman to write religious sonnets, Vittoria Colonna inspired famed artist Michelangelo with her faith, her poetry, and her appreciation of beauty.

Born to a Roman family of nobility, Vittoria married at age nineteen. A few years later, her husband died of military wounds; then an adopted nephew vanished at sea. In 1527 Vittoria retired to a convent and began writing sonnets about her husband's career, then about God.

Vittoria joined the Order of the Oratory of Divine Love in an effort to reform the church. After attending a meeting in a convent chapel in Rome, where Michelangelo was painting, she invited him to join a group of friends to discuss art and poetry. From then on, she inspired him with her sonnets, her godly lifestyle, and the notes of encouragement she wrote to him. She complimented the artist on his talent and challenged him to accept the divine calling on his life that she perceived. Michelangelo valued Vittoria's advice and counted on her to keep him on the right path so he would remain sensitive to the inspiration of the Holy Spirit while painting. He wrote eight sonnets and three madrigals to Vittoria and credited her for his salvation.

MY RESPONSE: Whom might I encourage with an uplifting note?

Laurette Levesque Connelly, 1928–

Our mouths were filled with laughter. . . . Then it was said among the nations, "The Lord has done great things for them."
Psalm 126:2

HER SERVICE: Writing and speaking

HER MESSAGE: When life takes you on an unexpected route, accept the detour and wave.

HER STORY: Laurette Connelly dishes out biblical teaching with doses of humor through her speaking and writing ministries. She has written two books and coauthored a third.

Laurette encountered her first life detour during the Great Depression when, at age fifteen, she had to work in a textile mill to help support younger siblings. Another detour came when she was twenty-two and journeyed to Washington, DC, in search of a better life. Laurette married and had six children. When her husband died at age fifty-four, Laurette traveled on, trusting God as her guide.

She remains flexible. Laurette once arrived at a retreat prepared to speak for four sessions only to learn that she was scheduled for five. Another time, while vacationing at a conference center where a speaker had failed to show up, Laurette graciously filled in. She shares life's journey with her friend Veda Boyd through their speaking ministry, Odds and Ends.

Laurette's attitude toward life's detours is demonstrated in the way she handled a wrong turn in Hershey, Pennsylvania. Laurette unexpectedly found herself in the middle of a parade with no way out. What did she do? She opened her sunroof and waved.

MY RESPONSE: What turns in life have broken my stride? How might I better adapt?

Why do you eat and drink with tax collectors and "sinners"?
Luke 5:30

HER SERVICE: Ministry to people in the entertainment industry

HER MESSAGE: Insiders have the power to influence people for Christ in any field.

HER STORY: Karen Covell and her husband, Jim, work as independent Hollywood producers. She uses her platform in a secular industry to share her faith.

The daughter of an actress, Karen grew up in a Chicago suburb. When it came time to choose a career, Karen felt called to work as a missionary—to the entertainment industry. Some criticized her Hollywood involvement, but Karen once received a note of thanks from a well-known playboy after she sent him a Christian book. She took a leave from MSNBC's celebrity-profile show, *Headliners and Legends with Matt Lauer*, to write *The Day I Met God*, a book of salvation testimonies. A lifestyle evangelism class the Covells taught in their home led the couple to coauthor *How to Talk about Jesus without Freaking Out*.

Karen lives by Christian principles and apologizes when she fails. She has seen women turn to Christ as a result of her testimony, and the Covells' prayer group attracts up to eighty people to pray for the entertainment industry. Karen sees Hollywood as the world's most influential mission field and encourages people to pray for entertainers. She uses film clips, music, and great Hollywood stories as a powerful ministry tool.

MY RESPONSE: In what arena might I offer an insider's testimony for Christ?

Water will gush forth in the wilderness and streams in the desert.
Isaiah 35:6

HER SERVICE: Mission work and writing

HER MESSAGE: As words that have inspired us flow from our hearts, others are refreshed.

HER STORY: Among devotional books, Lettie Burd Cowman's *Streams in the Desert* ranks as the all-time bestseller. She and her husband, Charles, founded the Oriental Missionary Society, now OMS International, an organization she served for almost sixty years.

In 1900 Charles Cowman was the first person ordained in the Pilgrim Holiness Church. The next year, he and Lettie journeyed to Japan as missionaries. Along with three fellow missionaries, the Cowmans pioneered Bible training centers. Through their efforts and a large team of Christian nationals, Bibles were placed in more than ten million Japanese homes.

In 1918 Charles suffered a stroke, and the couple returned to Southern California. During his illness, which led to his death in 1924, Lettie compiled *Streams in the Desert* using sermons, writings, and poems that had ministered to her. The book has sold more than six million copies and has been published in at least four foreign-language editions. Humbly published under the name Mrs. Charles E. Cowman, *Streams* and a companion book, *Springs in the Valley,* have had such an impact on readers that they are listed in *100 Christian Books That Changed the Century.* By simply passing along words that had encouraged her, Lettie Cowman has refreshed millions of souls.

MY RESPONSE: Whose soul might I refresh by sharing something that has inspired me?

Women who claim to be devoted to God should make themselves attractive by the good things they do.
1 Timothy 2:10 NLT

Her Service: Mission work

Her Message: We may feel insignificant, but God can feed a multitude with the crumbs we offer.

Her Story: For thirty-two years Sara Cox served with Campus Crusade for Christ (CCC). She taught at a lay institute, led women's Bible studies, and discipled women one on one.

Sara, who calls herself "a little gal from Georgia," accepted Christ at a Billy Graham crusade. She met and married Bob Cox in 1961. While Bob attended a Bible study led by a couple who had trained with CCC, he felt drawn to lay ministry. Before long the couple settled as field workers for CCC in Austin, Texas. Their first child, Christy, lived only eleven months. Her brief life and death drew Sara closer to God.

Bob's untimely death in 1976 left Sara feeling inadequate for ministry alone and frightened at the thought of raising financial support. But at Bob's memorial service, a man handed her a large check. She accepted the money as a sign that God would support and direct her.

Sara's long and fruitful ministry with single women was curtailed when she was diagnosed with hepatitis C, but she continues to pray for those she influenced who now minister to others. God has touched many lives through one woman who felt she had little to offer but offered what she had.

My Response: How might I share my faith with someone else?

March 17 *Crispina of Thagora,* birth date unknown–304

Others were tortured and refused to be released,
so that they might gain a better resurrection.
Hebrews 11:35

HER SERVICE: Martyrdom

HER MESSAGE: Renouncing Christ is worse than dying for Him.

HER STORY: Crispina of Thagora died as a martyr during the reign of Roman Emperor Diocletian.

We know little of the upbringing or conversion of Crispina other than that she was a highly educated wife and mother from a prominent family in North Africa. Crispina died during a ten-year period of intense persecution of Christians that began on February 23, 303, the day the Romans celebrated the Terminalia festival, when Diocletian boasted he would finally terminate Christianity once and for all. Christians were arrested and tortured. Some were beheaded. Others were drowned, hanged, thrown to wild beasts, or buried alive. They became martyrs, a term based on the Greek word for witnesses.

A judge pressured Crispina to renounce Christ. She refused. The judge called her stubborn and threatened to have her head cut off if she would not sacrifice to the Roman gods. Crispina accepted her sentence and thanked God for freeing her from the hands of her oppressors. She believed that renouncing Christ was worse than dying for Him. As a consequence of her resolute confession of faith, she was beheaded. Her legacy of faith, preserved in the *Acta Martyrum* (Acts of the Martyrs), lives on.

MY RESPONSE: How might I use difficult circumstances in my life to witness for Christ?

I will keep you and will make you . . . to open eyes that are blind . . . and to release from the dungeon those who sit in darkness.
Isaiah 42:6–7

HER SERVICE: Writing hymns

HER MESSAGE: Don't grieve over what you can't do; find something you can do, and do it!

HER STORY: Although Fanny Crosby was blind, she wrote more than eight thousand religious poems that offered spiritual insight. Many were set to music as hymns.

When Fanny was a baby, she was blinded when a man posing as a doctor applied a hot poultice to her eyes in an attempt to cure an eye infection. Fanny later considered the mistake to be God's way of ordaining her life's work. A precocious child who matured into a confident woman, Fanny memorized much of the New Testament. She gave her heart to Christ in 1850. Her husband, Alexander van Alstyne, a blind organist, contributed his expertise to Fanny's hymnology.

In "Saved by Grace" Fanny wrote of the joy of seeing Jesus face to face. It was said that the success of D. L. Moody's evangelistic campaigns might be attributed to Fanny's hymns. She also wrote under 204 pen names. Fanny was paid little for her compositions, but her reward came from hearing testimonies of those who accepted salvation through her words. Rather than focusing on her physical handicap, Fanny focused on God and made a difference for Him.

MY RESPONSE: How might I use a talent or skill to serve God?

When God, who set me apart from birth and called me by his grace, was pleased to reveal his Son in me so that I might preach him among the Gentiles, I did not consult any man.
Galatians 1:15–16

HER SERVICE: Preaching

HER MESSAGE: By responding in faith to a need, a woman may discover and be affirmed in her calling.

HER STORY: An itinerant preacher, Sarah Crosby traveled extensively, sometimes for months at a time, to speak at Methodist meetings. Great revival followed her five-month visit to Canterbury.

At age twenty, Sarah heard a sermon on being justified in Christ and accepted salvation. She married a year later, but her husband ridiculed her faith and eventually left her.

Two women asked for Sarah's help in running a school, and Sarah obliged. Soon after, she reluctantly accepted the responsibility of being a Methodist class leader, wondering if she was fit to lead the small group of believers who met for prayer and encouragement. To her surprise, attendance figures at her meetings climbed to more than two hundred. Again she agonized over whether it was permissible for her, a woman, to speak publicly to so many. In her heart, however, Sarah felt called to preach; and the invitations she soon received from Methodist societies in other towns affirmed her calling. By placing herself at God's disposal to meet the needs of the church, Sarah discovered God's place for her.

MY RESPONSE: How have I discovered and received affirmation of my calling?

I will go to the king, even though it is against the law. And if I perish, I perish.
Esther 4:16

HER SERVICE: Founded Home Interiors & Gifts, Inc.

HER MESSAGE: Be proactive, not reactive.

HER STORY: Mary C. Crowley founded Home Interiors & Gifts, Inc., as a business to honor God and bless people.

Mary was familiar with challenges. Her mother died when she was a baby, and her father and stepmother snatched her from her grandparents when she was seven. A teenage marriage ended in divorce and left her a single mother of two. Through it all Mary displayed a positive attitude. Then, in 1957, she lost a job because she refused to compromise her moral principles.

At first Mary reacted with tears. But then, characteristically, rather than agonizing, Mary organized. She took out loans, secured a charter, and created a company for women—all within ten days. Her company offered women products to enhance the décor of their home along with an opportunity to work from their homes. Mary's can-do philosophy was contagious—and it worked. By the end of the twentieth century, Home Interiors boasted retail sales of more than $675 million. Mary consistently gave God credit for His blessings to her—and shared them with her employees.

MY RESPONSE: In what area of my life do I need to be proactive?

Zacchaeus stood up and said to the Lord, "Look, Lord! Here and now I give half of my possessions to the poor."
Luke 19:8

HER SERVICE: Humanitarian work

HER MESSAGE: What Christ has done for us motivates us to do something for Him.

HER STORY: Dayna Curry witnessed for Christ in Afghanistan, where proselytizing is punished severely. She and coworker Heather Mercer became front-page news when they were imprisoned by the Taliban from August 3 to November 15, 2001.

Growing up in Tennessee, Dayna excelled in school and enjoyed church camp. But her life took a negative turn when her parents divorced. She dropped out of school activities and tried shoplifting. When she was seventeen, Dayna had an abortion. But while attending Baylor University, Dayna confessed her sins at a campus meeting. Gratitude for Christ's forgiveness motivated her to do something for Him. In 1999 she traveled to Afghanistan as a worker for Shelter Now International.

Although forbidden to talk about God, Dayna and Heather witnessed through their lives. They hired Afghanis for household jobs; they fed hungry street kids, hired them to shine shoes, and taught them printing. The women were arrested by the Taliban for telling local people about how Jesus had changed their lives. But after much prayer for them around the world, they were rescued by U.S. Special Forces. After being freed, Dayna and Heather founded Hope Afghanistan to continue assisting the Afghani people.

MY RESPONSE: How am I showing my appreciation for what Christ has done for me?

Lead me, O Lord, in your righteousness because of my enemies—make straight your way before me.
Psalm 5:8

HER SERVICE: Reigning as queen and befriending Reformers

HER MESSAGE: Whether we lead a home or a nation, we can base our decisions on God's best interests, not our own.

HER STORY: Jeanne D'Albret, queen of Navarre (a buffer state between France and Spain), remained true to her Christian convictions even when faced with strong opposition.

Jeanne ruled during a time of religious conflict between Protestants and Catholics. She supported the Reformers and declared Calvinism the religion of Navarre. She held Protestant services in her palace and decreed that churches with a majority of Protestants in attendance should become Protestant. If the two groups were equal, the facility should be used jointly.

Governing with God's best interests at heart rather than her own, Jeanne supported the study of theology with a grant to a college at Orthez. She also opened her palace for teaching theology and supported the spread of the gospel by having her chaplains translate the New Testament into the language of the Basques of Lower Navarre.

Letters to her son, Henry, tell of her incessant prayer on his behalf as he considered a marriage with political ramifications. Although he ignored her plea by marrying a French princess and wavering between Protestantism and Catholicism, as king of France Henry granted the Edict of Nantes, which established religious liberty.

MY RESPONSE: What decisions do I need to pray about?

March 23 *Clarissa Danforth*, ca. 1782–date of death unknown

Jesus said, "Go instead to my brothers and tell them, 'I am returning to my Father and your Father, to my God and your God.'"

John 20:17

HER SERVICE: Preaching

HER MESSAGE: If we are passionate about God, serving God becomes our passion.

HER STORY: In a day when women outside of Quaker circles rarely preached, Clarissa Danforth was recognized for her articulate sermons.

Raised in Vermont, Clarissa was well educated and experienced a life-changing conversion at age seventeen. From then on, the tall, dignified woman spoke at social meetings where women were permitted to express themselves. Her passionate explanations of Scripture were well received, and in 1814 Clarissa preached her first sermon. Soon she was invited to speak from the pulpit in churches across her home state and in neighboring states. For two years she ministered mainly in Rhode Island, where God used her to spark revivals that started new churches. One revival continued for sixteen months.

After returning to her hometown of Weathersfield in 1820, Clarissa led at least one hundred people to Christ. She then married and moved to New York. Even after she had a family, Clarissa preached as much as she could. Her passion for God developed into a passion for preaching.

MY RESPONSE: How can I use my passion for God?

It is God who works in you to will and
to act according to his good purpose.
Philippians 2:13

HER SERVICE: Mission work

HER MESSAGE: The garment of leadership may attract the lint of criticism.

HER STORY: Hannah Frances Davidson (called Frances) spent twenty-five years as a missionary to Africa under the auspices of the Brethren in Christ. She wrote a lengthy account of the denomination's work there.

In 1895 Frances, the first college graduate from her denomination, responded to a call to the mission field and, two years later, arrived in Matopo, Africa. Hannah assisted in services, organized a school system, served as Bible teacher and preacher, and nursed fellow missionaries in a wild and sometimes dangerous environment.

By mid-1903 tension had developed between Frances and a missionary couple assisting her. Frances pressed into the interior with another woman missionary. Later, tension arose between Frances and two men who were sent to assist at a mission station in northern Rhodesia. She resigned, indicating that the men resented a woman's leadership. A bishop sent to smooth things over told Frances she needed to place herself in subjection to the men. She pondered the validity of such advice but felt God had specifically placed her in charge of that ministry because she was an effective leader. The mission board refused her resignation, but later more tensions developed. Still, Frances did not let criticism distract her from the calling she felt God had placed on her life.

MY RESPONSE: How might I better prepare myself to handle criticism?

God is our refuge and strength, an ever-present help in trouble.
Psalm 46:1

HER SERVICE: Mission work

HER MESSAGE: Tragedies may happen—even to good women who serve God.

HER STORY: For twenty-one years, in spite of hardship, Emma Day served as a missionary in Africa alongside her husband.

Emma was born in Philadelphia, and after her mother's death was raised by an aunt. From girlhood she was devoted to God and worshiped in the Methodist Episcopal Church. After marrying the Reverend D. A. Day, Emma transferred to the Evangelical Lutheran Church, and the couple sailed for Africa. Although she was frail, Emma worked hard at Muhlenberg Mission and remained cheerful, a trait she believed contributed to one's well-being.

Soon, under Emma's tutelage, young African girls were wearing dresses they had made for themselves. Emma gave birth to two children in Africa, but both died. Another, born while on furlough, also died in Africa at the age of eight.

When Emma returned home alone in 1894 to recuperate from consumption, which she contracted in Africa, both she and her husband had premonitions that they would never see each other again, which proved true. Concerned about the people of Africa even in her illness, Emma wrote to her husband, urging him to continue the work. Consecrated to reaching the people of Africa for Christ, Emma never wavered from her mission in spite of difficult circumstances, hard work, and personal tragedy.

MY RESPONSE: How do I show my faith in God when I'm faced with difficult circumstances?

Dear brothers and sisters, stand firm and keep a strong grip on everything we taught you both in person and by letter.
2 Thessalonians 2:15 NLT

HER SERVICE: Founded a Catholic order

HER MESSAGE: If we don't show others how to serve God, their lives—and ours—will be diminished.

HER STORY: In order to offer young women, laywomen, and widows an opportunity to serve God, Jane Frances Fremyot de Chantal, along with her mentor, Francis de Sales, founded the Order of Visitation. With the primary purpose of teaching and caring for the sick, the order provided an avenue of service less demanding than the ascetic approach of self-denial demanded by other religious groups.

At age twenty Jane Frances married Baron Christophe de Chantal. Eight years later, her husband died in her arms following a hunting accident. She was left a widow with four young children. Said to be a beautiful woman sensitive to the spiritual life, Jane Frances found consolation in religion and in serving the sick and the needy.

Jane Frances wrote about the importance of dying to self and living for God. Her writings inspired others, including French mystic Jeanne Guyon. The Order of Visitation had established nineteen houses by 1622, and by the time of Jane Frances's death, there were several dozen such facilities. By blessing the lives of others, her followers found meaning and purpose in their own lives.

MY RESPONSE: Whom might I invite to join me in serving God by serving others?

March 27 *Joyce Branderhorst De Haan*, birth date unavailable

If I go up to the heavens, you are there; if
I make my bed in the depths, you are there.
Psalm 139:8

HER SERVICE: Medical mission work

HER MESSAGE: We are never so far from God that He cannot find us—and use us to draw others to Him.

HER STORY: After surviving addiction, Dr. Joyce Branderhorst De Haan contributed to a report on alcoholism and drug abuse for the Christian Reformed Synod and shed much-needed light on an emerging social issue.

Joyce wanted to become a missionary nurse, but a chapel speaker challenged her to become a doctor. She took his advice, and by 1953 she was treating dozens of families daily in Nigeria. Her ministry derailed when a kerosene heater exploded, severely burning her. Doctors gave Joyce alcohol to relieve the itching of her healing wounds, and she became addicted.

When her term ended, Joyce returned to the States. She married, had five children, and practiced medicine part time. But Joyce depended on pills to sleep and to wake up, and she continued to drink alcoholic beverages. Medical emergencies finally led her to seek help through Alcoholics Anonymous. One evening, when Joyce was overcome by guilt as she watched a beautiful sunset, God spoke to her heart, assuring her He had never left her. Joyce became medical director of Gateway Villa, a treatment center in Kalamazoo, Michigan. Her testimony has bolstered the confidence of others seeking to overcome addiction and renew their faith.

MY RESPONSE: Who might be encouraged by hearing of a victory I've gained in Christ?

The earth is the Lord's, and everything in it, the world, and all who live in it.
Psalm 24:1

HER SERVICE: Writing and teaching

HER MESSAGE: We are stewards of God's earth.

HER STORY: Joanne DeJonge has written more than one thousand articles, many for a children's page of the *Banner*, a magazine published by the Christian Reformed Church. She inspires others to be good stewards of God's earth through books based on devotional or natural-history themes.

Because women were not admitted to her denomination's seminary at the time she started college, Joanne chose to major in music and mathematics rather than pursue her dream of becoming a missionary. From 1965 to 1968 Joanne served in the Peace Corps on the island of Borneo, where she discovered God's tiny wonders—spiders and bugs.

When she married Wayne DeJonge, art director for the *Banner*, the couple chose not to have children so they could devote themselves to Christian service and conserve resources by leading a simple lifestyle.

Since her retirement, Joanne continues to write in addition to working as a National Park Service ranger. In both roles Joanne remains fully committed to conservation and stewardship.

MY RESPONSE: What changes might I make to be a better steward of God's earth?

You must be on your guard. You will be . . . flogged in the synagogues. On account of me you will stand before governors and kings as witnesses to them.
Mark 13:9

HER SERVICE: Martyrdom

HER MESSAGE: Women, too, may be called to share in the fellowship of Christ's suffering.

HER STORY: Phillipa de Lunz, a French Huguenot, was just twenty-two years old when tormentors cut out her tongue, strangled her, and burned her body. In spite of her suffering, her faith never wavered.

A beautiful woman, Phillipa was a widow when she was arrested and imprisoned for more than a year because of her interpretation of the Word of God. Even prominent visitors from Rome could not sway her: she refused to accept the church's teaching that the body of Christ was present in the sacraments. Additionally, critics condemned her for not sending for a priest when her husband died and for failing to baptize her child in the church, although the child had been baptized by the Huguenots.

Phillipa wore a bridal dress to her execution as a symbol that she was going to meet her Divine Spouse. On the way to her death, Phillipa spurned a priest's invitation to hear her confession, insisting that she had already received forgiveness for her sins from God. The king reportedly attended Phillipa's execution and witnessed her brave testimony.

MY RESPONSE: How might I strengthen my faith so that I am strong enough to face persecution?

All glory to God, who is able to keep you from stumbling, and who will bring you into his glorious presence innocent of sin and with great joy.
Jude 24 NLT

Her Service: Mission work

Her Message: God offers us security in Christ so we can offer that security to others.

Her Story: In 1983 Jeanne and George DeTellis founded New Missions, an organization in Haiti that now sponsors multiple churches, a medical clinic, a college, a missions-training center, and schools that educate six thousand children. In 1992 Jeanne hosted Haiti's first interdenominational women's meeting.

Because Jeanne knew her mother had wanted a boy, she wrestled with insecurity as a child. She dedicated herself to Christian service at the invitation of a student evangelist. At age eighteen Jeanne married that evangelist, George DeTellis. While George ministered to others, Jeanne's life revolved around her roles of pastor's wife and mother of four. After several miscarriages and stillbirths, Jeanne struggled with loneliness and heartache in spite of a bustling household.

A Women's Aglow mission trip to India revitalized Jeanne's interest in missions. She eventually earned a graduate degree in international development, and trips to Haiti opened the couple's eyes to urgent needs. After twenty-five years of pastoring, the DeTellises moved to Haiti. As God developed Jeanne's leadership skills, she discovered a deep security in Christ that met her emotional needs and motivated her to reach out to the poor and needy.

My Response: How can I overcome my own insecurities to reach out to others?

I will lead the blind by ways they have not known . . . ;
I will turn the darkness into light before them.
Isaiah 42:16

HER SERVICE: Ophthalmology

HER MESSAGE: God needs women to shine the light of the gospel on ethnic minorities.

HER STORY: Dr. Debra Dixon Deur served as medical director of the Lampstand, a free eye clinic in Arlington, Texas, where underprivileged patients are treated in the name of Christ.

Debra Dixon grew up attending church with her grandmother, but during college Debra pushed God away. The activism of the 1960s motivated her to take up nursing as a way of ministering to society.

As she contemplated becoming a doctor, Debra struck a bargain: if God would get her into medical school, she would serve Him. Debra entered medical school and was led to a deeper spirituality through involvement in a Campus Crusade ministry. She married Dr. Charles Deur in 1973 and opened an ophthalmology practice in Arlington, Texas. She prayed with patients before surgery if they wished and served on the board of The Luke Society, a nonprofit organization of Christian doctors dedicated to ministering to the needy. After giving birth to two children, Debra worked part time, wrote, and invested most of her time at the Lampstand. Eleven years after she opened her practice, she gave it up so she could devote herself to serving those of many ethnic backgrounds who visited the clinic.

MY RESPONSE: How might I minister to ethnic minorities in my community?

April

Lillian Dickson, 1901–1983

If you have faith as small as a mustard seed, you can say to this mountain, "Move from here to there" and it will move. Nothing will be impossible for you.
Matthew 17:20

HER SERVICE: Mission work

HER MESSAGE: God reserves power for those who unreservedly give themselves to Him.

HER STORY: Because of her unstoppable ministry, Lillian became known as "Typhoon Lil." She set up orphanages and leprosariums, carried food and medicine to mountain villages, and finally set up Mustard Seed, Inc., to oversee the work.

Straight from their honeymoon in the South Pacific, Lillian LeVesconte Dickson and her new husband, Jim, settled into a mission house in northern Formosa (now Taiwan), a Japanese island colony. Jim served as a school principal, then later headed a theological college. He held evangelistic meetings in the mountains and conferences on the island. Lillian supported his work by feeding as many as sixty people three times a day. She jokingly called herself the innkeeper's wife.

The Dicksons left the island when hostility with Japan escalated during World War II. Their Canadian mission board then sent them to British Guiana for five years. After returning to Taiwan, by then a province of the Republic of China, Lillian took an even greater hand in ministry through fund-raising as well as medical, charitable, and educational endeavors throughout Taiwan. Lillian admitted to doubters that while she could not meet every need, God certainly could.

MY RESPONSE: What might I do this week by relying on God's power instead of my own?

Woe to me if I do not preach the gospel!
1 Corinthians 9:16

HER SERVICE: Preaching

HER MESSAGE: The obedient heart of a gifted servant offers the most pleasing service to God.

HER STORY: The first woman radio preacher in the United States, Lou Agnes Diffee preached an hour on weekdays and four hours on Sundays. During the twenty years she served as pastor of Little Rock First Church of the Nazarene, membership grew from 297 to 1,163. Twenty-six men and women entered ministry under her leadership.

Agnes was born in Arkansas, where her family rarely attended church. She joined a Holiness church on her own and accepted Christ when she was fourteen. Two years later she preached at an Oklahoma revival, making her the country's youngest evangelist. But Agnes didn't want to be called a woman preacher. After college she taught school, preaching only occasionally. Then she developed such severe arthritis that she was confined to bed for forty days. Agnes promised God that if He would heal her, she would obey His calling to use her gift of preaching. God did His part, and Agnes kept her word.

Agnes became a bold and confident minister and a strong advocate of women's right and duty to preach. She was a strong example of church leadership, especially for women. She once said, "I urge young women to keep an ear turned to Heaven for the call of God to preach the gospel."

MY RESPONSE: How am I using my spiritual gifts in obedience to God?

Elizabeth Dirks, birth date unknown–1549

This is my defense to those who sit in judgment on me.
1 Corinthians 9:3

HER SERVICE: Martyrdom

HER MESSAGE: Scripture transforms, refreshes, and fortifies those who hide it in their hearts.

HER STORY: Elizabeth Dirks of the Netherlands was drowned in a sack for not informing on her fellow believers.

Raised in a convent from age twelve, Elizabeth took the vows of a nun. But as she read a Latin New Testament, she became convinced that monasticism was not biblical. She was imprisoned at the convent for a year but escaped, disguised as a milkmaid. Elizabeth joined the Anabaptists, who were considered heretics by many Catholics and Protestants. Anabaptists discounted infant baptism as a means of salvation and practiced adult baptism. The 1529 Diet of Speyer decreed death for Anabaptists.

Elizabeth was arrested by Catholic authorities on January 15, 1549. At her inquisition examiners tried to get Elizabeth to give up the names of those who had baptized her and those she had taught, but Elizabeth refused. Then they questioned her doctrine. Elizabeth insisted that she believed only the Word of God and quoted Scripture to answer their accusations. Screws were pressed upon her fingers until blood oozed from her fingernails. She fainted as iron screws were applied to her ankles, but then revived and held fast to her faith, strengthened by the scriptures she had memorized. To the end, Elizabeth held firm to the truth she'd found in God's Word.

MY RESPONSE: What scripture might I memorize that would offer a response to those who question my faith?

You received the Spirit of sonship. And by him we cry, "Abba, Father."
Romans 8:15

HER SERVICE: Speaking, writing, and praying

HER MESSAGE: If we neglect prayer, we neglect the most powerful tool for effective ministry.

HER STORY: Since 1991 Shirley Dobson has served as chairwoman of the National Day of Prayer Task Force, a movement that now includes more than forty thousand prayer events.

For many years Shirley had low self-esteem because she grew up in poverty, the daughter of an alcoholic father. Her mother, however, sent her to Sunday school, and Shirley embraced her heavenly Father. After her parents divorced, she prayed for a Christian stepfather and later for a Christian husband. Both prayers were answered, and Shirley became a lifelong advocate of prayer.

One day her husband, James Dobson, who has become a well-known psychologist and author, asked Shirley to tell his adult Sunday-school class how God had worked in her life so that others who had experienced traumatic childhoods might be encouraged. Shirley, who had hidden her wounds deep in her heart, balked—but she did agree to pray about it. As a result of that prayer, Shirley took a tentative step down the road to a public speaking ministry and has never looked back.

The Dobsons spearhead family and prayer ministries from Focus on the Family headquarters in Colorado. Shirley has authored and coauthored several books, including *My Family's Prayer Calendar: 365 Activities and Ideas to Help Families Pray Together.*

MY RESPONSE: How might I make prayer a more consistent part of my life?

Come with me by yourselves to a quiet place and get some rest.
Mark 6:31

HER SERVICE: Founding a ministry, writing, teaching, and psychology

HER MESSAGE: Those who care for others need others to care for them.

HER STORY: In 1992 Dr. Lois Dodds, a psychologist, and her husband, Larry, a physician, founded Heartstream Resources, Inc., a Central Pennsylvania ministry to cross-cultural workers wounded or depleted in Christian and humanitarian service.

Lois felt called to missions at age eleven. In 1970 the Dodds and their three children went to the Peruvian jungle as missionaries with Wycliffe Bible Translators and the Summer Institute of Linguistics. Larry treated 250 missionary families and locals while Lois counseled and edited. By the time they returned to their native California thirteen years later, Larry was suffering from burnout. He had fallen prey to faulty ways of thinking that left him feeling he could never do enough for others.

The couple later traveled the world as adjunct college professors, and they met many other missionaries with similar feelings. On donated land, the Dodds opened Heartstream with the goal of restoring missionaries who felt burned out. In a four-home hillside facility overlooking a peaceful river, the Dodds offer hospitality to twelve guests at a time for two-week intensive-care programs of counseling, instruction, and rest. The Dodds also train church missions committees so they better understand that those who care for others need others to care for them.

MY RESPONSE: How might I demonstrate care for a pastor or missionary today?

Follow justice and justice alone, so that you may live and possess the land the Lord your God is giving you.
Deuteronomy 16:20

HER SERVICE: Politics and public service

HER MESSAGE: Courage to stand for liberty and justice begins with faith in the God who stands for liberty and justice for all.

HER STORY: In 2003 Elizabeth Dole took the oath of office as a Republican senator from North Carolina. The only woman to hold cabinet posts under two presidents, Elizabeth also served as president of the American Red Cross for nine years.

Elizabeth learned humanitarian concerns from her parents, who taught her Christian virtues. The wife of former U.S. Senator Bob Dole, Elizabeth admits that at one time her political career crowded out spiritual matters; but she soon recognized her responsibility to bow to God's calling and God's will for her life.

Elizabeth views public service as a way to give back to a nation that has blessed her. She encourages young people to find their passion as she has found hers as a servant of the people and a strong supporter of liberty and justice for all. She publicly speaks of her faith in Christ. Fortified by her own morning devotional time, Elizabeth confidently faces the high-powered world of Washington, DC.

MY RESPONSE: How might I support a legacy of liberty and justice in my community?

April 7 *Sarah Platt Haines Doremus,* 1802–1877

Show me your faith without deeds, and I will show you my faith by what I do.
James 2:18

HER SERVICE: Advocating missions and volunteering

HER MESSAGE: Missionaries go, but those who stay can support them in many ways.

HER STORY: Sarah Doremus diligently supported missionaries. She served as the first president of the interdenominational Women's Union Missionary Society of America and hosted the headquarters in her home.

As a child Sarah had listened to her mother and others pray at women's gatherings for the salvation of people around the world. As an adult Sarah played a role in answering such prayers. She belonged to the Reformed Dutch Church, but she ministered to missionaries throughout the body of Christ. A New Yorker, Sarah married wealthy merchant Thomas Doremus, who supported her charitable activities.

Although she kept busy with nine children of her own plus others who were adopted, Sarah gathered women to sew clothes for missionaries and took gifts and food to those departing for and returning from foreign fields.

An administrator, fund-raiser, and hard worker, Sarah developed a Women's Prison Association and served as manager of a Bible tract society. She helped establish a school of industry, a children's hospital, a Presbyterian home for the aged, and the first women's hospital in the world. The Doremus Home in Calcutta bears tribute to an indefatigable woman who never served on the mission field herself but strongly supported those who did.

MY RESPONSE: How can I support missionaries in a tangible way?

Whatever is true, whatever is noble, whatever is right, . . . think about such things.
Philippians 4:8

HER SERVICE: Speaking and advocating for excellence in media

HER MESSAGE: By recognizing those who stand for what is right and good, we pave the way to a better future.

HER STORY: Mary Dorr worked hard to make the media more hospitable to inspirational programs promoting faith and values. She served as president of National American Women in Radio and Television.

A widow with five children in 1969, Mary taught media workshops and established a nationwide reputation as a speaker. In 1974 she became executive director of Religion in Media, a watchdog organization. Her responsibilities included offering daily devotionals on network stations.

At a party recognizing her as California's Mother of the Year in 1977, Mary heard a Hollywood producer claim that television success came by breaking five of the Ten Commandments every fifteen minutes. That comment sparked in Mary a vision for making a difference. That year, through Religion in Media, she started the Angel Awards to honor shows that make a positive impact on society by promoting what is right and good. In 1988 the organization's name was changed to Excellence in Media, and the Angel Awards program was expanded. It now offers scholarships to students who profess faith in God and their country.

By shining a spotlight on good programming that supports Christian principles, the awards help to build a better future for television viewers.

MY RESPONSE: Whom might I affirm with a note of recognition for good work?

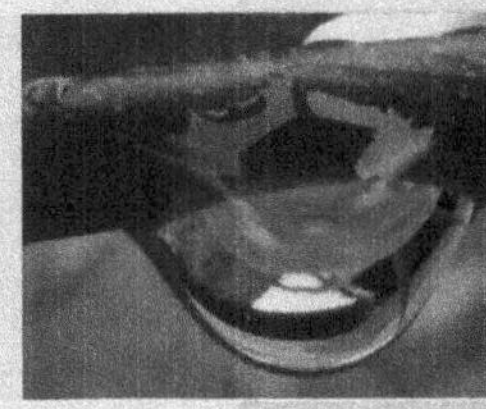

I press on toward the goal to win the prize for which God has called me.
Philippians 3:14

HER SERVICE: Athletics and advocating for the disabled

HER MESSAGE: Don't think about what you can't do; think about what God can do through you—and let Him do it.

HER STORY: Winner of two Olympic silver medals, twelve Paralympic medals, and more than one hundred national and international wheelchair races, Jean Driscoll was named 1991 Sportswoman of the Year by the Women's Sports Foundation. Jean won the wheelchair division of the Boston Marathon for the eighth time in 2000.

Jean was born with spina bifida. At fifteen she learned she would be confined to a wheelchair. Bitter at first, Jean found peace and a purpose for living as she attended church. She now views disabilities as just another physical characteristic, such as hair color, and sees limitations as opportunities for God to work through us.

After earning a master's degree in rehabilitation administration, Jean encouraged physical and spiritual growth in those to whom she ministered at Jean Driscoll Sports and Training Camps and through Joni and Friends' Wheels for the World. Her motto, "Dream big and work hard," inspires both athletes and nonathletes.

Now retired in Champaign, Illinois, Jean gives motivational speeches and promotes sports leagues for students with disabilities. Ranked number twenty-five on *Sports Illustrated*'s "Top 100 Female Athletes of the 20th Century," Jean tells about God's work through her in her book *Determined to Win.*

MY RESPONSE: What might I accomplish with a little determination?

Help these women who have contended at my side in the cause of the gospel.
Philippians 4:3

HER SERVICE: Trained women for missions and evangelism

HER MESSAGE: Women are vital to the work of the church.

HER STORY: Emeline "Emma" Dryer trained women for Christian service under the ministry of famed evangelist Dwight L. Moody.

Born in Massachusetts but orphaned in childhood, Emma went to live with an aunt in New York, where she took advantage of educational opportunities. Eventually she joined the faculty of Illinois State Normal University. After recovering from typhoid fever, Emma committed her life to Christian service.

In 1870, trusting God, Emma took a position in Chicago that offered no pay. There she met Moody, who recognized her deep faith, intelligence, and skill as a Bible teacher. At his invitation Emma led Bible studies at Moody Church and then opened and administered a school to train women as evangelists and Christian workers. In 1883 she began holding May Institutes, weekly meetings that included prayer and open discussions during which Emma urged women to participate in their children's education and to do community work as examples to their children. As Emma prepared women for vital work in the church, she also persuaded Moody to establish the Chicago Evangelization Society, which trained both men and women and eventually became Moody Bible Institute.

MY RESPONSE: How am I fulfilling my role in the church?

Susan Dyck, 1922–1998

We continually remember before our God and Father your work produced by faith.
1 Thessalonians 1:3

HER SERVICE: Mission work

HER MESSAGE: No matter how high people climb on the corporate ladder, they can't reach heaven without Christ.

HER STORY: Especially successful at leading businesspeople and their spouses to Christ, Susan Dyck served as a missionary to Japan from 1953 to 1985.

A Canadian, Susan taught an English class for high-school and adult students during her first term in Japan. She once invited adult students and their spouses to her home for dinner and laughed as they struggled with simple American customs, such as passing food. When one guest, the wife of a Buddhist engineer who attended Susan's class, returned home, she told her husband that she wanted to become a Christian so she could learn to laugh like Susan did. The woman accepted Christ, and she and Susan reached out to many other wives of her husband's employees.

While some might feel intimidated about approaching people of high financial or social standing, Susan found such people open to the gospel. She once led a woman to the Lord, and her husband, a superintendent of education and member of city council, came to church with her. Susan visited their home and led him to the Lord as well. She later learned he had been practicing witchcraft when she arrived.

MY RESPONSE: How might I witness to the people in my workplace?

Why do you judge your brother? Or why do you look down on your brother? For we will all stand before God's judgment seat.
Romans 14:10

HER SERVICE: Martyrdom and advocating for religious tolerance

HER MESSAGE: Intolerance cannot be tolerated.

HER STORY: Mary Dyer was hanged in Boston Common on June 1, 1660. She had been banished from Massachusetts Bay Colony twice previously but felt compelled to return to preach Quaker doctrine—even though she knew it would mean death.

Mary and William Dyer came to America from London in 1635 and joined Boston's First Church. Mary was reputed to have been an intelligent, attractive woman of means. She bore six children, but one child was stillborn and badly deformed. Some at the time interpreted such events as evidence of God's displeasure and judgment.

In 1652 the Dyers traveled to England on official business, and Mary converted to Quaker doctrine. By the time she returned to America four years later, persecution of the Quakers had commenced. On one occasion only her husband's plea (and friendship with the governor) spared Mary from the gallows, but she refused to accept a full reprieve on the condition that she would not preach. Determined to preach and to promote religious tolerance for Quakers, Mary kept returning to Massachusetts, though with each visit she risked death. Even as she was hanged, Mary refused to repent of her actions, stating she spoke out in obedience to God.

MY RESPONSE: In what ways am I intolerant of other Christians?

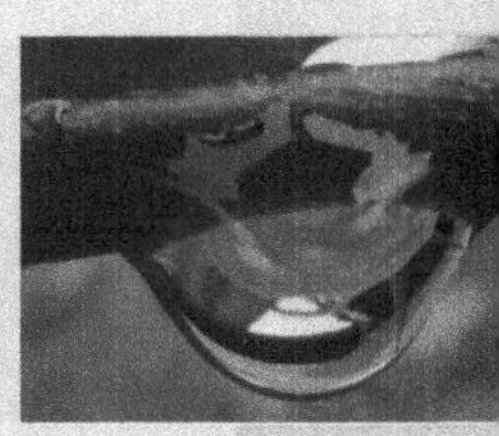

God, who has called you into fellowship with his Son Jesus Christ our Lord, is faithful.
1 Corinthians 1:9

HER SERVICE: Writing, speaking, and being a pastor's wife

HER MESSAGE: Invest time in developing a ministry, and it will stand the test of time.

HER STORY: Kristy Dykes has written six hundred articles and five works of Christian fiction. She was named the American Christian Writers' 1995 Writer of the Year and received the organization's 1999 Persistence Award.

While still in her twenties, Kristy felt God calling her to write. Armed only with library books, she taught herself to write. Eventually she earned a degree in mass communications and journalism. Her husband, Milton, felt the same call and assured her that God would someday use both of them in writing. Kristy honed her skill as a newspaper columnist, and her first nonfiction article was accepted for publication. But fiction was a tougher sell. Kristy persisted for seven years before successfully breaking into the Christian romance genre.

Kristy encourages new writers to take classes, join critique groups, send out articles, and view rejection as part of the process of becoming a writer. The novella collection *Sweet Liberty* includes Kristy's historical novella "Free Indeed" and reached thirteen on the top-twenty list at christianbook.com. Besides writing, Kristy supports her husband as pastor of Southside Assembly of God in Jacksonville, Florida. They have cowritten articles on marriage.

MY RESPONSE: In what area of ministry have I grown impatient for results?

If you suffer for doing good and you endure it,
this is commendable before God.
1 Peter 2:20

HER SERVICE: Being a pastor's wife

HER MESSAGE: We worship and serve an audience of One.

HER STORY: Sarah Pierpont Edwards, wife of theologian Jonathan Edwards, encouraged women's meetings in private homes, something just becoming acceptable in that day. The parishioners of the Congregational church her husband served in Massachusetts often criticized her conduct as a pastor's wife.

Jonathan and Sarah married when she was an attractive, well-mannered seventeen-year-old and he was shy and unpolished in social skills at twenty-four. Pastors' wives were required to sit facing congregations, so Sarah's reaction to sermons became Sunday dinner topics for parishioners. Her emotional reaction to one sermon when her husband was away caused consternation.

Even the days on which she bore children were gossip fodder. Six of the couple's eleven children were born, and thus were thought to have been conceived, on a Sunday—a day deemed inappropriate for sexual activity. When Sarah was asked by a town committee to itemize expenses, her critics noted that she wore an expensive brooch and dressed stylishly. They failed to note that she had the talent to duplicate dresses she saw in shops and remake old clothes for herself and her daughters.

But Sarah considered herself accountable to God alone. For the most part, she ignored community opinion and counted on her husband's trust and God's grace to see her through.

MY RESPONSE: How does my conduct please or displease God?

In perfect faithfulness you have done marvelous things.
Isaiah 25:1

HER SERVICE: Mission work

HER MESSAGE: God's servants may rest assured that results will come in God's time.

HER STORY: Gertrude Egede and her husband, Hans, were the first missionaries to Greenland after the Christian church, founded there as early as the tenth century, had died out. The Egedes labored for fifteen years—without seeing results.

Hans, a Norwegian pastor from Denmark, Gertrude, their four children, and several others arrived in Greenland in 1721. The locals rebuffed the Egedes' attempts at friendship and tried to kill the missionaries with magic. Sick and starving, Hans wanted to go home, but Gertrude insisted they persevere. Three weeks later a ship brought lifesaving supplies.

Gertrude suggested that Hans and their two sons move into Greenlander huts, beehivelike structures that housed multiple families and dogs. The huts had no ventilation and were heated with seal oil, a malodorous combination. In the summers Gertrude ran the colony while Hans hunted and fished with the Eskimos. In 1726, with starvation threatening the missionaries again, the Eskimos finally agreed to trade.

Gertrude died during a smallpox epidemic, and Hans later returned home in poor health. They never reaped the fruits of their labors. But the seeds were planted. Their son Paul, who had mastered the Eskimo language as a child, became an effective preacher and Bible translator. Many people were baptized in the religious revival that followed the Egedes' ministry.

MY RESPONSE: Am I faithful in Christian service even when I can't see results?

Remember the Lord your God, for it is he who gives you the ability to produce wealth.
Deuteronomy 8:18

HER SERVICE: Charitable work

HER MESSAGE: Possessions offer opportunities to bless others and God.

HER STORY: Elizabeth of Hungary built a house for lepers, fed nine hundred people at her palace gate during a famine, and nursed those with the worst diseases. Before her death at age twenty-four, possibly caused by exhaustion, she founded a chapel and took the vows of the Third Order of St. Francis.

Elizabeth was born in a castle and, at age fourteen, married Louis IV, Prince of the German state of Thuringia. During a famine in 1226, Elizabeth provided flour and urged bakers to bake bread around the clock. She also provided soup from her kitchen for monks and nuns to distribute. Her husband fully supported her generosity, which sustained many.

The following year Louis joined a Crusade and left his kingdom in the care of his brother. Louis died of a fever later that year, about the same time Elizabeth gave birth to their fourth child. Some people complained that Elizabeth had mishandled the kingdom's resources, and her unscrupulous brother-in-law put her out of her home. Eventually monies from her dowry were restored, and her son's succession rights were recognized.

At one point Elizabeth sold her jewels to raise funds for the needy. Throughout her brief life, she generously used her possessions to bless others and God.

MY RESPONSE: How might I use my resources to bless others and God?

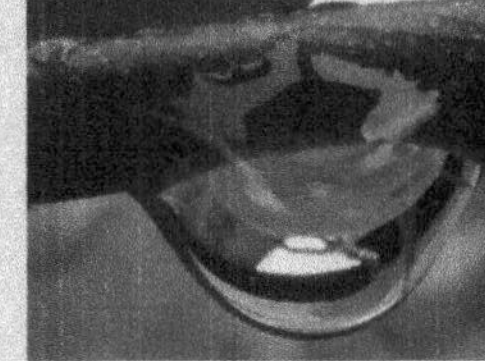

"I am the Lord's servant," Mary answered.
"May it be to me as you have said."
Luke 1:38

HER SERVICE: Mission work, writing, and radio ministry

HER MESSAGE: Life's blows knock us down, but God's grace picks us up.

HER STORY: Elisabeth Elliot has written at least five books, including *Through Gates of Splendor*, which tells of the death of her husband, Jim Elliot, at the hands of the Auca Indians. For many years she hosted *Gateway to Joy*, a daily radio broadcast.

Elisabeth was born in Belgium, where her parents served as missionaries. She met Jim at Wheaton College, where they both answered God's call to missionary service. They postponed marriage, however, until they were sure of God's plan for their lives. The couple was serving in Ecuador when Jim and four other American missionaries were slain in 1956.

Relying on God's grace to face the violent tribe that had killed her husband, Elisabeth and her daughter Valerie, just ten months old when her father died, returned to Ecuador to minister to the Aucas in 1958. After serving a total of eleven years as a missionary, Elisabeth returned to the States and married Addison Leitch, who died of cancer in 1973. She now lives in Massachusetts with her third husband, Lars Gren, who works with Elisabeth in her ministry. Through a long and fruitful career at home and abroad, Elisabeth has accepted her losses and steadfastly served God in many ways.

MY RESPONSE: For what past experience do I need God's present grace so that I might fulfill a future ministry?

Surely I spoke of things I did not understand,
things too wonderful for me to know.
Job 42:3

HER SERVICE: Mission work

HER MESSAGE: Don't complain about conditions permitted by a sovereign God.

HER STORY: Mary Ellis served as a missionary to the South Seas Islands for nine years.

An orphan raised by a godly guardian, Mary Mercy Moor kept the Bible under her pillow. After a serious illness, she consecrated her life to Christian service. In 1815 she married William Ellis, who was approved by the London Missionary Society. The couple's voyage to the South Sea Islands, made difficult by a surly captain and a boatload of convicts, might have been a harbinger of future challenges.

William set up a printing press to produce literature, and Mary taught the women bookbinding. Their son's frail health necessitated frequent trips across the island for medical help, and once he and Mary would have drowned had not islanders rescued them from a capsized canoe.

As William ministered throughout the region—one trip stretched to eight months—Mary cared for their four children. In time a spinal condition confined her to a couch. But whenever she had enough strength, she taught the women who came to hear her. Through it all, Mary refused to complain about conditions permitted by a sovereign God.

MY RESPONSE: In what circumstances do I need to be more accepting of God's sovereignty?

I have not come to call the righteous, but sinners.
Matthew 9:13

HER SERVICE: Acting, writing, speaking, evangelism, and social activism

HER MESSAGE: Ministering to people is more important than entertaining them.

HER STORY: Dubbed 1949's most promising starlet, Colleen Townsend Evans left behind a promising Hollywood career for a life of Christian ministry and public service. She has authored nine books, including a book on prayer.

Colleen Townsend began acting at the age of eighteen and was on her way to the top. She accepted Christ and joined the Hollywood Christian Group, dedicated to bringing well-known Christian speakers to the film community—an industry many Christians avoided. Not Colleen. She knew her colleagues needed a savior. In 1950 Colleen left Hollywood to speak at churches and Youth for Christ evangelistic crusades.

The Hollywood starlet married Louis Evans Jr. while he was in seminary. The Bel Air Presbyterian Church grew out of meetings the couple held in their Los Angeles home. Many Hollywood personalities who visited accepted Christ, and the Evanses rejoiced in the role they played in building God's kingdom.

Colleen has worked to advance human rights, racial reconciliation, and women's ministry. She has been a consultant to the White House on human rights and served on the boards of several prominent ministries. During the years Louis served at a Washington, DC, church, Colleen moved her four children to the inner city to build relationships with African Americans and introduce them to Christ.

MY RESPONSE: How might I introduce non-Christians to Christ?

You ought to say, "If it is the Lord's will, we will live and do this or that."

James 4:15

HER SERVICE: Preaching and developing ministry programs

HER MESSAGE: God grants seasons of ministry according to our seasons of life.

HER STORY: Neva VanderZee Evenhouse developed Coffee Break, an evangelistic Bible-study program designed to reach women in the community.

Neva's family moved from New York to Grand Rapids, Michigan, so she could attend a Christian high school. She married Robert Evenhouse the same year she graduated from nurses' training, and they settled in Chicago. The oldest of their four sons lived only six years. Once the other boys reached school age, Neva developed Coffee Break, the small-group ministry, for the Christian Reformed Church. She later partnered with a pastor to form a corporation, Discover Your Bible, which published Bible study materials.

In 1976 the Evenhouses returned to Grand Rapids. As Neva led workshops on her Bible study ministry, she yearned for broader outreach. Since her denomination did not ordain women, Neva enrolled in a Reformed Church of America seminary and was ordained at age fifty-one. She worked at a counseling center, as a minister of small groups, and as a solo pastor at a New York church before retiring in Grand Rapids. In each season of life, Neva found fulfillment by following the path God had laid out for her.

MY RESPONSE: What ministry might be tailor-made for my current season of life?

April 21 *Dorothy Millicent Knowles Fairley*, ca. 1908–1982

I know whom I have believed, and am convinced that he is able to guard what I have entrusted to him.
2 Timothy 1:12

HER SERVICE: Mission work

HER MESSAGE: The lives and ministries of Christian servants depend on prayer.

HER STORY: Dorothy Fairley and her husband, Don, spent more than forty years in missionary service, twenty of them in Gabon. She has also written a book, *In God's Plan, His Provision*.

In 1924, while on an outing on Oregon's Willamette River, Don Fairley rescued Dorothy Knowles from drowning. They began dating, but Don broke off the relationship to ponder God's direction for his life. While apart, Dorothy committed her life to missions. The couple reunited and eloped in 1926. After completing Bible school, they were appointed to serve in the French Congo by the Christian and Missionary Alliance.

Beginning in 1930 the Fairleys cleared land, built a home near Bongolo Falls, and worked to befriend tribesmen and roaming Pygmies. Wild pigs ruined their gardens, and leopards stalked their complex, but the Fairleys prayed for protection and help and persevered. Dorothy cooked over an open fire, entertained visitors, and translated the Scriptures. She played a portable organ for services, taught classes, and typed letters. When facing sickness and confrontations with tribesmen riled by the burning of fetishes, Dorothy prayed and trusted God. By the time the Fairleys left Bongolo, the church they had started seated one thousand worshipers, and Christianity had spread throughout the country.

MY RESPONSE: What missionary might I support with prayer?

He who finds a wife finds what is good
and receives favor from the Lord.
Proverbs 18:22

HER SERVICE: Being a pastor's wife

HER MESSAGE: A godly woman's influence spills over to her family and splashes out upon the family of God.

HER STORY: Macel Falwell, wife of well-known preacher Dr. Jerry Falwell, has supported her husband's pastoral ministry and his many radio, television, and public speaking ventures throughout their married life.

Macel Pate was playing the piano at a church in Lynchburg, Virginia, when she saw Jerry Falwell respond to an altar call in 1952. At the time Macel was engaged—to the man who would be Jerry's roommate in Bible college later that year. Before long, circumstances changed. Macel and Jerry fell in love and married in 1958.

As their three children grew, Macel spent time alone with each of them daily. She painted and played the piano with her daughter. She attended her sons' sporting events. She shared her faith during private devotions with each child and during the family's daily devotions. Although Macel shies away from the media spotlight, she articulately expresses opinions to her friends and acquaintances, especially on marriage and the family. She counsels women in her church and often accompanies Jerry during visitations. Recognizing his wife's great contribution, Jerry has said, "I would not be where I am today and doing what I am doing without Macel."

MY RESPONSE: In what ways am I a godly example to my family and my church?

"The Lord has done this for me," she said. "In these days he has shown his favor and taken away my disgrace among the people."
Luke 1:25

HER SERVICE: Teaching and mission work

HER MESSAGE: Pacesetting requires risk taking.

HER STORY: The first unmarried woman sent out as an "assistant" missionary by any American agency, Cynthia Farrar served for thirty-four years at the Marathi Mission of Bombay, India.

Cynthia was teaching school in Boston when the secretary of the American Board of Commissioners for Foreign Missions came looking for a mature Christian teacher with administrative skills. She fit the description and accepted his invitation. Though missionary wives had done a good job of teaching at Marathi Mission, an expansion called for the undivided attention of a single educator/administrator.

At that time Hindu men opposed educating girls and looked for any excuse to withdraw their daughters. Cynthia changed that. Soon girls from all levels of society eagerly enrolled and learned Christian truths along with their reading. In 1839 Cynthia organized schools in Ahmednagar at the request of locals and went on to run other mission schools after that one was closed.

Sponsors had feared Cynthia might fail and invite negative public reaction to single women missionaries. But she eventually won support from such important British residents as the governor. By risking failure to serve abroad as a single missionary, Cynthia paved the way for other single women to follow in her footsteps.

MY RESPONSE: In what way may God be calling me to be a pacesetter?

I was not disobedient to the vision from heaven.
Acts 26:19

HER SERVICE: Mission work

HER MESSAGE: By teaching children, we groom the next generation.

HER STORY: The first single woman sent from America to China by a missionary society, Lydia Mary Fay labored there for twenty-eight years.

Lydia was sent out from Albany, New York, by the Protestant Episcopal Church in 1850. In correspondence to a friend shortly after her arrival in China, Lydia told of the indifference of the idol-worshiping people and wondered how the small voice of the Spirit might touch their hearts.

Not one to dwell on the negative, Lydia opened a boarding school for boys in her Shanghai home so she could groom a new generation of Chinese teachers and preachers. She taught, did the housework, and managed the finances. Lydia also led a class for student teachers and looked after several schools for girls, all the while studying the Chinese language and modeling a deep spirituality for her students.

In time Lydia's boarding school grew into the Doane Hall and Theological School. At a twenty-fifth anniversary celebration, the school was turned over to the Episcopal Board. On that occasion a proclamation signed by the Chinese paid tribute to her literary scholarship. But the best honor for Lydia was the privilege of seeing some of the students she had trained enter Christian ministry.

MY RESPONSE: In what ways am I influencing the next generation for Christ?

We are weak in him, yet by God's power
we will live with him to serve you.
2 Corinthians 13:4

HER SERVICE: Mission work and Bible translation

HER MESSAGE: Our limitations need not define us.

HER STORY: Missionary Julianna Fehr served in Gabon for twenty-nine years. With the help of a native assistant, she translated the New Testament into the Getsogo language. She also developed the Theological Education by Extension program to train Christian leaders.

In Bible college Julianna's attempts to learn Greek were so dismal, she received credit for the class only after she promised the instructor she would never attempt to become a Bible translator. In 1965, under sponsorship of the Christian and Missionary Alliance, Julie was assigned to minister in Gabon.

While getting used to the bugs and biting flies of Guevede, Julianna visited village women and mimicked their words. She didn't let her previous struggle in learning Greek stop her from studying the difficult Getsogo language, and locals soon told her they had never heard a missionary speak their language as she did. Julianna later served at Mimonga, a government center, and in 1993 she became the first woman to attend the Billy Graham Center as a missionary scholar in residence. She died of cancer the following year—after interviewing people around the world to write a paper on how churches might support missions.

MY RESPONSE: What opportunities for ministry might I be missing because of limitations I perceive in myself?

Calling the Twelve to him, he sent them out two by two.
Mark 6:7

HER SERVICE: Mission work and evangelism training

HER MESSAGE: Train women to reach women.

HER STORY: While serving twenty years as a missionary to China, Adele Fielde trained more than five hundred women to reach other women for God. Her method became a model for other mission organizations.

Born in New York and raised as a Universalist, Adele converted to the Baptist faith when she became engaged to a missionary candidate. She traveled to China in 1865 to join him, but when she arrived, she discovered that her fiancé had died months earlier. Adele tried to fill his shoes. But being an outspoken woman, she also complained that her salary was only half that of a single male colleague. In addition, Adele danced and played cards—activities frowned upon by fellow Baptist missionaries. Although Adele tried to placate her critics by giving up socializing, she was dismissed.

On the journey home, however, Adele found herself consumed by a vision to reach women and appealed for reinstatement. Her request was granted. Back in China, Adele taught women a single Bible lesson and then sent them out in pairs to teach that lesson to others. When they returned, she taught them another Bible truth and again sent them out. In time Adele founded a Bible school for women. As other missionaries found her model effective and opened similar schools, such women became an important part of missionary work throughout Asia.

MY RESPONSE: With whom might I share a simple gospel message?

Lord, consider their threats and enable your servants to speak your word with great boldness.
Acts 4:29

HER SERVICE: Preaching and mission work

HER MESSAGE: With God the impossible becomes possible.

HER STORY: In 1657 Quaker missionary Mary Fisher walked alone at least five hundred miles to carry the gospel to the sultan of Turkey.

A servant in Yorkshire, England, Mary was converted and then imprisoned for sixteen months after she spoke of her Quaker faith to her parish priest. When freed, Mary and a friend preached at Sidney Sussex College. Town officials stripped the women to their waists and whipped them until they bled, yet the women continued to praise God. After a second imprisonment, Mary and another Quaker missionary sailed for America by way of Barbados and arrived in Boston in May 1656. But officials there imprisoned the women and burned their books. Someone bribed a jailer to feed them, so the women survived but were sent back on an outgoing ship.

Mary returned to England, but she felt called to take the gospel to the sultan of Turkey. The venture required a dangerous voyage, then a five-hundred-mile trek. Unfazed by the difficult journey ahead of her, Mary walked alone, across mountains and past shepherds, until she reached her destination. No evidence suggests that her evangelistic effort bore fruit, but the sultan respected her efforts, as did other Christians.

MY RESPONSE: To what difficult task has God called me?

God demonstrates his own love for us in this: While we were still sinners, Christ died for us.
Romans 5:8

HER SERVICE: Mission work

HER MESSAGE: Whether they appear godly or godless, people need the Lord.

HER STORY: Fidelia Fiske was the first single American female missionary to Persia, where she ministered for fifteen years.

The Secretary of the American Board for Foreign Missions, Rev. Dr. Anderson, remembered Fidelia, who had taught at Mount Holyoke Seminary in Massachusetts, as one of the most Christlike people he knew. But the girls and women Fidelia met in Persia were, before conversion, a sharp contrast. Fidelia doubted they could ever reflect Christ, but she started a boarding school so the girls could move away from the evil influences prevalent in their homes. She also visited their homes, inviting mothers to come to her room at the school for prayer.

Along with morality, Fidelia taught personal cleanliness. She knew that no matter how downtrodden or different they seemed, these people needed Christ just as those of her homeland did. The people responded to her teaching. Once an armed and arrogant tribal chief brought his daughter to the school and was converted on the spot. Fidelia sometimes awoke to find a girl by her bedside, waiting to pray for conversion. By the time the school had been open nineteen years, twelve revivals were credited to the prayer and fasting of its students and staff, and more than two-thirds of the students professed Christianity.

MY RESPONSE: For whose salvation might I pray and fast?

Even to your old age and gray hairs I am he,
I am he who will sustain you.
Isaiah 46:4

HER SERVICE: Philanthropy and preaching

HER MESSAGE: Even late in our lives, God offers opportunities for fruitful service.

HER STORY: Mary Bosanquet Fletcher began leading Methodist class meetings in England when she was eighteen and continued until her midseventies, a few months before her death.

Mary Bosanquet might have enjoyed the good life, but she turned her back on theatergoing and partying. At eighteen, using money inherited from her grandmother, she and a friend opened an orphanage and school for London's impoverished children. The women also organized a Methodist society.

Mary became an itinerant preacher; but sensitive to criticism against women preachers, she spoke from the steps leading to the pulpit and called her speaking "expounding." In 1781 Mary married a pastor, John Fletcher, who had also established a school for poor children. Together the couple preached and led classes. Their Dublin congregations increased a hundredfold.

John died just four years after their marriage. Mary continued her ministry activities for thirty more years, preaching to groups as large as three thousand and opening the first hospital in Vermont. At age seventy, Mary attended six meetings a week and preached at two of them.

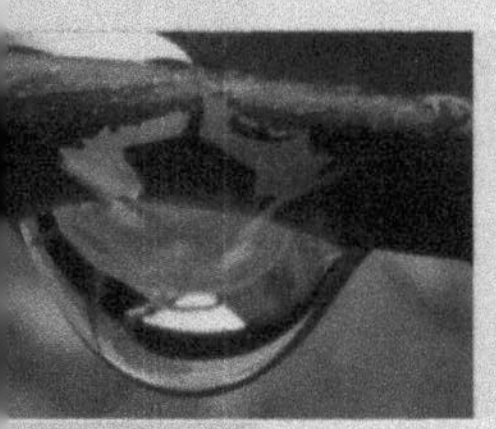

MY RESPONSE: What opportunities for Christian service might I discover during my senior years?

Just as the sufferings of Christ flow over into our lives,
so also through Christ our comfort overflows.
2 Corinthians 1:5

HER SERVICE: Writing poetry

HER MESSAGE: Pain can be a steppingstone to Christian service.

HER STORY: Seventeen of Annie Johnson Flint's poems appear in *The Best-Loved Religious Poems.* Many hymnals contain her poems set to music, such as "He Giveth More Grace."

Annie Johnson Flint's mother died when Annie's sister was born. Her father died when she was six, and a loving Christian couple adopted the girls. As a child Annie wrote poetry that showed a knack for observation. By age nine Annie had discovered her gift for poetry, and by the time she was twelve, she was setting her poems to music. She aspired to become a composer and concert pianist, but she became crippled by arthritis and could no longer play. It took many years for Annie to understand that her poems were not merely compensation for the loss of her music but were God's greatest gift and purpose for her life.

With joints swollen and fingers bent, Annie wrote a poem to a friend. "At the Place of the Sea" likened going through the Red Sea to going through struggles. In time it became her most widely read poem. At last, because of her pain, she wrote only a few lines at a time. But that pain became the vehicle of Annie's lasting ministry to others.

MY RESPONSE: How might I use my weaknesses to minister to others?

May

Margaret Askew Fell Fox, 1614–1702

Go quickly and tell his disciples: "He has risen from the dead."
Matthew 28:7

HER SERVICE: Leading Quakers, advocating for women, and writing

HER MESSAGE: Christ charged women to tell of His resurrection, so women should be free to evangelize.

HER STORY: Margaret Askew Fell Fox supported the fledgling Quaker movement and married its founder, George Fox. She wrote a tract supporting women's and men's equality in ministry, and her influence helped pass bills in London to safeguard religious freedom.

Margaret Askew married Judge Thomas Fell, and they had eight children. When itinerant pastor George Fox visited their home, Margaret and her daughters embraced his Quaker teachings. The Fells allowed Fox and other Quakers to use their home as a meeting place and refuge. After Judge Fell died in 1658, Margaret Fell and George Fox were put on trial for their religious activities. Margaret would be released if she promised not to use her home for Quaker meetings; she refused and was imprisoned for four years and threatened with the confiscation of her property.

Soon after her release she married Fox. Imprisoned two more times, Margaret wrote to the king, pleading for an end to the persecution of Quakers. In response James II issued the Toleration Act of 1689.

MY RESPONSE: With whom might I share the gospel?

In him we were also chosen . . . according to the plan of him who works out everything in conformity with the purpose of his will.
Ephesians 1:11

HER SERVICE: Mission work and perseverance

HER MESSAGE: Make the most of a post assigned by God.

HER STORY: Mabel Francis served as a missionary to Japan for fifty-six years. She received that country's highest civilian honor for her faithful ministry even during World War II.

A New Hampshire native, Mabel became a schoolteacher while still a teenager after being mentored by a young Christian man who then died of an illness. As she grieved, she felt called to evangelize by holding Sunday-afternoon services at her school. Mabel soon was invited to share the gospel in surrounding towns. At nineteen she entered Bible college.

Mabel went to minister in Japan in 1909. When other missionaries returned home because of the Great Depression's effect on missionary support, Mabel simply made the most of the post she considered assigned her by God. As she pedaled a bicycle to save expenses, she sometimes longed for a husband to share in the work, but she became convinced that singleness was God's plan for her. Tensions in Japan increased during the 1930s, and Mabel was placed under house arrest. She was, however, allowed to minister as long as she reported her activities to authorities. Through every circumstance, Mabel Francis persevered through difficult circumstances to share God's love.

MY RESPONSE: How might I make the most of my lot in life?

Lulu E. Frey, 1868–date of death unknown

Each of you should look not only to your own interests, but also to the interests of others.
Philippians 2:4

HER SERVICE: Founded a women's college

HER MESSAGE: Visionaries pull us out of ruts.

HER STORY: Lulu E. Frey went to Korea in 1893 as the youngest missionary sent out by the Woman's Foreign Missionary Society. She served as a principal at Ewha Hak-dang, an elementary school for girls, before building the school into Ewha College in 1910.

Born in Ohio, Lulu devoted her life to missions after reading a magazine article. Her father opposed her decision, however, so she ran a dress shop before attending a university, a training school for missionaries, and finally Moody Bible Institute in Chicago.

Another missionary, Mary F. Scranton, had launched Ewha school in 1886 at a time when Korean women received no formal education. Under Japanese occupation, the school was kept from becoming a college. But when Lulu came to the school, she recognized the Korean women's thirst for knowledge and noticed that families' expectations for women were growing. She wanted to groom national leaders with a Christian perspective, and no one could dissuade her.

Lulu expanded the faculty, curriculum, and facilities. Her persistent efforts led to the formation of Ewha College. Believing the higher education of girls was crucial to the development of the country, she stood her ground even though others thought her idea premature. Lulu proved to be the visionary needed to encourage the education of women in Korea.

MY RESPONSE: What is my vision for ministry?

I needed clothes and you clothed me, . . . I was in prison and you came to visit me.
Matthew 25:36

HER SERVICE: Reforming prisons

HER MESSAGE: To free people from a prison of sin, we must enter the prison of the sinner.

HER STORY: Elizabeth Fry traveled extensively to promote prison reform. Her success earned her recognition in her native England, throughout Europe, and in America.

The daughter of devout Quakers, Elizabeth married merchant Joseph Fry. She always tried to assist those who needed medicine and teach the needy how to care for themselves. In 1813, after giving birth to the eighth of her eleven children, Elizabeth went to Newgate Prison and asked to pray with female inmates. There she found three hundred women jammed into four small rooms. Three years later, she and eleven others formed an association to improve the conditions of women prisoners by offering clothing, employment, instruction, and Bible teaching. The group's goals also included separating the sexes in prison, female supervision for incarcerated women, and religious and secular education.

When Elizabeth visited prisoners, she led them through the Scriptures. Once freed from their prison of sin, transformed women transformed their physical prison into a peaceful community, astonishing authorities. Elizabeth's new approach formed the basis of prison reform. The House of Commons recognized her work, and Elizabeth became an internationally recognized authority on prison reform.

MY RESPONSE: How might I minister to someone who is sick or in prison?

Be very careful, then, how you live . . .
making the most of every opportunity.
Ephesians 5:15–16

HER SERVICE: Singing, songwriting, writing, and speaking

HER MESSAGE: Savor the moment.

HER STORY: Gloria Gaither has joined with her soul mate and writing partner, Bill Gaither, to produce more than seven hundred songs, hundreds of recordings, a dozen musicals, and a collection of books. Inductees of the Gospel Music Hall of Fame and Museum, the Gaithers have earned Grammy and Dove Awards and received the ASCAP Songwriters of the Century Award.

It all began with a special moment when Bill Gaither, an English teacher, dropped a pencil in front of a pretty college student sent to substitute for a French teacher. They soon were sharing their thoughts about politics, literature, and their love for God. Bill and Gloria also decided to share their hearts and lives. And since their marriage more than forty years ago, they've shared their souls through songwriting, with Bill usually providing the music and Gloria the lyrics.

Gloria strives to savor each moment. This attitude enables her to keep up with a busy speaking schedule, including serving as an advocate for family preservation and Christian higher education. Whether speaking, singing a worship chorus, brainstorming song lyrics, or chatting with one of her three children or five grandchildren, Gloria's goal is to extract from that experience whatever God has for her. She delights in the surprises and embraces the challenges of each day.

MY RESPONSE: How might I savor the moment—right now?

A generous man will prosper; he who refreshes others will himself be refreshed.
Proverbs 11:25

HER SERVICE: Funding a seminary

HER MESSAGE: Educate God's servants, and your investment will multiply as God's servants educate others.

HER STORY: Garrett Biblical Institute, now Garrett-Evangelical Theological Seminary, was named for benefactor Eliza Clark Garrett. Her foresight assured training for pastors and inspired other women to support theological institutions.

Eliza inherited the fortune of her husband, Augustus, who dealt in real estate and served as mayor of Chicago. The couple had accepted Christ under a Methodist Episcopal preacher, Peter Borein, who lamented his lack of formal schooling.

By the time of her husband's death in 1848, Eliza had developed a vision for educating pastors so that members of congregations might be properly taught. She also recognized a need to provide higher educational opportunities for women, since no such institution existed in that area. To this end Eliza drew up her will to specify that the bulk of her estate should be used to build a Bible institute. Any remaining money was to go toward establishing a college for women. Eliza died unexpectedly at the age of fifty. Her money and property were used to build the seminary. Garrett-Evangelical Theological Seminary, the school Eliza Garrett made possible, has for generations educated Christian men and women for fruitful ministry.

MY RESPONSE: What Christian college or seminary might I support?

Let's make a small room on the roof and put in it a bed and a table. . . . Then he can stay there whenever he comes to us.
2 Kings 4:10

Her Service: Being a pastor's wife and hostess

Her Message: Pass on God's blessings by hosting God's servants in your home.

Her Story: Catherine Livingston Garrettson created what became known as Traveler's Rest, a place for Christian men and women to rest from ministry. At a time when women ministering was not socially acceptable, Catherine conducted worship services, led prayer groups, and evangelized—all in her own home.

Catherine Livingston grew up in a prominent New York family. Three deaths in her family left her pondering eternity, and endless parties left her feeling empty. While reading the *Anglican Book of Common Prayer* in 1787, Catherine accepted Christ. To her family's dismay, a housekeeper introduced Catherine to Methodist teachings. Wealthy families at that time looked down on the Methodist church and frowned on associating with servants.

But Catherine developed a life of prayer and asceticism and sought God's direction for ministry. When Freeborn Garrettson, former slave owner turned Methodist preacher, visited, the two fell in love. They married in 1793. In marriage Catherine found the ministry that had eluded her as a single woman. By turning her elegant home into a retreat, Catherine found an acceptable avenue of ministry by offering hospitality to weary clergy and to famous and ordinary men and women alike.

My Response: What servants of God might I entertain?

Jesus spoke all these things to the crowd in parables.
Matthew 13:34

HER SERVICE: Drama and writing

HER MESSAGE: Drama breaks down barriers of age, religion, and location.

HER STORY: Just as Jesus spoke God's truths in parables, Dr. Jeanette Clift George sets those truths in drama. Her Houston-based A.D. Players tour the world, dramatizing the gospel message. A gifted speaker, Jeanette has written books, articles, and hundreds of scripts.

After earning a degree in drama at the University of Texas, Jeanette worked on stage and screen. She played the role of Corrie ten Boom in *The Hiding Place*. For an acting class she taught at Houston Baptist College, Jeanette wrote a script so students could express their faith in coffeehouses. Jeanette's After Dinner Players also performed in churches and schools. In 1979, twelve years after its founding, the group settled into the 220-seat Grace Theater, thanks in part to the efforts of Jeanette's husband, a civil engineer and businessman. The company became known simply as the A.D. Players.

Recognized as pioneers of this Christian art form, the A.D. Players offers family-theater workshops called "Moms and Pops and Tots." The troupe also produces videos for children and adults, including a Children's Bible Classics series. By performing in playhouses and theaters around the world, the group breaks down barriers of age, religion, and location, to reach people who otherwise might never darken the door of a Christian church.

MY RESPONSE: How might my church reach our community through drama?

Maria Regina Christina Zeller Gobat, 1813–1879

I was a stranger, and you invited me into your home.
Matthew 25:35 NLT

HER SERVICE: Mission work and hospitality

HER MESSAGE: We may not be able to host everyone, but we can host someone.

HER STORY: Maria Gobat found ways to minister in support of her husband, Samuel, bishop to Jerusalem for the Church Missionary Society. Known for gracious hospitality, Maria came to love many of the 1,400 students who attended schools under Samuel's supervision.

Maria's father, a pastor, ran a home for destitute children in Germany. Maria helped in any way she could. Otherwise a cheerful child, she grieved over her sinfulness and dedicated her life to Christian service. When Rev. Samuel Gobat visited Europe after pioneering missionary work in Abyssinia (now Ethiopia), he met Maria, and they married in 1834. While the couple endured illness, the deaths of children, and difficult travel situations, they remained true to God's calling.

The Gobats began ministering in Malta in 1836. Ten years later Samuel was appointed a bishop of the Church of England and sent to organize schools in Jerusalem. At times the Gobats used their own money to make up for a lack of funding. While Maria could not possibly become acquainted with all the students under Samuel's administration, she learned the names of the sixty children enrolled at a Mount Zion school and orphanage and ministered to them with a mother's heart.

MY RESPONSE: What student, needy person, or widow might I invite into my home?

If anyone sets his heart on being an overseer, he desires a noble task.
1 Timothy 3:1

HER SERVICE: Consulting

HER MESSAGE: If you don't need the paycheck, serve God instead of yourself.

HER STORY: Joyce Godwin was chief administrative officer of Presbyterian Healthcare Services (PHS) in New Mexico before her retirement at age fifty. Since then she has used her expertise in governance to serve as a board member for several large nonprofit organizations.

Joyce earned a master's degree in political science and public administration. Although she received a religious leadership award in college, she did not understand the gospel until she joined an inquirer's group. Then a colleague became her spiritual mentor and helped her to integrate her faith and work. During her years at Presbyterian Healthcare Services, Joyce hosted weekly Bible studies.

When the company downsized, Joyce became a sounding board for Christian employees seeking a godly response to their job loss. Through dialogue with them, she realized that a job loss leads people to consider new options, including missionary service. As she contemplated her own future, she joined those pursuing whatever future God might have for them. Since her early retirement, Joyce has taken short-term mission trips, many to missionary hospitals where she serves as a consultant for management problems. She was the first woman to serve as chairman of the Evangelical Council for Financial Accountability.

MY RESPONSE: Can I afford to stop working and start reaching the world for Christ?

Morrow Coffey Graham, 1892–1981

I have been reminded of your sincere faith, which first lived in your grandmother Lois and in your mother Eunice and, I am persuaded, now lives in you also.
2 Timothy 1:5

HER SERVICE: Mothering

HER MESSAGE: Mothers have the privilege of permeating the home atmosphere with the potpourri of prayer and Bible reading.

HER STORY: Internationally known evangelist Billy Graham credits the prayers of his parents, Morrow and Frank Graham, for his salvation and success in ministry.

On her wedding night, Morrow Coffey Graham began a family tradition of holding devotions with her husband. During the Depression years, Morrow's sister urged her to attend a weekly Bible class. As she and Frank read Christian books and studied the Bible, their faith grew, and devotional times in their North Carolina home became even more meaningful. While Morrow could hardly have imagined that her lanky son, who got up at 2:30 a.m. to milk cows, would one day leave his mark on evangelical Christianity, she faithfully provided a home atmosphere of prayer and Bible reading that nurtured the faith of Billy and her other children.

When Billy began working with Youth for Christ, Morrow worried about the pace of his ministry but committed him to God's care. As his ministry expanded and he preached to thousands, Billy Graham acknowledged the influence of his godly parents.

MY RESPONSE: How does my family sense the presence of God in my home?

Her children arise and call her blessed;
her husband also, and he praises her.
Proverbs 31:28

HER SERVICE: Being an evangelist's wife

HER MESSAGE: By sacrificing our own dreams, we may help others attain theirs.

HER STORY: Ruth Bell Graham, wife of international evangelist Billy Graham, tended her growing family as Billy traveled the world. She has authored nine books and nurtured their five children in the faith.

Ruth was born north of Shanghai, China, the daughter of medical missionaries. At age thirteen she was sent to school in North Korea, where she relied on Scripture to overcome homesickness. From childhood Ruth dreamed of living the single life in the Himalayas, but all that changed at Wheaton College when she met Billy Graham. When the couple married in 1943, she sacrificed her dream to follow his. Evangelistic crusades took Billy away from home for up to six months each year. While he was gone, Ruth ran the household, studied the Bible, and read books and magazines, looking for preaching illustrations.

For two years Ruth traveled with Billy, but his fevered pace wore her out. She returned to their North Carolina home to support him with prayer and her children by her presence. Ruth never served on the mission field as she had once dreamed, but by building a stable home on a foundation of faith, she helped Billy Graham become a leading evangelical influence of the twentieth century.

MY RESPONSE: How am I laying a foundation of faith that will support my family?

Those who hope in the Lord will renew their strength. They will soar on wings like eagles; they will run and not grow weary, they will walk and not be faint.
Isaiah 40:31

HER SERVICE: Mission aviation

HER MESSAGE: Just because something hasn't been done doesn't mean it can't be.

HER STORY: After writing a magazine article on the need for missionary aviation, Betty Greene was invited by a navy pilot to join him and others in forming the Christian Airmen's Missionary Fellowship, later called Missionary Aviation Fellowship (MAF). She was the first woman pilot to cross the Andes Mountains of Peru.

Betty took flying lessons at age sixteen and, after college, joined the Women's Air Force Service Pilots (WASPs) to fly military aircraft. She recognized the role planes could play in reaching people for Christ, a novel idea in that day.

MAF allowed Betty to show that just because planes had never been used to support missionary work didn't mean they couldn't be. She first transported missionaries and supplies to a jungle camp in Mexico, then flew across the jungles and deserts of Nigeria. She assisted the British MAF in East Africa, where a new law was required to permit a woman to fly in the Sudan. Betty once saved a little girl's life, even though it meant flying out of her way with darkness falling. Her service opened up ministry in the interior of what is now Irian Jaya.

MY RESPONSE: What new ways or materials could I use to serve God?

Your path led through the sea . . . though your footprints were not seen.
Psalm 77:19

HER SERVICE: Writing, speaking, and mission work

HER MESSAGE: Our expectations for ourselves may be higher than God's expectations for us.

HER STORY: Lillian Grissen has published five books, including *A Path Through the Sea*, the story of her triumph over depression. For several years she taught in colleges and served as associate editor of the weekly magazine of the Christian Reformed Church.

Lillian and her four brothers were born to Dutch Calvinist immigrants in Grand Rapids, Michigan. She longed to be a teacher, but her parents did not believe girls should be educated. As a teen she worked long hours in the family's bakery.

In 1952 Lillian, her husband, Ray, and their three children went to Lupwe, Nigeria, as missionaries. Ray supervised construction at a mission station while Lillian did bookkeeping and secretarial work, hosted visitors, taught Sunday school, and raised her family. But within two years Lillian was admitted to a Grand Rapids mental hospital, where she would remain for six months. Not until 1956 could she resume full care of her family. Lillian had been crippled by anger and collapsed under the weight of her own high expectations of herself and others. Through counseling and medication, she gained a healthier perspective of life, and in 1975 she earned a master's degree in journalism.

MY RESPONSE: What realistic and attainable expectations do I hold for my ministry?

You intended to harm me, but God intended it for good to accomplish what is now being done, the saving of many lives.
Genesis 50:20

HER SERVICE: Writing

HER MESSAGE: Outer struggles can build inner peace.

HER STORY: Jeanne Guyon left a legacy of forty books, including a seven-hundred-page autobiography and a twenty-volume Bible commentary. A Roman Catholic, she was known as a French mystic devoted to Quietism, the practice of losing oneself in contemplation of God. She emulated Christ by caring for the sick and needy and established two hospitals.

Born in Montargis, France, Jeanne Marie Bourvier de la Motte was married at age sixteen to Jacques Guyon, a prominent older man. This introduced a contentious mother-in-law into her life, but Jeanne believed the difficult situation was permitted by God for her good. Jacques died when Jeanne was just twenty-eight; they had already buried two of their five children. At each loss Jeanne viewed her sorrow as permitted by the hand of God. When smallpox left her face covered with pockmarks, she was able to rejoice in her inner peace. Jeanne eventually took an eight-year religious pilgrimage through France and Switzerland. She spent seven years in prison because of her beliefs. Her hymn "The Christian Life," written while imprisoned in the Bastille, tells of her inner peace in the midst of outward misery.

MY RESPONSE: How might I achieve inner peace in the midst of troubling circumstances?

There is no difference between Jew and Gentile—the same Lord is Lord of all and richly blesses all who call on him.
Romans 10:12

HER SERVICE: Christian education

HER MESSAGE: Christians should help break down barriers between genders and races.

HER STORY: From 1988 to 1996 Sheri Haan served as executive director of Christian Schools International (CSI), an organization that serves more than four hundred Christian schools in the United States and Canada.

Sheri's fifth-grade Christian schoolteacher listed occupations on the chalkboard and explained how each offered opportunities to stand for God. Something in that presentation clicked for Sheri, and she dedicated her life to helping children see themselves as God's creatures. After college, Sheri took a teaching job and married a year later.

In 1970, while pregnant with the first of her three children, Sheri wrote *Good News for Children*. That book garnered an invitation to write Bible course materials for CSI and for Christian Reformed Church publications. Eventually Sheri became director of operations and finally executive director of CSI. Some in her denomination were uncomfortable when a woman was named to a leadership position, but Sheri remained gracious and tried not to offend. In spite of requests to hire men or women for particular positions, Sheri insisted that all applicants be treated equally, with no discrimination against any race or gender.

MY RESPONSE: What barriers based on gender or race might I work to remove?

Do not let this Book of the Law depart from your mouth. . . . Then you will be prosperous and successful.

Joshua 1:8

HER SERVICE: Writing

HER MESSAGE: Serving God is more important than succeeding in a career.

HER STORY: When she committed her life to Christian writing, Robin Lee Hatcher was already well known for her romance novels. She had served as president of Romance Writers of America and received the 2001 Lifetime Achievement Award from that organization. Robin has written more than forty contemporary and historical novels and novellas. She received the 2000 Christy Award for excellence in Christian fiction.

Growing up in Idaho, Robin read voraciously, kept diaries, and wrote long letters. Christian books had led Robin to commit her life to Christ in 1976. Later, as a single mom with two daughters, Robin worked during the week and wrote on nights and weekends. In 1984 her first book was published.

Robin increasingly desired to write about her faith and used book plots to explore life's questions. When an editor cut a scene because of a reference to prayer, Robin decided that serving God was more important than a successful career and turned to Christian publishers. Since 1997 Robin's heroines have faced social issues in God's strength. Although the change threatened her financial security, Robin has never looked back—and has always paid the bills.

MY RESPONSE: How might I be compromising my faith to ensure financial success?

I will sing hymns to your name.
Romans 15:9

HER SERVICE: Writing hymns

HER MESSAGE: Serenity precedes service in the dictionary and in life.

HER STORY: Frances Ridley Havergal wrote dozens of hymns, including "Take My Life and Let It Be," "I Gave My Life for Thee," and "Lord, Speak to Me." She was a natural linguist with mastery of French, German, Italian, Latin, Greek, and Hebrew.

Frances was born in Worcestershire, England, and inherited a talent for singing, composing, and playing the piano from her father, an Anglican clergyman. Gifted and precocious, Frances could read by the age of three. At seven she was writing verse. She attended English and German boarding schools. As a serious Bible student, Frances memorized much of the New Testament and prayed three times a day. Described as a brilliant pianist, she played the music of Handel, Mendelssohn, and Beethoven. She also exchanged correspondence with American hymnwriter Fanny Crosby.

An illness forced Frances to give up writing during most of her twenties, but she resumed her passion as soon as she was able. Frances considered herself a channel through whom the Holy Spirit flowed to inspire her verses. Her service as a hymnwriter reflected her serene spirit and deep devotion to God.

MY RESPONSE: How might I develop greater devotion to God so I can better serve Him?

The words of the wise are like goads.
Ecclesiastes 12:11

HER SERVICE: Antislavery activism and social work

HER MESSAGE: God calls us to better the world.

HER STORY: Laura Smith Haviland helped organize the first antislavery society in Michigan. She and her husband ran that state's first Underground Railroad station.

While a child in Canada, Laura Smith was horrified to read about the cruel slave trade. She married Charles Haviland in 1825, and the couple settled in Michigan. There Laura was so outspoken for the antislavery movement that she and her husband withdrew from the Quaker church, made up of pacifists who tended to shy away from abolition.

In 1845 Laura lost her husband, parents, youngest daughter, and sister to an infectious skin disease and almost died herself. The untiring widow taught her seven remaining children plus some orphans. Her efforts led to the establishment of the first school to admit black children, the Raisin Institute. Although a woman's place was thought to be in the home, Laura felt God calling her to speak out and denounce slavery throughout the country. Once her children could manage on their own, she left home to help slaves escape to Canada. Towns were named for her in Kansas and Ohio, and a statue of Laura stands in Adrian, Michigan. A plaque below it reads: "A tribute to a life consecrated to the betterment of humanity." Laura combated slavery fearlessly and with a firm reliance on divine protection, devoting time and means to assist those escaping from bondage.

MY RESPONSE: What am I doing for the betterment of humanity?

In everything, do to others what you would have them do to you.
Matthew 7:12

HER SERVICE: Being First Lady

HER MESSAGE: You'll never know the joy that comes from putting others first until you think of yourself less.

HER STORY: The wife of the nineteenth president of the United States, Rutherford B. Hayes, Lucy Webb Hayes modeled Christianity to a watching nation.

From her childhood, Lucy Webb developed a concern for others. After her father's death, Lucy, her mother, and her siblings freed the family's slaves and continued to help them financially. She and Rutherford Hayes married in 1852, and during the Civil War Lucy spent two winters camping with Union forces under her husband's command. She ministered to the wounded, cheered the homesick, and comforted the dying.

Once in the White House, the Hayeses, who believed in temperance, refused to serve alcoholic beverages. Lucy's public stand against alcohol earned her the nickname "Lemonade Lucy," but she took the joking with grace and good humor. She was a popular hostess and much-admired First Lady who served as a positive example to her children and the rest of the nation. Lucy believed that the Golden Rule was the cornerstone of practical religion, and the couple gave generously to the church and held daily family prayers. Throughout her life Lucy found joy in putting the needs of others—in her nation and in her home—ahead of her own.

MY RESPONSE: In what ways have I put others' needs ahead of my own?

There is a time for everything, and a season for every activity under heaven.
Ecclesiastes 3:1

HER SERVICE: Singing, writing, and speaking

HER MESSAGE: We may minister to others during our darkest seasons—maybe even because of them.

HER STORY: Joyce Landorf Heatherley has experienced the song of spring, the fun of summer, the blight of fall, and the chill of winter—and has served God through every season. So far she has written twenty-six books, and at least ten million people have watched her video series, *His Stubborn Love*.

The daughter of a pastor, Joyce was encouraged to be all she could be. During college she sang with Christian music greats at Pasadena City Auditorium. After she married and gave birth to two children, she sang at women's clubs and gatherings. Then Dale Evans Rogers urged Joyce to give her testimony before singing at a Hollywood Christian Group meeting, and speaking became part of Joyce's ministry. She also hosted Christian radio shows.

But after the sunshine came the rain. Joyce wrote *Mourning Song* to share how she dealt with the deaths of her third child, a grandfather, and her mother. Joyce's marriage ended after thirty-two years, and her ministry almost screeched to a halt. But during her recovery, she penned *My Blue Blanket* and *Balcony People*, which became her best-selling book. By surviving personal heartache—or perhaps because of it—Joyce has inspired others to persevere in life's darkest seasons.

MY RESPONSE: Whom might I encourage by sharing how God picked me up when I was down?

Sow for yourselves righteousness . . . and break up your unplowed ground; for it is time to seek the Lord.

Hosea 10:12

HER SERVICE: Pioneering for Methodism

HER MESSAGE: Women are dreamers—*and* doers.

HER STORY: Barbara Heck organized one of the first Methodist congregations in America and later, the first in Canada. She designed the first Methodist church building in the Western hemisphere.

Born in Ireland of German ancestors, Barbara heard John Wesley preach when she was twenty-four. In 1760 she married Paul Heck, and they sailed for New York City along with others, including Barbara's cousin, Philip Embury, a preacher. In 1765 Barbara's brother and brother-in-law arrived. When she found the two men playing cards, she hurled the cards into the fire and insisted that Philip preach to them. When he hesitated because he had no church, Barbara organized one. She, her husband, a servant, and a hired hand became members of the first Methodist class meeting, a small group that met for study in Philip's home.

As the group grew, Barbara designed Wesley Chapel. The church soon drew thousands. When the denomination supplied a new minister, the Hecks and Emburys started another Methodist congregation in upstate New York. Philip died in 1775 in a hay-mowing accident. At the outbreak of the Revolutionary War, the families moved to Canada, where Barbara organized another Methodist class in 1785. Barbara dreamed of what might be—and worked until it was so.

MY RESPONSE: What dreams do I have? How can I make them come true?

We proclaim him . . . so that we may present everyone perfect in Christ.
Colossians 1:28

HER SERVICE: Ministering, advocating missions, writing, and speaking

HER MESSAGE: As women we have intrinsic worth because we were created by God.

HER STORY: Dr. Lana Heightley founded Women with a Mission to train women in Third-World nations for Christian leadership. She wrote the book *Presents from on High: Freeing Women to Walk in Their Gifts.*

Lana was born in California to a family of missionaries and pastors. Although in her teens she had a vision to do mission work, she didn't go to the field until she was forty-two. In the intervening years she married, had two sons, and worked as an executive assistant.

A graduate of Wagner Leadership Institute with a doctorate in practical ministry, Lana noticed that most overseas conferences were geared toward men. She also noticed a prejudice against women, who in some countries were still considered property. Her passion to help women discover their intrinsic worth in Christ and develop their spiritual gifts grew. In 1995 Lana recruited twelve women to offer her first Women of Destiny conference. Using her model of leadership training, women in India have now trained fifty thousand others. Lana has served with Aglow International and African Village Outreach. From 1986 to 2004 she made annual trips to the Philippines to participate in evangelistic crusades and conferences that reached more than 800,000 people.

MY RESPONSE: How can I help other women find their intrinsic value through Christ?

Wherever this gospel is preached throughout the world,
what she has done will also be told, in memory of her.
Matthew 26:13

HER SERVICE: Building churches

HER MESSAGE: To honor Christ, sanctify a place He touched.

HER STORY: Helena, mother of Roman Emperor Constantine, built some of Israel's most treasured holy places. She was canonized for finding what she believed was Christ's cross.

Helena was an innkeeper's daughter when Emperor Constantius I lifted her from her lowly surroundings. Though it seems Constantius divorced her for political reasons, their son Constantine remained loyal. When he came to power, he brought his mother to live at court and honored her with the title Augustus.

Helena's son was the emperor whose conversion turned the Roman world toward Christianity, and Helena soon became zealous for her newfound faith. On pilgrimages to the Holy Land, she tore down a pagan temple to excavate a cave believed to be Christ's tomb. On the same site, Helena believed she found the cross of Calvary, so she built there the Church of the Holy Sepulchre. She also built the Church of the Nativity over the site believed to be the manger of Bethlehem. Christians have worshiped there longer than at any other church in the world. In her seventies Helena directed the building of a church on Mount Calvary. She gave so generously to the poor that after her death, Constantine had gold coins struck in her honor.

MY RESPONSE: What place where the Spirit has touched me might I work to preserve for Christ's sake?

How great are your works, O Lord, how profound your thoughts!
Psalm 92:5

HER SERVICE: Bible teaching, founding a ministry and a college

HER MESSAGE: If we will work with God, we will see God at work.

HER STORY: Marilyn Hickey is recognized around the world through her television programs, books, audiotapes, videotapes, and crusades. Marilyn Hickey Ministries sponsors worldwide Bible and food distribution.

Marilyn attended church occasionally as a child and accepted Christ at a youth camp. She went to college to prepare for a teaching career. Then her mother, who had joined a Pentecostal group, and Wally Hickey, whom Marilyn was dating, began witnessing to her. A vision one night spurred Marilyn to commit herself and her career to God. After Marilyn married Wally, he began holding evangelistic meetings.

In 1960 the family settled in Denver, where Wally assumed a pastorate. Marilyn's love for language led her to study Hebrew and Greek. After returning from a 1978 retreat, she taught a Bible study that soon multiplied into twenty-two groups. Before long Marilyn was speaking around the nation—then around the world. *Outpouring* magazine gave her message a printed format, and Word to the World College in Greenwood Village, Colorado, passes on her mandate. As Marilyn committed herself and her career to God, she saw God work in her life and in her ministry.

MY RESPONSE: Am I willing to commit myself and my career to God?

"Get up," the Lord said, "and go into Damascus. There you will be told all that you have been assigned to do."
Acts 22:10

HER SERVICE: Mission work

HER MESSAGE: Effective ministry is not measured by length of service.

HER STORY: Susan B. Higgins served as a missionary to Japan for just eight months before her unexpected death.

Born the daughter of a pastor in America, Susan turned to God at age fourteen. By the time she began teaching in public schools, she had developed a reputation as a woman of the Word and of prayer. After a young niece and nephew died, Susan dedicated her life to serving God and responded to a call from the American Woman's Foreign Missionary Society. In 1878 she arrived at Yokohama, Japan, intending to devote many years to mission work.

The Japanese day school at which Susan taught grew from four to fifty-two students during her brief ministry. She also oversaw a women's outreach and taught a Bible class. Susan entered Buddhist shrines to pray for worshippers and visited humble dwellings, singing hymns to the lost. But soon new converts were singing hymns by Susan's bedside. As they choked back tears, she took up their refrain. Since she considered her call a divine appointment, she never measured her effectiveness by length of service or regretted going to Japan.

MY RESPONSE: What time constraints may be holding me back from effective ministry?

God had mercy on me, so that Christ Jesus could use me as a prime example of his great patience with even the worst sinners.
1 Timothy 1:16 NLT

HER SERVICE: Speaking and writing

HER MESSAGE: We are never so bad that God can't use us for good.

HER STORY: Author and speaker Liz Curtis Higgs has written more than two dozen books, including historical and contemporary fiction, nonfiction, and children's books. Her Parable Series for children received the Evangelical Christian Publishers Association (ECPA) Gold Medallion for Excellence, and *Bad Girls of the Bible* was an ECPA Gold Medallion finalist. One of only thirty women to be named to the Speaker Hall of Fame by the National Speakers Association, Liz serves as a columnist for *Today's Christian Woman.*

Though as a child Liz shared a special relationship with her parents, at times she missed the attention of her mother, who tended backyard flowerbeds for hours, and her father, who served on the borough council. As a teen Liz looked for acceptance elsewhere. In *Rise & Shine*, Liz writes of a lifestyle that included drugs, alcohol, and promiscuity. Her salvation, both physically and spiritually, came through colleagues at a radio station who introduced her to God. She joyously discovered that no one, not even a woman with her history, is so bad that God could not use her for good.

Liz has presented inspirational programs in every state and in several foreign countries.

MY RESPONSE: How might I be holding back from serving God because I'm not "good enough"?

Whatever your hand finds to do, do it with all your might.
Ecclesiastes 9:10

HER SERVICE: Ran a monastery

HER MESSAGE: Our pathway of service often becomes apparent as we complete tasks at hand.

HER STORY: Abbess Hilda ran an important monastery complex for men and women at Whitby in Yorkshire, England. Her institution produced five bishops, and she nurtured the work of the poet Caedmon, whose writings gave common people access to Scripture.

After political enemies killed Hilda's father, her mother fled the country, leaving Hilda with her great uncle, King Edwin. Hilda and the king were baptized on Easter Eve in 627. Six years later, the king died in battle, and Hilda fled to relatives in Kent. Sensing Christ's call, at age thirty-three she took vows at a French convent.

Edwin's successor, Oswio, asked a bishop to start religious centers in England, and the bishop invited Hilda to open a convent. A year later he asked her to establish a monastery for nuns and monks at Hartlepool. Hilda organized what became known as Whitby Abbey, where she raised Oswio's daughter, who became her successor. There, during the Dark Ages, monks and nuns studied, copied biblical manuscripts, and composed choral worship songs. By simply completing the tasks that lay before her, Hilda found her calling, fulfilled her vows, and contributed to the spread of Christianity.

MY RESPONSE: What opportunity for service lies before me?

This is what the Lord, the God of Israel, says: "Write in a book all the words I have spoken to you."
Jeremiah 30:2

HER SERVICE: Writing

HER MESSAGE: Regardless of our circumstances, we can count on God's promises.

HER STORY: Considering herself called of God, Grace Livingston Hill used her writing as an avenue to tell people about Christ. Her novel *The Witness* is listed in *100 Christian Books That Changed the Century*. Ten million copies of her books were sold during the twentieth century.

Early in Grace's career, her publisher advised her to take the gospel message out of her books if she wanted to write bestsellers. Grace ignored his advice and has attracted readers of multiple generations. She wrote of what she learned as the daughter of a Presbyterian minister, although at times her life lacked the happy endings of her stories. After only seven years of marriage, Grace's first husband, Rev. Frank Hill, died of infection following an appendectomy. Her second husband eventually deserted her. Grace lived through two wars and the Great Depression of the 1930s. Through it all she relied on God's promises and, through her pleasurable, faith-lifting stories, inspired her readers to do likewise.

MY RESPONSE: Which of God's promises do I need to hear—or share with someone—today?

Paul lived and worked with them,
for they were tentmakers just as he was.
Acts 18:3 NLT

HER SERVICE: Communications

HER MESSAGE: Your work is a calling.

HER STORY: Angie Hillman and her husband, Os, minister through Marketplace Leaders, an organization that helps people understand that work is a calling and a way to experience God. They provide resources at faithandworkresources.com, conduct seminars worldwide, and send out a daily e-mail devotional, Today God Is First (TGIF), to more than eighty thousand subscribers.

Angie's family moved from England to the United States when she was five. During college Angie discovered a love for communications and marketing and went to work in the corporate world. At twenty-nine she was floundering spiritually until a corporate vice president led her in the sinner's prayer. Rather than continuing to look for the right man to marry, Angie concentrated on falling in love with Jesus. Seven years went by before Angie dated again. Then she met Os at her church, and they married in 1998.

Always ambitious, Angie looked to God for career direction. For a time she worked as creative director for a nonprofit organization that distributes medicine to the world's poor. She codirected the 1996 Atlanta Host program, which housed twenty-two hundred Olympic athletes in homes provided by four hundred churches. Angie views her work as a calling and helps others find their calling through their work.

MY RESPONSE: Am I fulfilling the Great Commission in my workplace?

Dora Hofstra, 1907–1986

I will strengthen you and help you; I will uphold you with my righteous right hand.
Isaiah 41:10

HER SERVICE: Being a dorm mother

HER MESSAGE: Although our own strength is never sufficient, God's strength always is.

HER STORY: For thirty-six years Dora Hofstra served as a dorm mother at Rehoboth (New Mexico) Christian Boarding School for Navajo children. On duty around the clock, seven days a week, she cared for more than sixty girls per year.

Ironically, Dora had quit school after eighth grade because her mother was sickly. The family was keenly interested in missions, and Dora's mother urged her to heed the song "All the Way My Savior Leads Me." At first Dora resented her mother's persistence, but after hearing a radio speaker, she opened her heart to Christ and found peace.

In 1936 Dora was invited to serve as a housemother at a Christian school for Navajo children. She felt inadequate for the work, but she was urged to rely on God's strength instead of her own, and she accepted. Dora's work was not easy. Many of the Navajo schoolgirls knew little English and resented white people. The girls talked back to Dora until the school's director intervened and insisted they respect her. When Dora reached retirement age, she stayed on to host visitors for ten more years. She had truly found God's strength to be sufficient for her work.

MY RESPONSE: For what task do I need to rely on God's strength instead of my own effort?

June

Serve wholeheartedly, as if you were serving the Lord, not men.
Ephesians 6:7

HER SERVICE: Mission work

HER MESSAGE: The church plays an important role in turning seekers into servants.

HER STORY: Magdalene Hollis served at a homeless shelter and at churches in Grand Rapids and Kalamazoo, Michigan. The African American woman was also a missionary in the Christian Reformed Church.

When "Maggie" was seven, her mother died, and family members mistreated her so severely that she ran away. By 1970 she had been married, widowed, and remarried. Her family, which by then included eleven children, lived near a Christian Reformed Church in Grand Rapids, Michigan. Although she didn't attend, church members visited, took the children to Vacation Bible School, and baby-sat. Maggie eventually began attending services. When a daughter developed leukemia, Maggie's church family supported her with prayer and meals. When Maggie's husband became abusive, they divorced. As Maggie faced poverty, loneliness, and single parenting, she dropped out of church. But a pastor's caring concern revived her faith.

Maggie started dreaming of being a missionary so she could reach poor people with the gospel, and the church elders granted her wish. Through the love and outreach of church members, Maggie had grown from a seeker to a servant.

MY RESPONSE: How might I show care and concern to someone in my church?

Who shall separate us from the love of Christ?
Shall trouble or hardship or persecution?
Romans 8:35

HER SERVICE: Preaching

HER MESSAGE: There is no security in circumstances, but we are secure in God's hands.

HER STORY: The first Quaker convert and the first woman to preach as a Quaker, Elizabeth Hooton was imprisoned and persecuted in both England and America.

Elizabeth had been a Baptist, but in 1647 she heard a young shoemaker named George Fox preach Quaker doctrine in Nottingham, England. She embraced his teaching. Three years later the middle-aged mother was jailed for urging people to repent. After her husband's death, Elizabeth sailed for Boston in 1661. She expected to use her wealth to help persecuted Quakers, but she was taken before the governor and jailed with them. When unexpectedly released, Elizabeth fled to Rhode Island, then to a Quaker settlement in the West Indies.

Upon returning to Boston in 1662, Elizabeth was again imprisoned. Three times she was whipped and once left in the wilderness. Elizabeth returned to friends in Rhode Island, thanking God for counting her worthy of suffering for Him. By 1667 Elizabeth was back in England, interceding for imprisoned Quakers. In 1671 she accompanied George Fox and others to Jamaica.

MY RESPONSE: What is my attitude in suffering? Have I remained faithful?

Delight yourself in the Lord and he will
give you the desires of your heart.
Psalm 37:4

HER SERVICE: Writing

HER MESSAGE: Trust the God who made you; He will never fail you.

HER STORY: In 2001 Helen Kooiman Hosier received the Excellence in Media Gold Angel Lifetime Achievement Award for thirty-five years of writing and speaking.

Helen's father died five months before her birth in Iowa. As a child, when she snuggled on the shoulder of a friend's father, her friend pushed her away. When Helen cried for a father of her own, her mother introduced her to God, her heavenly Father. Unable to afford college, Helen went to work in Washington, DC, and later in California. There, alone and on her own, she opened her heart to Christ. She also married and had four children.

Helen's love of reading prompted her to sell Christian books door to door—and to open two Christian bookstores. Realizing God had given her a gift of writing, Helen wrote weekly columns in the *Church Herald* and later in *Christian Times*. When a publisher asked her to write a book, her career was launched. The book was her first of more than sixty.

Helen experienced dark nights of the soul when her twenty-three-year marriage ended. In 1974 she married Herman Hosier, a Christian radio program producer. Now widowed, she writes from her home in Texas to encourage readers to trust in the God who will never fail them.

MY RESPONSE: What has God entrusted to you that you can commit to Him?

He upholds the cause of the oppressed.
Psalm 146:7

HER SERVICE: Social work

HER MESSAGE: God offers freedom in Christ; we extend that grace when we offer freedom to each other.

HER STORY: After achieving recognition for writing the words to "The Battle Hymn of the Republic," Julia Ward Howe used her public platform to support women's suffrage and the abolition of slavery.

A prolific writer from childhood, Julia Ward was publishing essays in magazines by the age of sixteen. Her essays on notables such as Goethe, Schiller, and Lamartine ran in the *New York Review* and the *Theological Review*. Because women were not accepted in the world of literature, she did not use a byline on her early writings.

In 1843 Julia married Dr. Samuel Gridley Howe, renowned for his work at Perkins Institute for the Blind. Together they published the *Commonwealth*, an abolitionist newspaper. Julia supported groups such as the New England Women's Suffrage Association, the New England and General Federation of Women's Clubs, and the Association for the Advancement of Women. She supported women seeking careers in fields such as ministry, law, education, and science. In 1908 she was elected to the all-male membership of the American Academy of Arts and Letters. As president of the Women's International Peace Association's American division, Julia encouraged Christians, who experience freedom in Christ to unite to free oppressed people around the world.

MY RESPONSE: Who may need my support to experience true freedom?

He told them many things in parables.
Matthew 13:3

HER SERVICE: Writing poetry and plays

HER MESSAGE: To become the salt of society requires a dash of godly influence.

HER STORY: The writings of Hroswitha, Germany's first woman poet and playwright, were a godly influence during the Middle Ages, when secular literature sometimes focused on gaudy sensationalism. Hroswitha wrote eight narrative religious poems, two historical poems, three prefaces, and six comedies, along with other verse and prose. Her work is celebrated by members of the Hroswitha Club for women bibliophiles, with branches in five major American cities.

Leaving behind a life of nobility, Hroswitha entered a Benedictine convent to become a nun. There she was encouraged to use her talents to write. Hroswitha's works focused on the struggle between Christianity and paganism. Her drama *Dulcitius* tells the story of an evil man thwarted in his pursuit of three godly maidens. In Hroswitha's writing, Christian heroes and heroines emerge victorious in Christ's strength. Some critics see reflections of her plots in the writings of later playwrights, such as Shakespeare and Goethe.

Hroswitha worried that her pride would in some way prove a stumbling block. More than personal glory, she wanted her work to bring glory to God.

MY RESPONSE: How might I be a godly influence in my community?

When you are tempted, [God] will also provide a way out so that you can stand up under it.
1 Corinthians 10:13

HER SERVICE: Bible teaching

HER MESSAGE: Regardless of your age, circumstances, or physical strength, God can use you.

HER STORY: During the 1980s Juanda Huggins's Bible study grew from six women attendees to 179. Before she served the Word of God in her Texas home, Juanda served a catered dinner, complete with centerpieces.

Juanda married Charles Huggins when she was sixteen years old. A neighbor's knowledge of Scripture motivated Juanda to read the Bible, which transformed her life. Her family, which by then included two sons and a daughter, began attending church, and Charles also committed his life to Christ. At the request of a manicurist, whom Juanda had led to the Lord, she opened her home and taught women's studies. The group grew.

Through the years, Juanda's experiences—business ups and downs, children's personal problems, and her husband's illness and death—have enabled her to relate to the women who come to her Bible studies with their own heartaches. Juanda has survived kidney failure, two heart attacks, a stroke, and colon cancer. Yet even while at a dialysis center for treatment, she used the opportunity to lead a woman to the Lord. Despite her age, physical ailments, and difficulties, Juanda has remained active in her church and a faithful witness to Christ.

MY RESPONSE: In what way can I be a faithful witness to others?

He has sent me to bind up the brokenhearted, to proclaim . . .
release from darkness for the prisoners.
Isaiah 61:1

HER SERVICE: Founding a ministry, art, and evangelism

HER MESSAGE: When we develop relationships, we earn the right to be heard.

HER STORY: Dustee Hullinger founded and directs Gifted Hands, an art and evangelistic program that ministers to traumatized people.

Teen mission trips convinced Dustee she was called to Christian service. After college she worked as a flight attendant, then relocated to New York City in 1975. Colleagues invited her to Lamb's Manhattan Church of the Nazarene, where Dustee found a church home. In 1977 she married Jim Hullinger, the church's financial administrator.

Dustee ministered at the church's foot clinic, building relationships with street people. Eventually she joined the church's compassion ministries staff and founded Gifted Hands. Thirty-three programs, including courses on character and life-skills development, have evolved over the last eleven years. Under Dustee's leadership, volunteer artists weekly teach subjects such as jewelry making, cooking, and woodworking to two hundred people at seventeen locations. Those who attend workshops are given Bibles and invited to church.

Dustee has discovered a God-given ability to bring out the best in people. Whether she greets them at shelters, HIV/AIDS residences, or domestic violence centers, Dustee simply refuses to give up on anyone.

MY RESPONSE: What type of program might help my church bridge the gap between needy souls and God?

By the grace of God I am what I am,
and his grace to me was not without effect.
1 Corinthians 15:10

HER SERVICE: Writing

HER MESSAGE: Integrating our faith, our fancies, and our faculties produces fruit.

HER STORY: Angela Elwell Hunt has written more than one hundred books of various genres—fiction, nonfiction, and children's books. *The Canopy* won the silver medallion in *ForeWord* magazine's 2003 Book of the Year Award for religious fiction.

Angela Elwell grew up in a Christian home and put her faith in Christ at age six. During college, while touring with a music group, Angela kept a journal. The group's director read her account of getting stuck in a blizzard and suggested she switch her major from music to English. Weary from being on the road, Angela followed his advice.

After college Angela married, taught school, then spent a year writing church curriculum. A job as secretary in a communications department motivated Angela to try writing herself, and in 1983 she sent out business cards announcing her services. Over the next five years, the jobs came—as did two adopted babies. A picture book she entered in a contest launched Angela's career. Experiences in life and faith keep the ink flowing from her Florida home.

MY RESPONSE: What might I produce if I harness my faith and talents?

I now give my personal treasures of gold and silver for the temple of my God.
1 Chronicles 29:3

HER SERVICE: Philanthropy

HER MESSAGE: Funding God's work is more important than acquiring personal possessions.

HER STORY: Selina Hastings, who married the ninth Earl of Huntingdon, used her wealth to support England's fledgling Methodist movement. Lady Huntingdon helped preserve the Protestant movement by reuniting John and Charles Wesley with George Whitefield after their doctrinal rift.

The daughter of an earl, Selina began reading her Bible at age nine, after a playmate died. After marrying in 1728, she indulged in the life of a socialite. But after an illness, Lady Huntingdon turned her back on the social scene and dedicated her life to God. She opened her home for meetings, during which Church of England bishops listened from behind curtains in what was called Nicodemus's Corner.

Lady Huntingdon had seven children, but only one outlived her. After her husband died, she toured the British Isles with clergy to serve as a model of evangelism to the group of Methodists that became known as Lady Huntingdon's Connexion. An able administrator, Lady Huntingdon opened sixty chapels. She sold her jewels and moved to modest quarters to free funds for ministry. When she realized the need for evangelical training for church leaders, she opened a seminary, and she also sponsored missionaries to America.

MY RESPONSE: What sacrifice might I make for the gospel?

We have different gifts, according to the grace given us.
Romans 12:6

HER SERVICE: Mission work

HER MESSAGE: God can use every area of our expertise.

HER STORY: For more than forty years, Diane Huntzinger and her husband, Allyn, have served with Christar (formerly International Missions, Inc.), an organization that seeks to plant churches within Buddhist, Hindu, Muslim, and Asian communities.

Diane accepted Christ as a child in New Jersey. In college she majored in mathematics. Searching for God's will, she completed graduate work at Columbia Bible College, where she met Allyn.

A study on the Great Commission opened Diane's eyes to see that the call to Christian service was not just for a special few. When Allyn proposed, he already planned to go as a missionary to Iran, and Diane took that as God's direction for her life as well. They married in 1960. During their sixteen years in Iran, the couple developed a Bible correspondence ministry. Diane entertained frequent guests and, for a time, taught at a Christian school. Since 1979 Diane has concentrated on her area of expertise—mathematics—by serving in the finance department of the Christar home office in Reading, Pennsylvania, while Allyn serves as executive vice president. She has taught Sunday school for more than forty years and has served various churches as treasurer.

MY RESPONSE: How might I use my training to build God's kingdom?

Surely God is my salvation; I will trust and not be afraid.
Isaiah 12:2

HER SERVICE: Teaching

HER MESSAGE: Courage fortifies a heart resting in God.

HER STORY: After settling in the Massachusetts Bay Colony in 1634, Anne opened her home to discuss biblical teaching with other women, a first. Eventually men also attended the meetings. Her leadership helped lay the foundation for the later women's missionary society movement.

Anne, the mother of fifteen children, studied the King James Version of the Bible, released just before her marriage, and visited various churches in her search for truth. She favored Antinomianism, placing obedience to the Spirit above legal rules. Facing criticism for her beliefs, Anne's family came to America from England.

During her weekly home meetings, Anne expounded on the Sunday sermon and offered household helps and childcare hints. Attendance mushroomed from six to sixty. New England ministers, however, called Anne before a synod. Although, with her vast knowledge of the Bible, she ably defended herself, the ministers decreed that she should be confined to the home of one of her accusers' relatives for four months. In 1638 she was again tried for holding unorthodox opinions according to Puritan Calvinistic theology. This time she was ordered to leave the colony. Anne and her family moved to Rhode Island, but detractors followed, and she later moved to New York. Dogged by controversy and persecution, Anne relied on God's promise to be with her and courageously stood by her beliefs.

MY RESPONSE: What criticism do I need to face with courage?

The reason I left you in Crete was that you might straighten out what was left unfinished and appoint elders in every town.
Titus 1:5

HER SERVICE: Mission work

HER MESSAGE: The most effective servant draws others into ministry.

HER STORY: For more than forty years, Murilla Baker Ingalls demonstrated an amazing ability to involve people in God's work.

Murilla met her husband at a missionary meeting, and in December 1850 they were wed at her Wisconsin home. Six months later, they went to Burma as missionaries. Murilla plunged into the work. Her husband died about five years later, urging Murilla from his deathbed to continue ministering.

Murilla evangelized districts where no white woman had ever dared walk. She superintended ten pastors and organized churches and Sunday schools, mobilizing lay leaders. On Saturdays she trained local converts to join her on evangelistic tours into the jungle. By displaying Bible pictures in a marketplace booth, Murilla drew spectators and witnessed to them. When a railroad depot opened in Thongzai, Murilla distributed tracts. She set up a reading room at the depot and opened branch libraries at other train stations, staffing them with tract distributors. According to articles she wrote for a Baptist publication, nearly one hundred Buddhist priests turned to Christianity through her efforts, and some became preachers. Like a magnet, Murilla's contagious enthusiasm for the Lord's work drew others to labor beside her.

MY RESPONSE: What new Christian might I train to serve with me?

Jessie Inglis, birth date unknown–1889

Jesus grew in wisdom and stature, and in favor with God and men.
Luke 2:52

HER SERVICE: Mission work

HER MESSAGE: Effective Christians share Christ through their lives.

HER STORY: John and Jessie Inglis spent thirty-three years as missionaries in what is now Vanuatu, a group of South Pacific islands. After eight years, eight hundred islanders had converted to Christianity. All wore clothes Jessie had helped them make.

Born in Scotland, Jessie was well educated, then worked as a domestic for a large family, an experience that proved valuable on the field. In Vanuatu she learned the language as she taught local girls in a school she organized. She invited seven young women into her home to learn housework so she could teach them Christian virtues in the context of daily life. Jessie made Scripture memorization a priority, once promising cloth for a dress to the woman who could recite the first six chapters of Acts. She had to provide cloth for six dresses.

Jessie helped her husband translate the Bible and other books and financed publication of the Aneityunese Bible by selling arrowroot to New Zealanders. When she heard new mothers sometimes killed baby girls, Jessie promised them dresses if they brought these babies to her. Infanticide soon ceased. Jessie spent the last four years of her life in Scotland helping her husband print the Old Testament.

MY RESPONSE: Whom might I influence for Christ in my daily life?

*Teach the older women to be reverent in the way they live,
not to be slanderers . . . but to teach what is good.*
Titus 2:3

HER SERVICE: Women's ministry

HER MESSAGE: Women need other women.

HER STORY: Since 1997 Dr. Elizabeth Inrig has served as National Director of Women's Ministries for the Evangelical Free Church of America. She directs women's ministries at Trinity Evangelical Free Church in Redlands, California, where her husband, Gary, serves as senior pastor.

During Elizabeth's childhood in Vancouver, Canada, her mother mentored younger women. As Elizabeth watched them bake shortbread and discuss Scripture, she realized that women need other women to understand their problems, to learn to use God's Word, and to pray for each other. After college, Elizabeth taught school, then married and moved to Texas, where Gary attended Dallas Theological Seminary (DTS). Professors' wives helped Elizabeth further appreciate the God-given potential women have for ministering to other women. She also graduated from DTS, and in 2003 she earned a doctorate at Trinity International University.

Elizabeth now leads a team of women who help her teach more than five hundred other women through weekly classes and evangelistic outreaches. She developed a seven-day internship program that equips women to maintain women's ministries in their churches.

MY RESPONSE: How does my church help women build healthy relationships with each other and with God?

Everything got started in him and finds its purpose in him.
Colossians 1:16 MSG

HER SERVICE: Singing

HER MESSAGE: Once you find your purpose, focus on that.

HER STORY: Mahalia Jackson made more than thirty recordings of black gospel music. She was a prominent figure at civil-rights rallies and sang at Dr. Martin Luther King Jr.'s funeral.

Mahalia Jackson was born in New Orleans, the daughter of a Baptist preacher, and she grew up singing. She rocked to the music of a neighborhood church, clapped to the rhythmic beat of slave songs from the past, and delighted in the jazz music so popular in the region. After her mother's death when Mahalia was a teenager, she went to live with an aunt in Chicago. Mahalia became a popular soloist in storefront and tent churches, and her ministry spread across the United States. Some criticized Mahalia's energetic performances. In defense, she quoted passages from Psalms that encouraged clapping and shouting unto the Lord. She recorded her first song in 1930.

Once Mahalia found her purpose in life, she focused on that and refused to be drawn from her gospel roots, even though it meant rejecting lucrative offers from jazz recording companies. To Mahalia, the blues were songs of despair; but gospel songs brought deliverance. Her rich contralto voice, deep faith, and dedication brought her international recognition. She received a Lifetime Achievement Award from the Grammy committee.

MY RESPONSE: What is my purpose in life?

Whatever you do, whether in word or deed, do it all in the name of the Lord Jesus, giving thanks to God the Father through him.
Colossians 3:17

Her Service: Writing

Her Message: Like the little boy who gave his lunch to Jesus, we, too, can be used for God to do miracles if we give what is in our hands to Him and let Him use it.

Her Story: Neta Jackson and her husband, Dave, are an award-winning writing team who have delighted thousands of young readers with the Trailblazer Books—a forty-book series of historical fiction about great Christian heroes.

For many years the Jacksons have carried a passion for racial reconciliation in the church. Several years ago Neta became part of a culturally diverse women's Bible study, which she says "turned my life upside-down and rightside-up." Encouraged by Dave to write a novel inspired by this diverse group of "praying sisters," Neta took the plunge—and the Yada Yada Prayer Group novels were born. As readers devoured the novels, hundreds began forming their own Yada Yada prayer groups all over the country. Neta says gratefully, "Look at the miracles God can do when we give our talents and gifts back to Him."

Neta and Dave live in Evanston, Illinois, where they raised three children—Julian, Rachel, and foster daughter Samen Sang—and are enjoying six grandchildren.

My Response: What gifts and talents do I already have in my hand? How can I give them to Jesus to use?

The Sovereign Lord has given me an instructed tongue,
to know the word that sustains the weary.
Isaiah 50:4

HER SERVICE: Writing, speaking, counseling, and pastoral care

HER MESSAGE: Education plus experience equals ministry.

HER STORY: Joy Jacobs has written three books, including devotional books on Old and New Testament women. She has coauthored a devotional book for couples and a book on singles and sexuality. A popular retreat speaker, Joy is heard on *The Counselor's Notebook* radio program and serves as director of pastoral care at Daybreak Christian & Missionary Alliance Church in Mechanicsburg, Pennsylvania.

Joy majored in English literature at Messiah College, where she met Bob Jacobs of the Jacobs Brothers Evangelistic Association. They married in 1966. Although she had accepted Christ as a child, at age twenty-nine Joy developed a deeper appreciation of Christ's work when an outbreak of chickenpox on her face reminded her of inner sin.

Because of her husband's travel, Joy gave up teaching and concentrated on writing, church work, and raising three sons. Joy took graduate courses to equip herself to counsel others who, like her, had been sexually abused as a child by a family member.

On her fifty-seventh birthday, Joy learned that she had cancer and needed a thyroidectomy. Fortunately, her voice was spared. Joy's education and the unique experiences of her life have made her an effective writer, speaker, and counselor.

MY RESPONSE: What unique perspective and training enables me to empathize with others?

I have brought you glory on earth by completing the work you gave me to do.
John 17:4

HER SERVICE: Mission work

HER MESSAGE: Missionaries don't go because there's nothing else to do; they go because there's nothing else worth doing.

HER STORY: Alma and Gerhard Jacobson spent twenty-five years as missionaries to China.

Born to Mennonites in Ohio, Alma Amstutz was four years old when her father died. After college she taught school, then ministered at Chicago's Hebrew Mission. After a yearlong courtship, she eloped with Gerhard Jacobson. In 1918 the couple and their nine-month-old daughter sailed for Dongxi, China. While overseas, the family grew to include three more girls; an infant son died soon after birth. The Jacobsons spent months apart while Gerhard visited outlying regions. Spiritual warfare was intense. The girls saw apparitions; Gerhard confronted demon possession; and several times the family lost their belongings in conflicts. Despite great danger, Alma once felt God prompting her to visit Gerhard, who had gone to Taiping on missionary work. She revived his faith, which had sunk to a low point in the city's oppressive spiritual atmosphere.

Alma might have had a safer, more comfortable life teaching in a one-room Mennonite schoolhouse, but once she considered the call to mission work, she considered it the only thing worth doing.

MY RESPONSE: To what person or people might God be asking me to go?

It is like a mustard seed, which a man took and planted in his garden. It grew and became a tree, and the birds of the air perched in its branches.

Luke 13:19

HER SERVICE: Founding a ministry

HER MESSAGE: Small tasks, when committed to God, may bring big results.

HER STORY: A. Wetherell Johnson served as a missionary in China but is best remembered for founding Bible Study Fellowship (BSF), an international lay Christian organization that offers classes and publishes her notes and Bible-study questions.

In 1950, during a time of political unrest, Johnson and other missionaries were evacuated from China. Though a native of England, she came to the United States for six months, eagerly anticipating her return to China. At first she traveled and spoke extensively. Then illness sidelined her. As she rested, five women asked her to teach them from Colossians. Johnson almost shrugged off their request, believing that women in America had ample opportunities to study in their churches. But God spoke to her heart, asking her to do this small thing—and she did. She insisted, however, that the women study and answer questions on their own.

The Bible-study group grew, and soon other groups formed. Several years later, Johnson's lessons formed the basis for incorporating BSF. She never would have dreamed that by completing the small task of teaching neighborhood women, her influence would be carried around the world.

MY RESPONSE: To what small task might God be calling me?

[God] comforts us in all our troubles, so that we can comfort those in any trouble with the comfort we ourselves have received from God.
2 Corinthians 1:4

HER SERVICE: Writer and ministry founder

HER MESSAGE: Hollows carved in our hearts by hurts allow us to catch everyday blessings others might take for granted—and pass them on.

HER STORY: Barbara Johnson has sold more than five million books. *Where Does a Mother Go to Resign?* is ranked in *100 Christian Books That Changed the Century*. She and her husband, Bill, founded Spatula Ministries, a California-based nonprofit organization to support struggling parents. Barbara has been named speaker emeritus of Women of Faith conferences.

Barbara has had more than her share of grief. Her husband was once severely injured in an accident. Although he had been brain damaged, he recovered. Two years later, the couple's son Steve was killed in Vietnam, and the Johnsons began ministering to other parents who had lost sons in the conflict. Five years later, when son Tim was killed in an accident with a drunk driver, the couple's ministry grew. In June 1975 Barbara stumbled upon a cache of homosexual magazines in son Larry's room. That incident birthed Spatula Ministries, humorously named to indicate it helps scrape distraught parents off the ceiling with a spatula of love.

A fourth son, Barney, completes the family. In 2001 Barbara was diagnosed with a malignant brain tumor; *Plant a Geranium in Your Cranium* tells how she has coped with the diagnosis and its effects on her life. Barbara's husband died in 2003.

MY RESPONSE: How might I proclaim God's goodness to me during a hurtful experience?

While Jeremiah dictated all the words the Lord had spoken to him, Baruch wrote them on the scroll.
Jeremiah 36:4

HER SERVICE: Book publishing

HER MESSAGE: Stories cross boundaries between generations and offer fresh insight into Christian themes.

HER STORY: As she intends, Carol Johnson's publishing clients' names are far more easily recognized than her own. Editorial vice president at Bethany House Publishers since 1979, Carol has brought the writings of Larry Christenson, Janette Oke, Beverly Lewis, and many other Christian authors to a world of readers.

Books were precious commodities when Carol grew up in Borneo, where her missionary parents supervised a Bible school and indigenous churches among the Dyacks. With new books scarce in the jungle, she reread many favorites, such as *The Pilgrim's Progress.*

When the Indonesian Revolution forced the family to return to the U.S., Carol eventually enrolled at Bethany College of Missions in Minnesota, where she met her future husband, Gary Johnson, who was managing the campus bookstore.

As members of Bethany Fellowship, which included the college, mission, and publishing efforts, Gary became president of Bethany House Publishers and Carol served as librarian until the appointment to her present position. The books, fiction and nonfiction, that Carol has acquired span audiences and ages and offer readers new perspectives on spiritual truths.

MY RESPONSE: What illustration from our postmodern world might I use to help someone understand the Scriptures?

He said to the paralytic, "Get up, take your mat and go home."
Matthew 9:6

HER SERVICE: Ministry to the disabled

HER MESSAGE: Tragic circumstances may draw us closer to God—and to discovering God's plan for our lives.

HER STORY: In 1998 Carmen Jones founded Solutions Marketing Group to help corporations employ, serve, and market to people with disabilities.

When she was a college junior, Carmen was in an automobile accident that left her a paraplegic. While recuperating, she cried out to God, and her faith deepened. She now views the accident as part of God's plan for her life. After two years of working in a counseling job, Carmen moved to Washington, DC, to work as a government program manager. After switching jobs twice more, Carmen saw the need for a link between companies and the disabled community. By founding a company to provide that link, she found God's plan for her life.

Carmen relies on the Scriptures for encouragement and strength. She insists on keeping her word, even when it costs her company extra money. She hosts Bible studies, sends inspirational cards, and prays with coworkers. Through it all, Carmen considers herself a partner with God, ministering in His name to people with disabilities.

MY RESPONSE: How have I noticed God at work in my life? What one step might I take to discover God's plan for my life?

Jesus Christ is the same yesterday and today and forever.
Hebrews 13:8

HER SERVICE: Mission work

HER MESSAGE: God remains the same in good times and in bad.

HER STORY: Ann Hasseltine Judson and her husband, Adoniram, were the first American missionaries to work in the Far East. They established the Burma Mission and worked together in Bible translation.

Ann grew up in Massachusetts and prayed for a place to serve God. She taught school for a few years, then married Adoniram Judson, a Congregational minister who felt God calling him to India. Soon the Judsons lived in a teakwood house surrounded by gardens in Rangoon. With olive skin and brown hair, Ann made a pretty picture in colorful Burmese dress. But the Judsons' world shattered when their son died of a fever. Though grieving, Ann wrote that God remained the same and could be trusted in times of affliction as in times of mercy.

In 1822 an illness forced Ann to spend time in America. After returning to Burma, war broke out with the British, and Adoniram was imprisoned for two years. A pregnant Ann tried to supply him with food. After that baby's birth, Ann, the baby, and two adopted Burmese children slept in a filthy room of a jailer's hut for months while caring for Adoniram, who was recuperating from a tropical fever. After the war, the Judsons went to lower Burma, where Ann died of a fever.

MY RESPONSE: How might I prepare myself to trust in God's faithfulness during times of suffering?

What do you have that you did not receive? And if you did receive it, why do you boast as though you did not?
1 Corinthians 4:7

HER SERVICE: Writing and mission work

HER MESSAGE: Respect the work of those who preceded you in ministry.

HER STORY: Emily and her husband, Dr. Adoniram Judson, served as Baptist missionaries in Burma for four years before his death.

Emily Chubbuck taught school and published books under the pen name of Fanny Forrester. She used her earnings to provide for her ill parents, and her generosity caught the eye of widower Adoniram Judson, who invited Emily to write a biography of his second wife, Sarah Hall Boardman Judson. While collaborating on the book, the two fell in love and married.

Going to Burma to join her husband's mission work was challenging. Emily wrote of frogs hopping from clothes and lizards dropping from ceilings. The couple's first child, Emily Frances, was born in 1847. Adoniram died at sea in 1850, but four months passed before authorities notified Emily. Meanwhile, her second child, Charles, was born and died ten days after his father's death. Emily returned to America in 1851. Respectful of the hard work on the mission field endured by Adoniram's previous wives, Emily completed Sarah's biography while in Burma and, after Adoniram's death, continued to raise Sarah's three children.

MY RESPONSE: To whom might I express appreciation for the groundwork of my ministry?

Because the Sovereign Lord helps me, I will not be disgraced. Therefore have I set my face like flint, and I know I will not be put to shame.

Isaiah 50:7

HER SERVICE: Mission work

HER MESSAGE: Serving God requires sacrifice.

HER STORY: Sarah Hall Boardman Judson served as an American Baptist missionary in Burma.

Sarah and her first husband, George Boardman, had three children on the mission field. They pioneered work at Moulmein along with missionaries Adoniram and Ann Judson, and Sarah founded a girls' school among a mountain tribe. Later, her oldest child, Sarah Ann, was killed in a tribal rebellion. Besides translating religious tracts, Sarah wrote hymns and other religious literature. When George died in 1931, Sarah continued to minister alone.

In 1934 Sarah married missionary widower Adoniram Judson. Their family grew to eight children as they continued their mission work. In 1845, before Sarah had finished translating *The Pilgrim's Progress* into Burmese, she was struck with dysentery. Weary and ill, she, Adoniram, and three of their six surviving children sailed for home. After twenty years of sacrificing safety and comfort to serve God, Sarah died on the island of St. Helena.

MY RESPONSE: What am I willing to sacrifice to serve God?

When the righteous thrive, the people rejoice;
when the wicked rule, the people groan.
Proverbs 29:2

HER SERVICE: Ruling as queen

HER MESSAGE: God's grace is there for the asking—grace to change a lifestyle or to rule a nation.

HER STORY: The revered Queen Kaahumanu ruled the Hawaiian Islands with a firm hand. After her conversion, she influenced Hawaii for Christ.

Kaahumanu's husband, King Kamehameha, died in 1819. She then became coruler with her stepson. When he also died, Kaahumanu became Queen Regent on behalf of the stepson's younger brother.

Even before Christian missionaries arrived in 1820, Kaahumanu fought to improve the status of women, who were not even permitted to eat with men. Kaahumanu resisted the gospel for four years, yet during that time she implemented a code of law based on the Ten Commandments. She took Elizabeth as a Christian name at her baptism in 1825. Her subjects noticed the difference God's grace made in her life and called her "the new Kaahumanu." God's grace also made a difference in the nation. As queen, Kaahumanu demolished pagan idols and refused admittance to Roman Catholic missionaries, fearing their statues would reignite idol worship. She destroyed sugarcane fields, crucial to the manufacturing of rum, and visited the islands of her domain to promote Christianity and literacy.

MY RESPONSE: For what task might I pray for an extra measure of God's grace?

If one person falls, the other can reach out and help. But people who are alone when they fall are in real trouble.
Ecclesiastes 4:10 NLT

HER SERVICE: Founding a ministry

HER MESSAGE: In an age of independence, Christian women still need each other.

HER STORY: In 1991 Marsha Kallander founded the Heavenly Hearts Prayer Partner Ministry to help Christian women connect.

Raised in Washington, Marsha accepted Christ at age twelve. The following year her parents separated, and the Lord became Marsha's anchor during this difficult time. In 1981 she married Kirk, a navy dentist. His career necessitated frequent moves, and Marsha missed the neighborhood connections women usually make. In an age of independence, Marsha knew Christian women still need friendships in Christ, maybe more than ever. Instead of fretting, she prayed—and devised a plan.

Two Christian women could meet weekly for one hour to exchange a list of two items of praise, two prayer requests, and two areas in which they want to be held accountable. Each woman would share for fifteen minutes, then they would trade lists and pray for one another.

Marsha tested her idea by partnering with an acquaintance, and their friendship blossomed. Since then many other women have followed Marsha's pattern, and many have become more comfortable with the idea of praying aloud.

MY RESPONSE: What might I do to connect with women in my community?

It was he who gave some to be . . . teachers, to prepare God's people for works of service.
Ephesians 4:11–12

HER SERVICE: Education, evangelism, and women's rights

HER MESSAGE: Women have worth and dignity and the right to an education.

HER STORY: Dr. Helen Kim was the first Korean woman to lead an institution of higher education, serving as dean and then president of Ewha College in Seoul, Korea.

Born near Seoul to a wealthy merchant's family that had converted to Christianity, Helen attended a school established by an American missionary. Ewha Hak-dang was the first school to offer Korean girls a basic education. Helen's schooling there formed the basis of her lifelong effort to ensure that women are treated with worth and dignity and receive an education. After college Helen taught at the school and at Ewha College, then went to America to further her own education. At Columbia University she became the first Korean woman to earn a doctoral degree.

Helen kept Ewha College open during World War II, and the school became Ewha Womans University in 1945. During the Korean War, faculty and students fled the campus. Helen ran a "Campus in Exile" on a hillside, determined that women should continue their education. For three years the women lived in huts and used orange crates for shelving.

MY RESPONSE: How might I help a young woman become all God wants her to be?

Heal the sick who are there and tell them,
"The kingdom of God is near you."
Luke 10:9

HER SERVICE: Medical practice

HER MESSAGE: Women can partner with God to bring health and healing.

HER STORY: Dr. Sally Knox, a respected breast surgeon, serves on the medical and teaching staffs at Baylor University Medical Center in Dallas, Texas.

Sally grew up in Bartlesville, Oklahoma, and accepted the Lord at age nine. As she matured in the faith, Sally felt sure of one thing: God's call to the field of medicine. That surprised Sally's friends. She lacked the aggressive style and confidence they thought she would need. While training, Sally, too, wondered if she could handle the demands of a surgeon's life. Besides, she wanted a family. Nevertheless, Sally enjoyed surgery and felt called to partner with God to bring health and healing to women.

Sally tries to live by godly business practices based on the book of Proverbs. She takes a day of rest each week as possible, offers to pray with patients, and works to provide resources for patients without insurance. In a world where colleagues may assume she would champion abortion, Sally is a staunch pro-lifer. She also supports medical and church-related mission work in Russia and Eastern Europe.

MY RESPONSE: How might I minister to someone who is sick?

He will wipe every tear from their eyes.
Revelation 21:4

HER SERVICE: Supporting missions, advocating adoption, and writing

HER MESSAGE: The sunshine of God's love dispels the darkness of the past.

HER STORY: Executive director of outreach ministries at Azusa Pacific University in California, Carolyn Koons has taken more than 100,000 students and adults on mission trips around the world. She founded Mexico Outreach, which has helped more than ten thousand young people minister. Carolyn shares the story of her abusive past in *Beyond Betrayal*.

Carolyn's family moved around the western United States. Her alcoholic father cursed at his daughter, beat her, and even threatened to shoot her. In her early teens Carolyn ran wild, drank, and stole. At fourteen she was left with friends of the family, who also turned out to be abusive. While living in California with a brother, Carolyn, then a high-school junior, attended a church youth group. She accepted Christ and became active in the Baptist church. She eventually graduated from Azusa and joined the faculty.

On a mission trip to Mexico, Carolyn met Tony. The eight- or nine-year-old boy was accused of murdering a baby brother three years earlier, though prison officials suspected his parents of the crime. Eventually Carolyn adopted Tony and introduced him to the healing power of God's love that had removed the darkness from her own past.

MY RESPONSE: How might God's love shine through me to someone today?

July

They can train the younger women to love their husbands and children.

Titus 2:4

HER SERVICE: Women's ministries

HER MESSAGE: Only a woman can both teach and model godly womanhood; if we don't do it, it won't get done.

HER STORY: In 1984, while ministering to women at Northwest Bible Church in Dallas, Vickie Kraft and her husband, Fred, founded Titus 2:4 Ministries. The program encourages churches to provide relevant women's ministry programs and urges older women to teach and model God's Word to a younger generation.

Both chiropractors, Vickie and Fred first worked together, then entered full-time ministry to serve with Child Evangelism Fellowship and eventually the Luis Palau Evangelistic team. Vickie graduated from Dallas Theological Seminary when she was fifty-seven. A pacesetter, she developed a program called Heart to Heart during her tenure as a minister to women. To participate, women commit to meet monthly for one year. They complete Bible studies, go shopping, minister, or just go to lunch together. The goal is to build a friendship by contacting each other weekly, praying for each other, and becoming aware of each other's needs and sensitivities.

Convinced that only a woman can both teach and model godly womanhood, Vicki speaks to women at retreats and conferences, urging them to mentor other women. One of her books, *Women Mentoring Women*, has been translated into ten languages.

MY RESPONSE: How might I build a mentoring relationship?

Do your best to present yourself to God as one approved, a workman who does not need to be ashamed and who correctly handles the word of truth.
2 Timothy 2:15

HER SERVICE: Founding a ministry, scholarship, and advocating for women

HER MESSAGE: Read scriptures in context, in light of society, and in light of other scriptures.

HER STORY: Dr. Catherine Clark Kroeger is founder and former president of Christians for Biblical Equality, a group supporting women in ministry of all types, and she is the president of a new organization, Peace and Safety in the Christian Home, a network of Christians addressing any aspect of domestic abuse.

Catherine and her husband, a pastor, have served in Presbyterian churches in several states. She has five children and has been a foster mother to forty young people, many from troubled backgrounds. Once her children were in school, Catherine dedicated herself to studying biblical mandates regarding women. She earned a doctorate in classical studies in 1987, then taught in colleges and seminaries, including Gordon-Conwell Theological Seminary in Massachusetts. She insists that her students read scriptures in context, in light of society, and in light of other scriptures. Catherine has organized and chaired various meetings of evangelical scholars on women's issues.

In many scholarly writings, Catherine has explored the seeming contradictions of Scripture regarding women. She explains that Paul's statements that seem to prohibit women from teaching may actually be meant to silence false teachers, since all Christians are encouraged to use their spiritual gifts.

MY RESPONSE: How might I interpret Scripture more accurately?

The prayer offered in faith will make the sick person well; the Lord will raise him up.
James 5:15

HER SERVICE: Healing ministry, preaching, and writing

HER MESSAGE: The human mind cannot explain divine activity.

HER STORY: Kathryn Kuhlman became known for the miraculous healings that took place during worship services she led. Thousands attended, and many claimed healing after she prayed.

At a little church in Concordia, Missouri, fourteen-year-old Kathryn sobbed in remorse over her sins. A few years later she set out in ministry with her sister, Myrtle, and Myrtle's husband, an evangelist. Later, a woman named Helen Guilford became Kathryn's pianist and traveling companion, and the two developed a church/radio ministry in Denver. The ministry ended in 1938, when Kathryn married. After several years, however, the couple divorced.

In one of Kathryn's services in Franklin, Pennsylvania, in 1946, a woman was suddenly healed of a tumor. Soon a man, blind for twenty-two years, received sight. In 1948 Kathryn moved her meetings to Pittsburgh's Carnegie Hall. The red-haired woman with the slow drawl insisted that the human mind could not explain divine activity, and anyone yielded to the Holy Spirit might invoke the same miracles. She declined to be called a preacher, claiming she simply shared her experiences. Kathryn wrote *Nothing Is Impossible with God* and founded the Katherine Kuhlman Foundation for the purpose of saving souls.

MY RESPONSE: What divine activity have I seen that I cannot explain?

Each of you must put off falsehood and speak truthfully to his neighbor.
Ephesians 4:25

HER SERVICE: Mission work and writing

HER MESSAGE: To encourage others, write openly and honestly.

HER STORY: Isobel Kuhn and her husband, John, served as missionaries among the Lisu tribe with China Inland Mission. She founded the Rainy Season Bible School. A prolific author, she did not sugarcoat her experiences.

Isobel came to the mission field through honest dialogue with God—after a university professor's remarks made her question her faith. Isobel and her husband were both headstrong, arguing over household help and the wording of prayer letters. Isobel wrote candidly of their conflicts, but she also shared how they persevered by God's grace. She wrote about converts who later rejected the faith and about the pain of sending her young daughter away to school.

In 1950 Isobel left the country amid guerrilla warfare, but John stayed. He was later transferred to North Thailand, an assignment Isobel accepted reluctantly. It meant learning another language and facing new challenges and trials at the age of fifty.

Isobel was diagnosed with breast cancer several years later and returned to the United States. There she spent the final two years of her life writing open and honest accounts of life on the mission field so that others might be encouraged to work through their challenges.

MY RESPONSE: What am I trying to keep others from seeing about God or about me? How might my transparency help others?

Marilyn Kunz, 1927–1999
Catherine Kay Schell, 1926–

All Scripture is God-breathed and is useful for teaching, rebuking, correcting and training in righteousness.
2 Timothy 3:16

THEIR SERVICE: Founding a ministry

THEIR MESSAGE: Home Bible studies offer spiritual food, a sense of community, and support.

THEIR STORY: Marilyn Kunz and Catherine Kay Schell cofounded Neighborhood Bible Studies, which now furnishes study materials to groups around the world.

Marilyn, who held a master's degree in Christian education, met Kay, a nurse, when both counseled at a Billy Graham Crusade. The women later moved into a suburban New York City community where there were few evangelical churches. Christians there had been motivated by an evangelistic crusade to reach out to neighbors who felt threatened by invitations to church. So Marilyn and Kay began to write Bible study guides based on inductive questions Christians could use to lead home Bible studies. Within five years, people in two hundred groups had found spiritual food, a sense of community, and support through Marilyn and Kay's Bible study materials. As people relocated, the movement spread.

Neighborhood Bible Studies incorporated in 1965. The studies urge leaders to keep the focus on the chapter under study, to avoid drifting off the topic, and to view the Bible as the final authority. Kay credits Marilyn for being the visionary and the writer of clear inductive questions. Kay edited and revised their series of thirty guides.

MY RESPONSE: Whom might I invite to my home for Bible study?

My frame was not hidden from you when
I was made in the secret place.
Psalm 139:15

HER SERVICE: Founding a counseling and pregnancy care center

HER MESSAGE: Every person is precious from the moment of conception.

HER STORY: Millie Lace founded Concepts of Truth, Inc., a ministry that offers professional counseling to children, youth, and adults and free pregnancy care to women. Concepts of Truth offers post-abortion women's Bible studies, a national help line, and counseling for crisis pregnancies.

Millie and Dail Lace already had a three-year-old son when Millie got sick during a second pregnancy. After taking a drug to shrink a tumor, she was told that her life and the baby's well-being were in danger. Insisting that the baby's heart was not yet beating, her doctor urged her to get an abortion. Afterward Millie suffered physical complications and intense emotional pain. For twelve years she begged God's forgiveness. Then she heard a woman testify of God's healing after a similar experience. Millie realized she had been duped into thinking it was in her best interest to eliminate what some considered a blob of tissue. She came to understand that every person is precious—from the moment of conception.

Now a licensed professional counselor, Millie helps women overcome shame and grief and find God's peace. She counsels girls to remain chaste.

MY RESPONSE: How might I promote respect for life?

God did not give us a spirit of timidity, but a spirit of power, of love and of self-discipline.
2 Timothy 1:7

HER SERVICE: Social reformer

HER MESSAGE: The Holy Spirit equips us for the ministry to which we are called.

HER STORY: Realizing women form a key force in shaping a country's moral atmosphere, Beverly LaHaye founded and serves as chairperson of Concerned Women for America (CWA). The Washington DC–based group boasts five hundred thousand members, many involved in local chapters, and since 1979 has grown to become the largest public-policy women's organization in America. Beverly has written and coauthored several books, including *The Spirit-Controlled Woman.*

When she was a toddler, Beverly's father died. Her mother remarried, but Beverly suffered from a poor self-image. After marrying Tim, a pastor, Beverly took a backseat, raising their four children, teaching Sunday school, and hoping no one would ask her to do more. Then she heard a talk on the power available through the Holy Spirit, and Beverly asked God to empower her. With that prayer, she gained victory over the timidity and anxiety that had plagued her. Tim followed suit, and the borders of the couple's ministry expanded. In 1971 they founded Family Life Seminars.

Beverly hosted a radio show for more than ten years, *Concerned Women Today*. Today CWA can be heard on the Internet at www.cwfa.org. CWA personnel speak before government leaders on issues, such as the sanctity of human life, pornography, and the protection of marriage.

MY RESPONSE: How might I seek the fullness of the Holy Spirit?

They went around to all the towns of Judah and taught the people.
2 Chronicles 17:9

HER SERVICE: Christian education and writing

HER MESSAGE: God has made our minds ready to learn—if we're appropriately taught.

HER STORY: Marlene LeFever's books include *Creative Teaching Methods* and *Learning Styles*. As director of educational ministries and publisher development with Cook Communications Ministries, Marlene speaks at conferences that draw thousands. She directs international institutes for Christian publishers.

Marlene's love for teaching the Bible developed as she listened to her mother tell Bible stories. Marlene earned a master's degree in Christian education at Wheaton College. Wanting to encourage children's creativity instead of yawns, she wrote curriculum as a missionary schoolteacher in Japan. Marlene discovered that God had made her students' minds ready for learning—they just needed to be appropriately taught.

Her research into learning styles has helped thousands of teachers do a better job of teaching learners of all ages "the way God made them, not the way we wish he had made them, and not the way we used to think he made them." Her books suggest teaching methods to reach four styles of learners: imaginative, analytic, common sense, and dynamic. Marlene suggests that learning styles also play a role in matching volunteers to appropriate ministries, in patterning worship experiences, and in getting along with our family members.

MY RESPONSE: How might an understanding of learning styles help me reach others for Christ?

I am going to send you what my Father has promised; but stay in the city until you have been clothed with power from on high.

Luke 24:49

HER SERVICE: Mothering

HER MESSAGE: With God as our partner, we can accomplish much.

HER STORY: Evelyn LeTourneau was named American National Mother of the Year in 1969 for "mothering" hundreds of young people.

Evelyn eloped—marrying R. G. LeTourneau—before she turned seventeen. Her first child was born in 1918 but died the next year, an experience that caused the LeTourneaus to reevaluate their lives and ministry. R. G. began teaching Sunday school, and Evelyn picked up his teenage students. In 1929 R. G. founded LeTourneau, Inc., which prospered while developing the world's largest earthmoving equipment. R. G. made a point of employing homeless boys. Evelyn mothered and sometimes housed twenty or more of them, leading many to the Lord.

In 1935 the couple established the LeTourneau Foundation to channel 90 percent of their income into Christian work. Evelyn purchased Bethany Camp in Indiana for summer ministry to youth. The couple eventually settled in Texas, where they founded LeTourneau University. R. G. once asked Evelyn to serve hot tamale pie to eight thousand people; she ordered two thousand pounds of ground beef, cooked it, and dished it out. With God as her partner, she accomplished a great deal.

MY RESPONSE: How can I include God as a partner in every aspect of my life?

All men will hate you because of me, but he who stands firm to the end will be saved.
Mark 13:13

HER SERVICE: Martyrdom

HER MESSAGE: Dying for Christ inspires others to live for Christ.

HER STORY: Joice Lewes died a martyr's death for embracing the Protestant faith.

Joice grew up attending a Catholic church in Stafford, England. Her first husband, the father of her two sons, died in battle. She then married Thomas Lewes, a wealthy man. A few years later, when she heard of a minister who was martyred for his faith, Joice asked a godly neighbor about the religion that inspired such devotion. Joice embraced reformed Christianity and stopped attending Catholic services. When her husband demanded that she return, she did—but turned her back on a priest sprinkling holy water and was reported to the bishop.

Thomas forced a man to eat the document he was carrying summoning Joice to report for questioning. Both Thomas and Joice were charged and appeared before the bishop. After Joice explained her position, Thomas was excused, paid bond for Joice, and was told to bring her back in a month. He complied, and she was then sentenced to death by fire. Priests offered to hear a final confession, but Joice refused. She lifted her hands and died gracefully. Her faith never wavered, even at the stake. Dying for Christ, she strengthened the faith of friends and challenged them to live for Christ.

MY RESPONSE: How might I strengthen the faith of friends?

Put on the full armor of God, so that when the day of evil comes, you may be able to stand your ground.

Ephesians 6:13

HER SERVICE: Mission work

HER MESSAGE: Those who proclaim peace often face spiritual warfare.

HER STORY: Lelia Lewis served as a missionary in Bali with her husband, A. Rodger Lewis, for more than four decades. They planted three churches, and Lelia's Christian education expertise helped start a national Christian education movement.

After marrying in 1948, the couple studied at Nyack College, then accepted a New England pastorate. The daughter of missionaries, Lelia started her own missionary assignment—with her husband—in Bali in 1953. They had requested a post that lacked a gospel witness.

Lelia taught children, including her own five, in her home and attracted marketplace crowds with flannelboard stories. But the peace of the gospel contrasted sharply with the atmosphere of the island, which showed evidence of spiritual warfare. People decorated gargoyles on buildings with flowers, considering them island gods. Many believed the souls of the dead wandered about after bodies were cremated, so they stayed indoors then, hiding in darkness. At times Lelia fearlessly held people who coughed up objects while being delivered from demon possession. The couple continued in active ministry in Bali until 1994, then settled in Carlisle, Pennsylvania.

MY RESPONSE: How might I dress in spiritual armor before sharing the gospel?

We know that we have passed from death to life, because we love our brothers.
1 John 3:14

HER SERVICE: Shopping for missionaries

HER MESSAGE: See a need and meet it.

HER STORY: In 1999 Marcie Lind started Mom's Missionary Shopping Service. Since then she has purchased countless items for missionaries and shipped them around the world from her home in Fargo, North Dakota.

Marcie grew up on a Minnesota farm. When her oldest child served as a missionary on the island of Bonaire, Marcie recognized the need for a missionary shopping service. Upon retiring from a nursing career, she offered her services—first to missionaries from her own church and later to other churches and mission organizations.

Missionaries notify Marcie of specific needs by e-mail, telling her their preference for shipping. They request items such as clothing, books, school supplies, computer software, hardware, and toiletries. Whatever the request, Marcie shops locally, on the Internet, and through catalogs. She buys the items and mails them to the missionaries, noting the total cost, including shipping. Marcia adds no service fees. She spends fifteen to twenty hours per week shipping everything from heartburn remedies to replacement truck windows. By seeing a need and meeting it, Marcie has developed a ministry that reaches far beyond her North Dakota home.

MY RESPONSE: What need do I see? How can I meet it?

All your words are true; all your righteous laws are eternal.
Psalm 119:160

HER SERVICE: Leading an abbey

HER MESSAGE: A knowledge of Scripture undergirds and strengthens our spiritual gifts.

HER STORY: Lioba served as an abbess in Bischofsheim, Germany, and had authority over other regional Benedictine nunneries.

Lioba's mother dreamed she gave birth to a church bell, and an aged nurse told her it meant her daughter must be dedicated to God. So the baby was named Lioba, "beloved," and reared by the abbess of an English monastery. As a young woman Lioba became well versed in theology and church law. It was said that nuns read the Scriptures to her even as she slept. Lioba was a cousin of Bishop Boniface, "the apostle of Germany," who requested that she help him establish a monastic community. She began work in Germany in 748. Boniface granted Lioba access to the monastery of Fulda, where she prayed and consulted with monks, a privilege most unusual for women at that time.

Her reading, intelligence, and knowledge of Scripture equipped Lioba to work as an administrator and counselor. Using her spiritual gift of leadership, she trained nuns to serve as superiors in other convents. Church bishops visited Lioba, seeking her wisdom and counsel. When she dreamed of drawing a purple thread from her mouth, an elderly nun told her it represented divine wisdom.

MY RESPONSE: What portion of God's Word will I memorize?

Teach these great truths to trustworthy people who are able to pass them on to others.
2 Timothy 2:2 NLT

HER SERVICE: Speaking and writing

HER MESSAGE: By serving as mentors, we offer God's grace to those who need to be transformed and equip them to pass on the faith.

HER STORY: Florence Littauer and her husband, Fred, founded what has become known as Christian Leaders, Authors and Speakers Services (CLASServices, Inc.) to teach communication skills. Her book *Personality Plus* has sold more than a million copies.

A Depression-era child, Florence set goals for herself: get an education, gain financial security, and marry. She reached her final goal when she wed Fred Littauer in 1953. In 1965, at a Christian Women's Club luncheon, Florence accepted Christ. Fred soon followed suit, and the couple's priorities changed. Marriage classes they taught in their home flourished. Then, in the fall of 1980, a study of 2 Timothy 2:2 led the Littauers to develop what has become an international ministry based in Albuquerque, New Mexico. The gifted communicators wanted to teach what they had learned about speaking so that others might minister more effectively.

Although Fred died in 2002, Florence and her daughters lead a professional team of speakers and writers at CLASSeminars, who mentor participants in effective communication. Those who attend are challenged to step forth as transformed communicators with the potential to transform the world for Christ.

MY RESPONSE: How might I equip someone to equip others?

If you are a teacher, do a good job of teaching.
Romans 12:7 NLT

HER SERVICE: Teacher training

HER MESSAGE: Training transforms teaching.

HER STORY: For forty years Rita L. Lobdell has inspired children's teachers to teach God's Word more effectively. As a faculty member of the Child Evangelism Fellowship (CEF) Leadership Training Institute in Michigan and Missouri, Rita trained church leaders, missionaries, and volunteers throughout the United States. From 1978 to 2004 Rita served as state director of education for CEF of Eastern Pennsylvania; she continues as associate state director.

Rita committed her life to Christ as a child in Indiana and soon spoke of becoming a missionary. Her Christian service began as a Sunday-school teacher, but Rita quickly became frustrated with rowdy students who cared little about God's Word. Then a few hours of training transformed Rita's teaching. She learned how to share the gospel in ways that appealed to children, and she learned how to challenge Christian children to live out their faith. Kids in her class became excited about God's Word, and Rita became excited about helping others excel at teaching the Bible.

In Pennsylvania Rita has developed curriculum to reach children for Christ, conducted teacher training, and conceived a training program for CEF staff members. Those who experience her training tell her they use her principles to teach their own children. Many of her trainees have gone into full-time Christian ministry.

MY RESPONSE: How can I help someone—even myself—become a better teacher?

As iron sharpens iron, a friend sharpens a friend.
Proverbs 27:17 NLT

HER SERVICE: Supporting reform

HER MESSAGE: God uses our strengths and gifts to complement those with whom we serve Him.

HER STORY: The First Lady of the Reformation, Katherine von Bora Luther proved a suitable partner for Reformer Martin Luther of Germany.

Sent to a convent when she was about nine years old, "Katie" took vows six years later. After reading Martin Luther's writings, she and other nuns appealed for his help to leave the convent. He sent a merchant to deliver barrels of smoked herring, and twelve nuns escaped in the empty barrels. Eleven were returned to their families or married off, but Katie, a spunky woman with a quick tongue, seemed hard to place.

At twenty-six, Katie offered to marry Luther, who was forty, and the former monk accepted. He was generous; she was a fiscal planner. He was sickly; she nursed him. He opened his doors to relatives, orphans, and seminary students; she offered hospitality. Katie managed the family's finances, ran a small brewery, and operated a farm. A bright woman, she asked theological questions that challenged Martin's thinking. In every way, Katie's strengths and gifts complemented those of her Reformer husband.

MY RESPONSE: What might I do to support those who serve God beside me?

Teach what is in accord with sound doctrine.
Titus 2:1

HER SERVICE: Education and advocating missions

HER MESSAGE: A well-rounded education must be grounded in Christianity.

HER STORY: In 1836 Mary Lyon founded Mount Holyoke Female Seminary in Massachusetts. She inspired dozens of women to serve as missionaries.

Born and raised in Massachusetts, Mary Lyon grew up in a period when girls were usually taught only practical household crafts. Mary began teaching at age seventeen, and she had a fervor to see pupils converted to Christianity. More than one hundred colleges were open to men when Mary raised thirty thousand dollars to open the first college for women. Offering a well-rounded education grounded in Christianity, Mary required women to bring a Bible, an atlas, a dictionary, and two spoons. Eighty women enrolled the first year.

During her childhood, Mary had heard of missionaries such as William Carey, and she organized her hometown's first missionary society. At Holyoke she maintained faithful communication between students and missionaries. During the school's first twelve years, almost five hundred of its sixteen hundred pupils converted to Christ under Mary's influence. What's more, each graduating class included one or more women who became foreign missionaries. Her pupils carried the gospel to people all over the United States, including Cherokee villages, and to several foreign countries.

MY RESPONSE: How might I add a Christian perspective to the education of children I know?

It is God who arms me with strength and makes my way perfect.
2 Samuel 22:33

HER SERVICE: Medical missions

HER MESSAGE: Whether we need a thimbleful or a bucketful, God's grace is available to God's workers to do His work.

HER STORY: Serving with her husband as a South Seas medical missionary, Mrs. R. B. Lyth learned languages, assisted in Bible translation, and nursed the sick. She once risked her life to save islanders captured by cannibals.

Miss Hardy was a woman of refinement when, in 1836, she married R. B. Lyth, a minister and a doctor. Few would have thought the new Mrs. Lyth could survive jungle life. But she learned the languages of the islanders and, as her husband treated patients, assisted and taught others how to care for the sick. Later she taught women to sew and knit while her husband trained new converts and sent them out to villages to preach.

Once, when the husbands of Mrs. Lyth and her colleague, Mrs. Calvert, were away, islanders prepared to kill and eat prisoners of war. The two women courageously walked by the death drummer into the house of an old king to present a whale-tooth offering and plead for mercy for the condemned. Five women were saved through their efforts. Mrs. Lyth found that God's grace was always available for doing God's work—whether she needed a thimbleful or a bucketful.

MY RESPONSE: For what task must I pray for God's grace today?

Lucy Mabery-Foster, birth date unknown–2002

From him the whole body . . . grows and builds itself up in love, as each part does its work.
Ephesians 4:16

Her Service: Education and writing

Her Message: Accept opportunities to use your spiritual gifts—but don't demand them.

Her Story: In 1990 Lucy Mabery-Foster became the first woman to teach on the faculty of Dallas Theological Seminary (DTS). A professor of pastoral ministries, Lucy also served there as a counselor and therapist. She wrote *Women in the Church*, one of books in the the Swindoll Leadership Library Collection.

Even as a teenager Lucy was encouraged by a Sunday-school superintendent to use her gift for teaching. Later the Texas native taught school, and for twenty years she taught a "Through the Bible" course that drew more than one hundred women weekly. In 1983 she earned a Master of Arts degree in biblical studies, the only course of study open to women at DTS. After she earned a master's degree in theology, the conservative seminary invited her to become the first woman to join the faculty—and she accepted.

Lucy advised her students to serve within frameworks available to them and to wait for God to open doors rather than pushing through themselves. She urged women to leave uncomfortable ministries, but to avoid creating church splits. By accepting the opportunity to use her spiritual gifts in a groundbreaking way, Lucy served as a positive role model for Christian women everywhere.

My Response: What opportunities are open for me to use my spiritual gifts?

He is always wrestling in prayer for you, that you may stand firm in all the will of God, mature and fully assured.
Colossians 4:12

HER SERVICE: Mission work

HER MESSAGE: It's better to take risks than to risk missing out on God's will.

HER STORY: Eleanor Macomber, only the third single woman ever sent out by the Baptist Mission, convinced superiors to let her move into the jungles to evangelize the Karen tribes of Burma.

Eleanor first worked for four years among the Ojibways, a Native American group, in Michigan. She went to Burma in 1836. Willing to take chances rather than risk missing out on God's will, she soon let it be known that she had no intention of staying at the main station in Moulmein.

A male missionary accompanied Eleanor to Dong Yhan and arranged for the construction of a house. Although native leaders were holding a drunken party when she arrived, they responded well to the indomitable woman. Soon twenty locals attended church, and converts evangelized surrounding tribes. Even Adoniram Judson, a missionary with conservative views about women in missions, visited Eleanor's work and baptized three daughters of a tribal chief. As time passed, other congregations formed. Eleanor was so respected that a Karen chief protected her when Burmese Buddhists tried to burn down her house.

MY RESPONSE: What opportunities for ministry might I miss if I refuse to take risks?

An unmarried woman or virgin is concerned about the Lord's affairs.
1 Corinthians 7:34

HER SERVICE: Founding a monastery

HER MESSAGE: People, positions, and possessions grow less important to us as Jesus Christ grows more important.

HER STORY: Three of Macrina's nine siblings became bishops in the early church and were strong advocates of Christianity. After her brother Basil the Great visited religious communities in Egypt, he and Macrina founded similar monasteries, one for men and one for women, at Pontus in northeast Asia.

Macrina was educated by her mother, a woman who spurned the prevalent form of teaching in that day, which was to use poetry, and taught from Scripture instead. Macrina persuaded her mother to allow the family's servants to live as their equals, and she gave her own inheritance to minister to the poor. As Jesus grew more real to Macrina, people, positions, and possessions grew less important. Heaven was so real to her that when her fiancé died, she considered him waiting for her and remained single.

Macrina lived a life of self-denial and died in such poverty that her brother Gregory, Bishop of Nyssa, covered her with his own cloak at her funeral. At her monastery for women, Macrina taught the Bible and built a hospital. She and the other nuns prayed continuously and sang praises to God.

MY RESPONSE: How does my life show that Christ is important to me?

Blessed are they whose ways are blameless, who walk according to the law of the Lord.
Psalm 119:1

HER SERVICE: Founding a convent

HER MESSAGE: To study and pray, come away from the hustle and bustle.

HER STORY: Patterning it after Egyptian monasteries, Marcella founded the first religious community for women of the Western church in Rome. She lived by Psalm 119:1, being careful about appearances in her own life and urging others to live ascetic, devoted lives.

According to writings of the early church father Jerome, Marcella chose to remain a widow after her husband died prematurely. Jerome stayed at Marcella's house for three years as he translated the Bible into the Latin Vulgate. She invited women to hear him speak, and her home became known as a place of study and prayer away from the hustle and bustle of Rome. Marcella continued to correspond with and question Jerome about the Scriptures after he left Rome.

At her convent Marcella wore a coarse brown dress and spent much time in prayer and Bible study. When the Goths attacked Rome, they demanded treasure from her; but she had given her wealth away, and although they beat her, it was said she felt no pain. She begged for mercy for a younger friend, and their captors sent the two to the Basilica of St. Paul for safety.

MY RESPONSE: Where might I establish a quiet place for study and prayer?

He came as a witness to testify concerning that light,
so that through him all men might believe.
John 1:7

HER SERVICE: Ruling as queen and befriending Reformers

HER MESSAGE: By providing a platform for Christians to speak, we influence our family, our neighborhood, and our nation.

HER STORY: Best remembered for her support of the Reformers at a crucial time in church history, Margaret reigned as Queen of Navarre, at one time a kingdom in southern France.

As a young woman Margaret was influenced by Jacques Lefevre d'Etaples, known as the pioneer spirit of the Reformation. She invited him and other Reformers to preach at her palace and shared in communion with them. Her second husband once slapped her face when he heard of her religious activity, but in time he became supportive of the Reformers and offered protection to the persecuted Protestant Huguenots.

An outspoken advocate of religious freedom, Margaret freed French hymnwriter Clement Marot when he was imprisoned on charges of heresy. By providing a platform for church reformers to speak, Margaret influenced her family and her nation. Her daughter, Jeanne, continued her mother's legacy of faith; and her grandson, Henry IV, issued the Edict of Nantes, which protected religious freedom in France.

MY RESPONSE: Whom might I invite to speak in my home at a summer tea or a Christmas coffee? Whom might I invite to attend?

My Father, if it is possible, may this cup be taken from me. Yet not as I will, but as you will.
Matthew 26:39

HER SERVICE: Writing

HER MESSAGE: Until we accept God's will for our lives, our lives are out of God's will.

HER STORY: *100 Christian Books That Changed the Century* lists two of Catherine Marshall's books. *A Man Called Peter* tells the story of her husband, who served as chaplain to the United States Senate. *Christy* offers a fictionalized account of the experiences of Catherine's mother, a schoolteacher.

Raised in West Virginia, Catherine met Peter Marshall, a pastor who would also be her husband, when she went to college. In 1943 Catherine developed a lung infection. For three years she was confined, so Catherine poured her struggles with prayer and faith onto the pages of her journals. She finally relinquished her life to the will of God and experienced peace and, eventually, healing.

Peter died of a heart attack in 1949 at age forty-six. To assuage her grief, Catherine, who had always wanted to write, compiled his sermons in *Mr. Jones, Meet the Master*. With that she launched her writing career. In 1959 Catherine married Leonard Earle LeSourd, a *Guideposts* magazine editor. She accepted as God's will the responsibility of mothering his three small children.

MY RESPONSE: What circumstances that I cannot change might I accept as God's will for my life?

Never get tired of doing good.
2 Thessalonians 3:13 NLT

HER SERVICE: Missions

HER MESSAGE: God grows the harvest, but we plant seeds and cultivate the crop.

HER STORY: The first woman missionary of modern times, Hannah Shepherd Marshman spent forty-seven years in Bengal.

The Marshmans left England for the Danish settlement of Serampore in 1799. Hannah's husband was responsible for running a school, but much of that responsibility fell to Hannah. Besides offering a Christian education to women and children, Hannah bore twelve children, though only six survived. For a while she cooked and cleaned for two men who worked with the couple. By running a boarding school, Hannah earned nearly $100,000 dollars for missionary work in the region that stretched from the Persian Gulf to the Pacific Ocean.

Eurasians and East Indians who were evangelized at Hannah's school went home as missionaries to their own people. She formed a Serampore Native Female Education Society in 1824 so the work might continue. That year the society directed 14 schools with 260 students. In a letter, Hannah praised God for protecting her when she stepped on a snake. She told of being too tired even to read after she tucked the schoolgirls into bed—but Hannah's efforts at planting and sowing the Word of God yielded a great harvest.

MY RESPONSE: How might I plant seeds of faith?

Let your light shine before men, that they may see your good deeds and praise your Father in heaven.
Matthew 5:16

HER SERVICE: Visiting homes

HER MESSAGE: Small gestures ease pain.

HER STORY: An angel of compassion, Ella Mavretic has made and taken hundreds of pumpkin rolls to people who need encouragement.

Ella's caring nature developed naturally. Hobos marked the fence of her childhood home to signal that her mother could be counted on for a handout. After Ella grew up and married, she and her husband were touched by gestures of kindness when they experienced severe trials. In 1972 their home was flooded. Then two operations to correct Ella's overbite went awry, necessitating a third. Tragically, a son, David, committed suicide at fifteen.

Ella's healing from grief and loss began with a craving for chicken corn soup. Unexpectedly, three strangers brought food—including her favorite soup. In gratitude for how others ministered to her, Ella began visiting others. She rings the doorbells of the sick or grieving, offering her trademark pumpkin rolls and leaving behind copies of poems she has found comforting. Sometimes she mails pumpkin rolls to distant states. At least one man came to know the Lord after reading the literature and letters Ella sent him. Her small gestures of support and friendship have eased the pain of many in her Central Pennsylvania congregation, her community, and beyond.

MY RESPONSE: Whose life might I touch with a small gesture of kindness?

God blesses the people who patiently endure testing. Afterward they will receive the crown of life that God has promised to those who love him.
James 1:12 NLT

HER SERVICE: Philanthropy and administration

HER MESSAGE: The difficulties of life serve a valuable purpose if they draw us closer to Christ.

HER STORY: Lady Darcy Maxwell generously supported Methodist and Anglican causes and founded a boys' school.

Educated at home, Lady Darcy attended the Church of Scotland. She married at age seventeen, but just a few years later her husband and their only child died of illness. Lady Darcy's intense grief launched her on a search for spiritual peace. In 1764 she joined the Methodist society and met John Wesley, who assured her that God was using the difficulties of life to draw her closer to Christ. Lady Darcy enthusiastically embraced Methodism. She rose at four in the morning to attend Methodist preaching sessions held at five o'clock. When she returned home, she led her household in prayers. She devoted an hour each morning to intercessory prayer and prayed before and after dinner. In the evenings Lady Darcy read, often books of divinity or theology. Her schedule revolved around prayer meetings and preaching sessions.

For forty years Lady Darcy supervised her boys' school as eight hundred students passed through its doors. She also ran two Sunday schools, paid pastors' salaries, generously contributed to charitable causes, and became known as a skillful counselor.

MY RESPONSE: What experience might draw me closer to Christ?

Is the one who made your ears deaf?
Psalm 94:9 NLT

HER SERVICE: Serving as Miss America

HER MESSAGE: We must step out in spite of obstacles if we want to experience God's surprises.

HER STORY: Heather Whitestone won the Miss Alabama contest, then captured the 1995 Miss America title. She has coauthored three books.

At eighteen months of age, Heather was given a medication that saved her life—but destroyed her hearing. Her mother, Daphne Gray, wanted her daughter to experience life to the fullest, so she taught Heather to read lips and sent her to public school. Daphne focused on five points that Heather later turned into a program to challenge young people to reach their potential: STARS—Success Through Action and Realization of your dreamS.

Heather made Jesus her role model in high school. In spite of her hearing impairment, she competed for college scholarships in talent shows. During the Miss America contest, Heather performed ballet to the tune of "Via Dolorosa" and became the first woman with a disability to win the crown. In 1996 she married John McCallum. The couple operates Heather Whitestone, Inc., which supports Heather's advocacy for the deaf and hearing-impaired communities. In 2002 Heather received a cochlear implant so she could hear her two sons' voices. Heather never lets her disability prevent her from using her abilities and experiencing some of God's most joyful surprises.

MY RESPONSE: What might be keeping me from experiencing God's joyful surprises?

Whoever sows sparingly will also reap sparingly, and whoever sows generously will also reap generously.
2 Corinthians 9:6

HER SERVICE: Philanthropy

HER MESSAGE: God's projects may suffer if we fail to release our resources for His work.

HER STORY: Nettie Fowler McCormick used her wealth to support worthy causes around the world.

Nettie met her husband, Cyrus H. McCormick, on a visit to Chicago. They held many philanthropic meetings in their brownstone home while raising their children. Nettie considered her vast estate a sacred trust, so she hosted missionaries at home and funded their work abroad.

She gave more than four million dollars to the McCormick Theological Seminary in Chicago and funded a building at a college campus in Iran. She also donated to a hospital in Siam, helped fund the first women's hospital in Persia, and gave generously toward theological education in Korea. Nettie paid to improve water supplies, buy agricultural equipment, and build school facilities around the world. If she had not given so generously of her resources to support God's work, many projects would have suffered.

MY RESPONSE: To what worthy cause might I make a significant (for me) contribution?

"I will restore you to health and heal your wounds," declares the Lord.
Jeremiah 30:17

HER SERVICE: Songwriting, being an ordained minister, and writing

HER MESSAGE: God can turn painful memories into beautiful ministries.

HER STORY: Named 1998 Songwriter of the Year by the American Society of Composers, Authors, and Publishers, Terri McFaddin also won an American Music award and two Grammy awards. She has cowritten theme songs for two movies: *Big*, starring Tom Hanks, and *Men in Black*, starring Will Smith. She is a popular speaker and has written three books: *God Made Me Beautiful*, *Only a Woman*, and *Sapphires and Other Precious Jewels*. Her books encourage women to recognize their worth.

At age twenty-two Terri married Adam McFaddin. They soon had a house and two daughters. After seven years of marriage, Adam developed terminal cancer. He died three years later. Faced with losing her home, Terri turned to alcohol and tranquilizers. During this time she discovered strength in songwriting. Overwhelmed by fear and depression, Terri had neglected her mail. But a close friend encouraged her to open just one envelope each day. The first she opened contained a check for $10,000 for the release of her first song by the Jackson 5. By 1975 Motown Records was paying Terri eight hundred dollars a week. After several hit records, she earned enough money to purchase a home in the Hollywood Hills of California.

Still struggling with depression, Terri began work on a gospel-music project. In 1978, after visiting a church, she accepted Christ. As Terri gradually recovered from phobias and anxiety attacks, she started a Bible study support group called Help for Hurting People. She later organized Women's Discipleship Group and also conducts a popular Internet Bible study, www.wdgonline.org. Terri went on to earn a master of theology degree at Fuller Theological Seminary and recently married Charles Solomon. They reside in Los Angeles, California.

MY RESPONSE: What is one step I might take to heal from a painful memory?

He has sent me . . . to bestow on them
a crown of beauty instead of ashes.
Isaiah 61:1, 3

HER SERVICE: Writing and speaking

HER MESSAGE: God helps us triumph over tragedy.

HER STORY: Cheryl McGuinness wrote *Beauty Beyond the Ashes* and launched a speaking ministry by that name to share how God helped her cope with the death of her husband. Tom McGuinness, copilot of American Airlines Flight 11, was killed when his plane crashed into New York City's World Trade Center on September 11, 2001.

Cheryl grew up in Massachusetts and accepted Christ at a youth camp. She and Tom dated in high school and married in 1983 after she graduated from college. In 2000 Cheryl, weary of juggling her career and a family that included two children, quit her job. Tom, an airline pilot, transferred to Portsmouth, New Hampshire, and the family looked forward to spending more time together. Then came the tragedy of 9/11.

In the days that followed, Cheryl sensed God's comfort and love through His people. She learned to trust God for healing. And she focused on the cross of Christ so she could forgive the perpetrators of the attack. As she accepted God's help to triumph over her tragedy, she committed her life to supporting others going through crises.

MY RESPONSE: How has God helped me through a hard time? Whom might I encourage by sharing my story?

August

When they saw the courage of Peter and John . . . they were astonished and they took note that these men had been with Jesus.
Acts 4:13

HER SERVICE: Christian education

HER MESSAGE: Discipleship is the natural result of sound Christian education.

HER STORY: Christian educator Henrietta Mears inspired more than four hundred people to enter full-time Christian service.

Dream Big, Henrietta's motto and the title of her biography, says a lot about the Christian educator who dressed in big hats and dreamed big dreams. She had once considered becoming a missionary, but instead she directed Christian education at Hollywood Presbyterian Church in Hollywood, California. Within a few years "Teacher" had attracted a class of five hundred college students.

Henrietta opened her home to the Hollywood Christian Group and led many entertainers to the Lord. When Henrietta couldn't find biblically accurate Sunday-school curriculum, she wrote her own and eventually founded Gospel Light Publications. She also opened Forest Home, a retreat center for young students, and established Gospel Literature International (GLINT), which continues to publish her books and curriculum in more than one hundred languages.

Instead of leading Henrietta to the mission field as she had first expected, God led her to the people of Tinseltown. She offered sound Christian education and nurtured disciples, including Billy Graham and Bill Bright, who became giants of the faith.

MY RESPONSE: What might I do to support the Christian education program of my church?

The Sovereign Lord will wipe away the tears from all faces.
Isaiah 25:8

HER SERVICE: Humanitarian work

HER MESSAGE: Faith springs from soil watered by our tears.

HER STORY: Heather Mercer survived more than three months of imprisonment by the Taliban in Afghanistan for teaching Christianity in a Muslim country.

Heather attended high school in Virginia and threw herself into activities, but she failed to measure up to her own high standards. Her parents divorced, and she rebelled by breaking their rules. Then Heather accepted Christ. She promised that if Christ healed her hurting heart, she would follow Him anywhere. That path led to Afghanistan.

All went well for a few months. Then one day a strange man took Heather, her colleague Dayna Curry, and six other aid workers to a reform school converted into a prison. In October 2001 the United States launched Operation Enduring Freedom against terrorists in Afghanistan. At times, as bombs fell, Heather hid under a bunk and cried with despair. U.S. Special Forces rescued her on November 15. *Prisoners of Hope* tells Heather and Dayna's story of danger, tears, hope, and victory. They founded Hope Afghanistan to continue ministry to the Afghani people so that someday faith may spring from the soil watered by their tears.

MY RESPONSE: What step might I take to nurture faith in those involved in a situation that has brought me to tears?

The body is not made up of one part but of many.

1 Corinthians 12:14

HER SERVICE: Planting churches

HER MESSAGE: Church ministry takes a team effort.

HER STORY: Elizabeth Meson and her husband, Lorenzo, served as church planters in Argentina for more than twenty years before coming to the United States in 2000.

Elizabeth treasures her memory of the first woman she led to the Lord at her kitchen table. But then the mother of five tried to live up to people's expectations of the perfect pastor's wife and soon felt overwhelmed. When no one volunteered to direct Sunday school, Elizabeth accepted the task—and struggled with the responsibility. Through prayer and study she realized that others, too, were accountable to use their spiritual gifts. Convinced that God had gifted someone in the area in which she lacked expertise, Elizabeth cancelled Sunday school—and a director soon stepped forward.

Wherever she serves, Elizabeth tries to avoid the pitfall of thinking she has to do it all. She knows that church ministry takes a team effort. Just as God calls Elizabeth to minister to women, God calls people to lead worship, to teach Sunday school, and to join in the many other tasks required to fulfill the Great Commission. Church ministry takes all of us doing our best.

MY RESPONSE: What's my role on the team? How might I improve as a team player in my church?

I commend to you our sister Phoebe, a servant of the church in Cenchrea.
Romans 16:1

HER SERVICE: Church leadership, social work, and writing

HER MESSAGE: Deaconesses extend Christ's hands into the world.

HER STORY: At the 1888 Methodist Conference, Lucy Jane Rider Meyer was instrumental in gaining approval for the creation of a deaconess order. She was involved in the founding of more than forty humanitarian organizations, including a hospital and a children's home. Seated in 1904, Lucy was among the first women delegates at a Methodist general conference.

Lucy founded the Chicago Training School for City, Home, and Foreign Missions, now part of Garrett-Evangelical Theological Seminary. She earned a medical degree and, in 1887, founded in Chicago the first of many deaconess homes to minister to the poor. As editor of the *Deaconess Advocate,* Lucy rose as a leader in the deaconess movement. By 1939 more than one thousand Methodist deaconesses served in various ways. The goals of the lay order include alleviating suffering, eradicating injustice, and facilitating the development of full human potential. Deaconesses extend Christ's hands to those who are marginalized. They may work in a church-related vocation or in a helping profession. Current ministries focus on issues related to prison, environment, refugees, immigration, health care, education, homelessness, women and children, youth and families, senior adults, peace with justice, working poor, and a wide variety of church and community ministries.

MY RESPONSE: How might I extend Christ's hands in my neighborhood?

I praise you because I am fearfully and wonderfully made.
Psalm 139:14

HER SERVICE: Founding a ministry and speaking

HER MESSAGE: God designs each woman as a unique bundle of traits, talents, spiritual gifts, and experiences, and uses her for a wonderful purpose.

HER STORY: In 1999 Christie Miller founded the Northwest Christian Speakers Bureau to train and unite speakers for service. Her own speaking ministry, Fresh Look Ministries, takes her across the United States to address topics relevant to women's struggles.

When Christie attended a women's retreat that she felt failed to address the real needs of women, she secretly created a set of her own talks. To her delight, people started asking her to speak. That was when she realized that God was going to use her unique traits, talents, and spiritual gifts to help her reach other women. Her curious nature gave her a hunger for God's Word, and painful challenges drove her deeper into Scripture. God was faithful to reveal what Christie calls treasures of truth for women, and Christie now shares the results of her studies with audiences. Her book *Married But Walking Alone* addresses the differences in couples' spirituality.

Christie's God-given creativity helped her to run Creative Youth Theater and Drama Outreach Team, for which she writes plays. And her experience in a family business has equipped her to organize her ministry. The mother of two teaches part time and thrives on reading and listening to tapes, gleaning ideas for ministry.

MY RESPONSE: For what special purpose has God designed me?

[Apollos] began to speak boldly in the synagogue. When Priscilla and Aquila heard him, they invited him to their home and explained to him the way of God more adequately.
Acts 18:26

HER SERVICE: Ministering

HER MESSAGE: Churches are best served when men and women serve Christ together.

HER STORY: Dianne Miller is the first and only woman on the five-member Core Vision leadership team of Northwest Bible Church in Dallas, Texas.

Although communication styles may differ—women may open conversations with small talk while men plunge directly to the topic—Dianne has found that churches are best served when men and women serve Christ together. Dianne believes that, generally speaking, men, who were given the task of caring for the earth, continue to be task oriented; and women, who were given the privilege of childbearing, continue to be concerned with relational connections and with creating beauty and order.

In keeping with her belief, when the church staff plans an event, Dianne makes sure matters such as childcare, food, and the décor of the area are considered. She serves as a voice for women with concerns they might not share with men, such as proper accommodations for nursing mothers. Although married, Dianne empathizes with single women and widows who feel excluded if activities, such as lighting Advent candles, focus only on families. She has found that men and women complement each other in the home—and in the church.

MY RESPONSE: How do men and women share in the leadership of my congregation?

Yet for your sakes he [Christ] became poor, so that you through his poverty might become rich.
2 Corinthians 8:9

HER SERVICE: Mission work

HER MESSAGE: To bring the lost to Christ, identify with them.

HER STORY: Petra Malena "Malla" Moe spent half a century in Swaziland, South Africa, working as a missionary with the Scandinavian Alliance Mission.

Malla was born in Norway but joined her sister in Chicago in 1884. After hearing a missionary speaker, Malla took a two-week Bible course and set out for Africa with seven others. A converted Zulu man, Johane Gamede, helped her bridge the cultural gap and became her lifelong ministry associate.

To closely identify with those she was trying to reach, Malla moved into their native *kraals*, enclosures that housed the huts of several families. Though Malla sometimes offended colleagues with her outspoken, domineering ways, the Africans loved her and wept when she left for furloughs. She was unconventional and assertive in evangelism, once hanging on to a man's arm as she prayed aloud for his salvation. He repented on the spot. In 1898 Malla established the Bethel Mission.

At age sixty-five Malla set out on evangelistic campaigns in her "gospel wagon," a horse-drawn covered wagon that carried her and helpers to places never before reached with the gospel. She appointed local pastors to head the congregations she established and oversaw their training and development.

MY RESPONSE: How might I better identify with someone I want to reach for Christ?

[Love] always protects, always trusts, always hopes, always perseveres.
1 Corinthians 13:7

HER SERVICE: Mission work

HER MESSAGE: We cannot evaluate eternal results from an earthly perspective, but we can obey God and reach out in love.

HER STORY: Under hostile conditions, Mary and her husband, Robert, evangelized the Bechuana tribe of South Africa for fifty-one years.

Mary Smith was fascinated by mission reports as she studied at a Moravian School near Manchester, England. When Robert Moffat, an aspiring missionary, came to work on the Smith farm, he and Mary discovered their mutual interest. Robert left for the mission field in 1816, and Mary followed three years later. They married in Cape Town and moved six hundred miles inland to Kuruman. As Robert preached and translated the New Testament, Mary taught the women to sew, garden, and understand the Scriptures.

Local tribesmen stole water by diverting it from the Moffats' irrigation ditch, and they stole vegetables the Moffats managed to raise. Mary, with nine children, tried to solicit household help. But local women refused to learn how to wash clothes and could not be trusted to care for the children. Refusing to evaluate eternal results from an earthly perspective, Mary simply obeyed God. Showing the love of Christ, she taught the women to dress modestly and in time opened a sewing school. As the Bechuanas converted, their lifestyle changed, and the Moffats joyously held their first baptism service in 1829.

MY RESPONSE: How might I obey God and show His love to the unlovely?

Those who sow in tears will reap with songs of joy.
Psalm 126:5

HER SERVICE: Mothering

HER MESSAGE: God answers a mother's fervent prayers for her children's salvation.

HER STORY: Monica's son, Augustine, became Bishop of Hippo and one of the church fathers.

Monica was born to a Christian family but married Patricius, a pagan Roman official. Although the marriage was not happy, she showed patience and humility when faced with a disagreeable mother-in-law or a hot-tempered husband, and her husband converted late in life. It's said that before Augustine's birth, Monica consecrated him to God. She warned him of sin's consequences, but to no avail. Augustine took a mistress at age sixteen and joined a heretical sect called the Manicheans. Monica once asked a bishop to counsel her son. He refused but assured her that her tears were not in vain. Monica must have felt as though the heavens were brass as year after year she begged God to save her wayward son.

One day, while in a garden, Augustine cried out to God. As he heard a child sing, "Take up and read; take up and read," he picked up a Bible and was soon convicted of his sin. He later wrote of how Monica had wept over his spiritual waywardness. He was baptized on Easter in 387. Before her death, Monica had many conversations about God with Augustine. Although many years had passed, God answered the fervent prayer of a mother for the salvation of her son.

MY RESPONSE: For whom might I intercede for salvation with tears?

"Neither this man nor his parents sinned," said Jesus, "but this happened so that the work of God might be displayed in his life."
John 9:3

HER SERVICE: Writing, social work, preaching, and teaching

HER MESSAGE: God heals bodies and spirits in each generation.

HER STORY: A charter member of the Assemblies of God, Carrie Judd Montgomery published a journal, *Triumphs of Faith*, which focused on themes of the Pentecostal and Holiness movements. Her book *The Prayer of Peace* offered patterns of prayer for physical healing. She also wrote *Under His Wings*.

Born in Buffalo, New York, Carrie credited the prayers of Holiness preacher and faith healer Elizabeth Mix for her healing of injuries that had left her an invalid after a childhood fall. Carrie's testimony of healing formed the foundation of her ministry, which later included preaching. In 1880 Carrie moved to California, where she married George C. Montgomery, a wealthy businessman. The couple dedicated themselves to the support of Christian social and missionary work. They worked in close affiliation with the Christian and Missionary Alliance and the Salvation Army, and their efforts supported the founding of a California orphanage, a missionary training school, and a home for missionaries on furlough. Carrie traveled around the world to observe and write about the newly emerging Pentecostal movement, with its emphasis on the anointing of the Holy Spirit and healing.

MY RESPONSE: For whose healing—spiritual or physical—might I intercede?

You will be my witnesses in Jerusalem, and in all Judea and Samaria, and to the ends of the earth.
Acts 1:8

HER SERVICE: Bible translation, preaching, and mission work

HER MESSAGE: Support God's work abroad, but don't neglect God's work at home.

HER STORY: Dr. Helen Barrett Montgomery was the first woman to translate and publish the Greek New Testament in everyday English, a work called the Centenary Translation. In 1910 she became the first woman to lead a major denomination when she assumed the presidency of the Northern Baptist Convention (now American Baptist Churches in the United States).

Helen and her husband, William Montgomery, dedicated their lives to Christian service and gave generously to their church, Lake Avenue Baptist Church, in Rochester, New York. Helen once sent her sister a gift of twenty-five dollars, suggesting that the only way to keep things, such as money or talents, was to give them away. To observe mission activity, Helen traveled with Lucy Peabody, a mission organizer, to Europe, Asia, and Egypt. Concerned for women's rights, the two women raised funds to build women's colleges abroad. Although Helen also held offices in various mission organizations, she and William also faithfully taught Sunday school in their local congregation.

MY RESPONSE: How might I better support both world missions and my local congregation?

They have devoted themselves to the service of the saints.
1 Corinthians 16:15

HER SERVICE: Ministry of support

HER MESSAGE: A vision for ministry prompts a sacrificial attitude.

HER STORY: In 1862 Emma Revell married Dwight L. Moody, known as one of the greatest evangelists of all times. She strongly supported his vision for ministry.

Emma was born in London but moved to Chicago as a child. When she was fifteen, she met Dwight Moody in a Baptist Sunday-school class: he was recruiting workers for his exploding Sunday schools, and she agreed to teach. After marriage, Emma focused on Dwight's ministry. He founded three Christian schools, preached to a hundred million people, won a million souls, and inspired thousands of preachers. Emma protected Dwight from interruptions, helped with correspondence, and raised their three children, mostly while living in hotels and the homes of supporters during Dwight's frequent speaking engagements. When their house burned during the great Chicago fire of 1871, Emma alone helped her sons escape—Dwight was at church preaching.

Emma never complained about sacrificing for the sake of ministry. Dwight's colleague, Ira Sankey, said of her, "Amid all that has been said about what has made Mr. Moody so great a man . . . one of the greatest influences of his life came from his wife. . . . She more than any other living person is responsible for his success."

MY RESPONSE: What can I do to support some worthy ministry?

Where your treasure is, there your heart will be also.
Matthew 6:21

HER SERVICE: Mission work

HER MESSAGE: It's a partnership: Missionaries give of their lives; worshipers give of their means.

HER STORY: While serving as a missionary to China, Charlotte "Lottie" Moon sent letters home, challenging women to support missions. The Lottie Moon Christmas offering now raises millions of dollars each year for missions.

Many people thought Lottie foolish to pursue missions instead of marriage. But Lottie wanted to make a difference. She became one of the first Southern women to earn a master's degree. Forsaking genteel life on a Virginia plantation, Lottie followed her sister, Edmonia, to China as a missionary. The sisters evangelized, offered hospitality, and supplied missionaries with books.

Lottie, an attractive woman, dressed in plain Chinese clothes. On soles made from scraps of garments, she walked fearlessly, even in dangerous places. She once traveled 115 miles in a mule litter to a previously unreached village and ministered there nine years, until funding supported more missionaries. Lottie viewed her work as a partnership with worshipers at home. She repeatedly wrote letters challenging the Southern Baptist Women's Missionary Union to send more funds. Lottie endured a severe famine with the Chinese people, giving all she had to alleviate their suffering. She herself weakened and eventually died of starvation on Christmas Eve.

MY RESPONSE: How much can I give to world missions?

Faith by itself, if it is not accompanied by action, is dead.
James 2:17

HER SERVICE: Writing, social work, and philanthropy

HER MESSAGE: Faith blossoms into good deeds.

HER STORY: Hannah More influenced British society with her writing, her philanthropy, and her dedicated community service.

The plays Hannah More wrote as a young woman were critically acclaimed. After she was converted at age thirty-five, she attended meetings of the Clapham Sect, a group of intellectuals dedicated to combining faith with works. And work she did. Hannah learned of illiteracy and poverty in mining villages, so she and her four sisters began offering Sunday-school classes. She noticed mothers poorly equipped to care for their children, so she started home-economics classes for girls and clubs for mothers. Hannah promoted literacy and distributed clothing, Bibles, tracts, and prayer books. Through many visionary activities and good deeds, she led the way for other single women who wanted to live out their faith in practical ways within their communities.

With pen in hand, Hannah joined parliamentarian William Wilberforce in his quest to abolish the slave trade. Rather than hiding behind a male pen name, as was customary to make a woman's writings more socially acceptable, Hannah signed her works. At her death, her fortune was disbursed to religious and charitable organizations.

MY RESPONSE: What works have blossomed from my faith?

A man will leave his father and mother and be united to his wife, and they will become one flesh.
Genesis 2:24

HER SERVICE: Writing

HER MESSAGE: When marriage gets humdrum, humor and playfulness start things humming.

HER STORY: Marabel Morgan's book *The Total Woman* is listed in *100 Christian Books That Changed the Century.* Her marriage-enrichment program by the same name drew many football players' wives and sparked a movement of women's study groups.

A Miami housewife with two daughters, Marabel set out to revitalize her marriage to Charles O. Morgan Jr. when their union failed to meet her expectations of marital bliss. She noticed weaknesses in communication and explored ways to rekindle romance. In 1974 the resulting book sold more copies than any other fiction or nonfiction project. Marabel appeared on *The Donahue Show,* which publicized one of her suggestions—dressing in clear plastic wrap to greet a husband. *People* magazine listed her as one of the twenty-five most influential people in America in 1975.

At one time, one hundred instructors taught Marabel's marriage-enrichment classes, and *The Total Woman* paved the way as a "crossover" book, reaching both Christian and secular markets. Marabel followed up on the book's success by writing *The Total Woman: Total Joy* and *The Electric Woman.* The latter explained how only God, not spouses, can meet our deepest needs.

MY RESPONSE: How might I surprise my husband or family with a playful diversion?

Whenever the spirit from God came upon Saul, David would take his harp and play. Then relief would come to Saul; he would feel better, and the evil spirit would leave him.
1 Samuel 16:23

HER SERVICE: Hymnwriting and composing

HER MESSAGE: When we live in tune with God, the music of our lives blesses and refreshes others.

HER STORY: Lelia Naylor Morris wrote the lyrics of more than a thousand hymns, and many tunes as well. "Nearer, Still Nearer," for which she wrote both words and music, became one of her most famous hymns.

Born in Pennsville, Ohio, Lelia came to know Christ in early youth. She married Charles H. Morris in 1881, and the two were active in a Methodist Episcopal Church. Lelia used her literary and musical gifts to write hymns for the Holiness camp meetings at which she and her husband ministered. Always in tune with God, Lelia kept a pad and pencil nearby. She jotted down inspirational thoughts while cooking dinner, washing dishes, and working around the house.

When her eyes began failing in 1913, Lelia's son constructed a twenty-eight-foot-long blackboard with staff lines so she could continue to write music. With help from family and friends and a conviction that noble poetry springs from a noble life, the gifted woman refreshed and blessed others within the body of Christ.

MY RESPONSE: How might I become more conscious of the song of God's Spirit in my daily life?

Devote yourself to the public reading of Scripture, to preaching and to teaching.
1 Timothy 4:13

HER SERVICE: Teaching and speaking

HER MESSAGE: Effective teaching is based on the Word of God and illuminated by our experiences.

HER STORY: Elizabeth Ritchie Mortimer, a Methodist teacher and speaker, cared for John Wesley as he lay dying.

Elizabeth Ritchie felt stifled by her Methodist parents. At age twelve she went to live with a family friend, who denigrated Methodism and offered Elizabeth a full social life. When she returned home four years later, she was led to Christ. Elizabeth struggled mightily with what her friends would think of her. She experienced such joy in her salvation, however, that she soon witnessed to neighbors, prayed for an ailing brother, and taught children the gospel.

In the decade following her conversion, she developed into a counselor and Methodist class leader who led small groups in study. Elizabeth found that her teaching was most effective when based on God's Word and illuminated by her own experiences. She related well to others and enjoyed visiting surrounding areas to speak at Methodist meetings. In the process, she became friends with John Wesley.

MY RESPONSE: To whom might I teach God's Word by sharing an illustration from my life?

A kindhearted woman gains respect.
Proverbs 11:16

HER SERVICE: Mission work

HER MESSAGE: Sometimes it takes a woman to reach a woman.

HER STORY: By promoting education, Hannah Lacroix Mullens parted the curtain that separated Hindu women from society.

Hannah was the daughter of missionaries serving with the London Missionary Society. She was so fluent in Bengali that she was teaching children by the time she was twelve. Hannah accepted Christ at age fifteen, and from then on she taught family servants as well. At nineteen Hannah married Joseph Mullens, a fellow missionary. One day she stumbled upon a surprising way to part the curtain that separated Hindu women from the rest of society. It all began when a native man admired the needlework on slippers Hannah had made. She subsequently visited his wife and spoke of Christ. As a woman teaching needlework, Hannah was able to gain access to the women who, in that society, were mostly confined to their own apartments.

When a physician lamented the death of a local teacher, Hannah suggested opening a school. She ran a girls' boarding school in Calcutta, India, at a time when girls were held in low esteem and married off as young as ten years of age. Over the years, enrollment in Hannah's school grew from fourteen to sixty. Hannah was able to reach a segment of Hindu society to which no male missionary would have had access.

MY RESPONSE: To what woman might I witness for Christ?

Drunkards and gluttons become poor,
and drowsiness clothes them in rags.
Proverbs 23:21

HER SERVICE: Prohibition

HER MESSAGE: To stop abuses, save souls.

HER STORY: Carrie Nation's efforts led to the 1920 passage of the Eighteenth Amendment prohibiting the manufacture, sale, and transportation of intoxicating liquors in America.

Nearly six feet tall, Carrie Nation presented a formidable figure in her fight against alcohol. And she knew no fear. Convinced that the key to eliminating alcoholism was to save the souls of alcoholics, Carrie and supporters of the Women's Christian Temperance Union entered bars and liquor houses to hold gospel services and lecture drunkards on the evil of their ways. Those services usually ended in physical confrontations: women smashed liquor bottles and wielded hatchets. In fact, Carrie sold souvenir hatchet pins to raise money for her campaigns.

At times the spunky woman went home black and blue, but her injuries only strengthened her resolve. In a society where the definition of manliness included wife-beating and drunkenness, Carrie believed something needed to be done. Her tactics sometimes landed her in jail, but she refused to post bond. Instead she preached to inmates and triggered revivals. Some Christians may not have agreed with Carrie's methods, but they applauded her message. Both men and women respected her work to protect people from the ravages of alcoholism.

MY RESPONSE: How might I reach people in a pleasure-oriented culture?

The Lord is my light and my salvation—whom shall I fear?
Psalm 27:1

HER SERVICE: Nursing

HER MESSAGE: One can make a difference for many.

HER STORY: Tending British soldiers wounded in the Crimean War, Florence Nightingale changed the profile of nursing. She proved the need for improved sanitary conditions in hospitals, reformed the nursing system, and saved the lives of thousands of soldiers as well as countless lives in generations to follow.

Florence felt called by God and wanted her life to count. Though nursing was considered an improper occupation for well-educated women, Florence trained as a nurse and was ready when duty called during the Crimean War. Arriving at a hospital in Turkey, she was appalled at the lack of sanitation and basic care. Through careful recordkeeping, she showed that seven times more men died from disease than from their original injuries. In spite of initial resistance, Florence demanded and won hospital reform.

Florence worked as many as twenty hours a day and became known as the "Lady with the Lamp" because she checked on patients by lantern's light. With a strong stomach and an iron will, but little concern for herself, Florence personally nursed those most ill. When the war ended, she founded the Nightingale Home for Nurses in England to pass on her revolutionary nursing ideas. Her fortitude in the face of many who opposed her made a huge difference for countless patients.

MY RESPONSE: What can I do to help others?

You must go to everyone I send you to
and say whatever I command you.
Jeremiah 1:7

HER SERVICE: Writing

HER MESSAGE: God's invitations may lead to occupations.

HER STORY: Diane Noble has authored more than twenty books, including novels, novellas, and nonfiction for women. She previously wrote under the pen name of Amanda MacLean.

With a love for words, Diane read her way through childhood. In college she pursued various courses of study—psychology, history, music, and art—before settling on English. But it took twenty years for the Lord to nudge Diane into writing Christian fiction. Her years of occupational indecision were not lost, however, for she incorporates those early studies and experiences into plots for historical fiction and contemporary romantic suspense books.

God's invitation to write books first came when a Christian publisher asked Diane, a magazine columnist, to develop a gift book for mothers. Later, while she worked as an editor for a Christian relief organization, another author encouraged her to write fiction from a Christian perspective. After submitting proposals, Diane was offered a book contract. Then her company's headquarters moved, but Diane and her husband stayed behind in California. She took that move as a definite invitation from God to focus on what she loved doing best—writing Christian fiction full time.

MY RESPONSE: What invitations has God given me that might lead down a new life path?

I give him to the Lord. For his whole life
he will be given over to the Lord.
1 Samuel 1:28

HER SERVICE: Mothering

HER MESSAGE: The legacy of a mother's faith stretches far beyond her family.

HER STORY: Nonna was the wife, mother, and grandmother of men who served as bishops in the early church.

Nonna won her husband, Gregory the Elder, to Christianity from a sect called the Hypsistarians. From then on he supported and supplemented her efforts to use their resources for God and went on to serve as Bishop of Nazianzus for forty-five years. They likely lived in the region of Cappadocia. According to one son, Gregory of Nazianzus, Nonna dedicated him to the Lord before birth and later shared her vision for his godly future by placing his hands on the Bible in an act of consecration. At a school in Caesarea, Gregory befriended a man who became Saint Basil the Great, a friendship that affected the developing theology of Christianity. Gregory studied theology in Alexandria and, like his father, became a bishop. Nonna's daughter, Gorgonia, also embraced the faith, and her two sons became bishops.

Gregory credited his mother for saving his life by praying for him during a storm at sea. He promised to dedicate his life to God if saved and kept that promise. Through her husband and progeny, the legacy of Nonna's faith stretched far beyond her family.

MY RESPONSE: How might I encourage someone's future in Christ?

You and I may be mutually encouraged by each other's faith.
Romans 1:12

HER SERVICE: Women's ministries

HER MESSAGE: Lead women to Christ, then lead them to one another.

HER STORY: Colleen Nordlund serves as vice president of CRISTA Ministries, a large evangelical parachurch organization based in Seattle, Washington. She directs CRISTA Women's Ministries, which strives to engage, encourage, and equip women to glorify God and enlarge God's kingdom as described in Romans 1:11–12.

Colleen felt called to minister in a way that would support Christian leaders. However, in her ministry she defines "leaders" as "influencers" and believes God calls every Christian to be an influencer for Christ. Touchpoints, groups of local women's ministry directors meeting for prayer and encouragement, is one practical outlet for developing influencers. With a goal of connecting women with resources for life, Touchpoints combines the work of various individuals and organizations to provide biblical teaching applied to contemporary challenges.

Through what she calls "kingdom collaboration," Colleen builds community among believers. Relationship with Christ remains the main focus of the ministry; then relationships with others provide support for service and outreach. Colleen emphasizes prayer in every area of ministry as the key to achieving that ministry's goals. CRISTA also offers support and encouragement for pastors' wives. The CRISTA Women's Ministries Web site, www.womensministries.org, connects women with resources to enrich their lives and ministry.

MY RESPONSE: How might I network with other women for prayer, encouragement, and support?

Even if my father and mother abandon me, the Lord will hold me close.
Psalm 27:10 NLT

HER SERVICE: Writing

HER MESSAGE: Rather than eliminate difficulties, God walks with us through our challenges.

HER STORY: Janette Oke ignited the market of Christian fiction when she wrote *Love Comes Softly*, a romance in a prairie setting. More than twenty million copies of her books have been sold.

Janette's mother descended from Puritans, and her father, a Canadian prairie farmer, from German immigrants; so Janette grew up listening to stories of pioneering the Canadian wilderness. After marrying, she experienced her own heartaches and struggles. The Okes' first child, a boy, and later a grandchild, died of sudden infant death syndrome. As the couple raised three more sons and a daughter, Janette relied on her faith and her family to cope with death, celebrate life, and conquer daily challenges. Through it all she experienced the underlying message of her books: rather than eliminate difficulties from our lives, God walks with us through them.

Janette incorporates life's experiences and challenges into her characters' lives, but she waited until her children were teenagers before launching her career as an author. She writes two or three books each year, some in partnership with T. Davis Bunn. Her books have won numerous awards, including the President's Award of the Evangelical Christian Publishers Association.

MY RESPONSE: With whom might I share a story of how God has walked with me through a challenge?

I have set before you an open door, and no one can shut it.
Revelation 3:8 NKJV

HER SERVICE: Pastoring and social reform

HER MESSAGE: Search for a ministry where you can most effectively use your spiritual gifts and talents.

HER STORY: Anna Oliver was the first woman to graduate from a North American theological seminary and one of the first to pastor a mainline congregation.

Anna taught school in Connecticut, then, following the Civil War, volunteered with the American Missionary Association to teach black children in Georgia. She dealt with poverty, disease, and inadequate facilities, but when she learned that her male supervisor earned eight hundred dollars while she earned only $135, Anna resigned in protest. She moved to Ohio, where women had more rights.

Feeling called to ordained ministry, Anna changed her name from Snowden to Oliver to keep from embarrassing her family: in those days women were discouraged from becoming preachers. She enrolled in theological school in Ohio. There women were discouraged from speaking in public—except when the school needed her as a spokesperson for temperance—so she transferred to Boston University. After earning her degree in 1876, she led congregations in New Jersey and New York. She campaigned unsuccessfully for the ordination of women in the Methodist Episcopal Church. Convinced of a calling to do a great work, Anna always searched for the position that would allow her to use her spiritual gifts and talents most effectively.

MY RESPONSE: How might I more effectively use my spiritual gifts and talents?

Will you not revive us again, that your people may rejoice in you?
Psalm 85:6

HER SERVICE: Writing

HER MESSAGE: Christian novelists can penetrate hearts to revive relationships and renew faith.

HER STORY: The recipient of a Career Achievement Award in inspirational fiction, Catherine Palmer has written more than forty books, including *The Happy Room*, based on childhood experiences in Africa. She won a Christy Award for her novel *A Touch of Betrayal* and was a finalist for *Wild Heather*.

Catherine grew up as a missionary kid in Africa. With only a sister for a playmate, Catherine loved telling stories. As a teenager she jotted them down. She later married, worked as a schoolteacher, and in her spare time wrote a historical novel. But her book proposals were rejected—until her mother-in-law suggested Catherine rewrite the novel as a romance. The result won a writer's contest award and launched Catherine's career.

A committed Christian, Catherine tried to reach a secular readership with stories of faith; however, some Christians criticized her line of work. After talking to another author with similar goals, Catherine switched to a Christian publisher. She now freely expresses a message of faith that may still reach unbelievers. Letters from readers tell her that her work penetrates women's hearts—in the privacy of their own homes—in ways that revive relationships and renew faith.

MY RESPONSE: What Christian book can I pass on that might touch someone's heart?

You were washed, you were sanctified, you were justified in the name of the Lord Jesus Christ and by the Spirit of our God.

1 Corinthians 6:11

HER SERVICE: Social work and advocating holiness

HER MESSAGE: Consecration leads to sanctification and erupts in social action.

HER STORY: Phoebe Palmer was credited with bringing 25,000 people to Christ. The Holiness movement she promoted paved the way for Church of the Nazarene and some Pentecostal groups, such as the Church of God.

In 1835 Phoebe's sister experienced what she called "entire sanctification" and founded the Tuesday Meeting for the Promotion of Holiness in her home, shared by Phoebe and her husband, Walter. Phoebe experienced sanctification two years later. In her leadership of the meetings, which continued for more than twenty years, Phoebe maintained that consecrating one's life to God led to sanctification, a lifestyle of holy living. And in Phoebe's life, that sanctification erupted in social action. She distributed tracts in slums and visited prisons. She founded Five Points Mission, which became a forerunner of settlement houses that offered education and training to the poor. She wrote eighteen books of practical theology, inspiration, and poetry. For eleven years she edited one of the most popular religious magazines of the time, *Guide to Holiness*.

In evangelistic meetings Phoebe and Walter promoted the sanctification experience across the eastern United States, Canada, and the British Isles.

MY RESPONSE: What have I accomplished by dedicating my life to Christ?

He will judge the world in righteousness and the peoples with equity.
Psalm 98:9

HER SERVICE: Civil-rights activism

HER MESSAGE: Do not condone anything that diminishes the dignity of God's children.

HER STORY: By refusing to give up her bus seat to a white man, Rosa Parks took a stand that made her the "mother of the civil-rights movement" in America.

While growing up near Montgomery, Alabama, Rosa attended a private school for black girls. Prayer and Bible reading were woven into the fabric of her life.

On December 1, 1955, after working all day as a seamstress, Rosa sat in the eleventh row of a bus, behind the rows reserved for whites. When a white man later boarded the crowded bus, the driver demanded that the African Americans in Rosa's row rise so the white man would not be humiliated by having to sit next to blacks. Rosa's three companions stood. She remained seated—and was arrested because of it. Through her actions she showed that she refused to condone anything that diminished the dignity of those created by God. Her quiet determination to stand for equal rights made a huge impact on society, sparking a boycott of buses that spurred the civil-rights movement and elevated Martin Luther King Jr. to prominence. In 1956 bus segregation was ruled illegal by the Supreme Court, thanks in part to Rosa Parks's courageous stand.

MY RESPONSE: What behavior am I allowing that might diminish someone's dignity?

August 29 *Sally Parsons*, ca. 1775–date of death unknown

I will praise you among the nations, O Lord;
I will sing praises to your name.
Psalm 18:49

HER SERVICE: Preaching

HER MESSAGE: No matter where we swim, love for God bubbles to the surface.

HER STORY: Sally Parsons preached independently in New England in the late 1700s. Her successful ministry caught people's attention at the New Hampshire Yearly Meeting of the Freewill Baptists, and the group provided her with a horse, saddle, and bridle so she could broaden her outreach.

Sally had come to Christ as a teenager during a 1792 revival. Her mother was happy about Sally's newfound faith, but her father ordered her out of their home. She knelt outside, asking God to forgive him, then moved in with a neighbor. The young woman's love for God soon bubbled forth in her life. She told everyone she knew of Christ's love. Rough New England frontier pioneers gathered to hear what she had to say—and responded to the gospel. Once Sally had a horse, she carried the gospel beyond her region to the towns and villages of New Hampshire.

Eventually Sally's family came to Christ, including her contrite father. To make up for his hastiness in condemning her faith, he promised her a dowry. Sally married another Freewill Baptist minister, and in recognition of her ministry, the denomination gave up any claim to Sally's horse.

MY RESPONSE: What neighbor, friend, or relative might I introduce to Jesus?

"In him we live and move and have our being." As some of your own poets have said, "We are his offspring."
Acts 17:28

HER SERVICE: Writing and poetry

HER MESSAGE: Talent is a gift from God; technology, a tool from God; and personal contacts, our assigned territory.

HER STORY: Frances Gregory Pasch has published more than two hundred devotions and poems in denominational magazines and booklets. She recycles those writings as weekly e-mail devotions to one hundred people. She also creates and sends more than three hundred Easter and Christmas cards each year.

Frances had considered herself a good Christian from childhood. Yet she was unsure how to respond when her son Brian asked if she had a personal relationship with Christ. Participating in Bible studies and reading the Bible led her to make a commitment to Christ. When people asked about the difference they saw in her, she shared the gospel. Frances had never written poetry, but she discovered that she could effectively share her love of God through poems. Some were published in her church newsletter, and in 1990 she began writing verses and enhancing them with clip art for holiday cards.

After discovering her talent with words, Frances considered how she might also use today's technology to reach people for Christ. She now sends weekly e-mails to what she considers her God-assigned "territory." Frances includes insight from her personal devotions, writings relating to specific holidays, or works that have been published elsewhere.

MY RESPONSE: How am I using my talents and technology to reach my "territory"?

Ask the Lord of the harvest, therefore, to send out workers into his harvest field.
Matthew 9:38

HER SERVICE: Outreach

HER MESSAGE: Passion for Christ and compassion for neighbors drives Christians to action beyond church walls.

HER STORY: As executive director of Metro-Link, an interfaith group in Dallas, Texas, Marion Pattillo links those who need a hand with those who can lend a hand. The ministry challenges believers to live out their passion for Christ by showing compassion in their communities.

As a teenager Marion taught Spanish-speaking adults to read. As an adult she discovered that most churches expected missionaries to deal with social issues, such as hunger and housing, but believers themselves seemed reluctant to minister outside the church. Metro-Link has changed that attitude. Organizers and about three hundred volunteers from two suburban churches visited South Dallas, an area marked by poverty, crime, and unemployment, weekly for more than two years. They prayed, picked up trash, and offered to do odd jobs for homeowners. They developed relationships by attending funerals and providing meals. In the third year of the program, Metro-Link formed a ministry partnership with an inner-city church to assist them with their projects in the same neighborhood. Volunteers now lead Bible studies, teach computer skills, renovate housing to offer transitional living to people such as hurricane victims, and teach children to read.

MY RESPONSE: What could my church, class, or home group do to show Christ's love in our community?

September

Keep your lives free from the love of money.
Hebrews 13:5

HER SERVICE: Building monasteries

HER MESSAGE: Our children's security comes from a legacy of faith, not a legacy of wealth.

HER STORY: According to the early Christian scholar Jerome, Paula was the first Roman woman to choose the hardship of life in Bethlehem as a service to Christ. Paula began life as a wealthy Roman aristocrat, yet in the three monasteries she built in the Holy Land, she slept on a mat of goat's hair.

After her husband's death, Paula was won to Christianity by a friend who hosted Bible classes taught by Jerome. Paula began living simply and spending long hours in prayer. She later journeyed with her daughter Eustochium and Jerome to the Holy Land: both women had aided Jerome in his Latin translation of the Bible, and he wanted them to see the places Jesus had walked.

As Paula toured the Holy Land, she gave money to the poor. She then built monasteries to offer women a place to retreat for prayer, Bible study, and service. Relatives worried that Paula would have nothing left to leave her children, but she assured them that her children would be left with the mercy of God. She knew their security came not from a legacy of wealth but from a legacy of faith.

MY RESPONSE: What legacy am I leaving?

I live in eager expectation and hope that . . .
I will always be bold for Christ.
Philippians 1:20 NLT

HER SERVICE: Mission work

HER MESSAGE: Take advantage of every opportunity to promote the vision God gives you.

HER STORY: Lucy Waterbury Peabody was tireless when it came to raising money for missions. As head of the Women's Baptist Foreign Missionary Society, a position she held for twenty-eight years, Lucy formed the Central Committee for the United Study of Foreign Missions to educate church women about foreign-missions needs.

Lucy and her husband, Norman Waterbury, served in India as American Baptist missionaries. Five years later, following her husband's death, Lucy returned to New York. At a meeting, she spoke about foreign missions and met Helen Barrett Montgomery, a Bible translator, who became her partner in fund-raising. Lucy once collected $2,942,555 after getting John D. Rockefeller Jr. to pledge a million dollars if she could match it two to one. She used the money to fund seven schools for women abroad, including a medical school in India.

Lucy married importer-exporter Henry Wayland Peabody, who died two years later. She again devoted her time and finances to promoting missions. She organized rallies across the United States and promoted the vision God gave her at every opportunity. During one two-month period, she, Helen, and their associates gave about two hundred speeches, which raised more than a million dollars for missions.

MY RESPONSE: With what person or group might I share my vision?

Ruth Stafford Peale, 1906–

A word aptly spoken is like apples of gold in settings of silver.
Proverbs 25:11

HER SERVICE: Supporting, encouraging, publishing, and writing

HER MESSAGE: We serve God as we encourage—and sometimes challenge—His servants.

HER STORY: Ruth Stafford Peale cofounded *Guideposts* magazine and Guideposts Publishers with her husband, Norman Vincent Peale. She held many positions, including CEO, at the Peale Center for Christian Living. Ruth wrote two books on marriage and established the Ruth Stafford Peale Center in Syracuse, New York. But her most significant role may have been as wife of a man whose theology influenced the twentieth century.

The daughter of an Ohio Methodist preacher, Ruth postponed her own education to help finance an older brother's. That delay meant that she met Norman as an incoming student during her senior year at Syracuse University. They married a few years later.

Ruth faced challenges from the start. Norman spoke eloquently from the pulpit but showed indecision at home. His creativity suffered if things were out of place, so Ruth kept an orderly house. She countered his depression with optimism and took on church responsibilities to free him for preaching and writing. When Norman's tenure at Marble Collegiate Church in New York City languished on the heels of the Depression, Ruth told him to trust the God about whom he preached. Throughout their marriage Ruth encouraged—and sometimes challenged—her husband, and their church eventually flourished.

MY RESPONSE: What servant of God might I encourage—or challenge—today?

Encourage one another and build each other up.
1 Thessalonians 5:11

HER SERVICE: Writing

HER MESSAGE: We sometimes need encouragement to recognize our own gifts.

HER STORY: Judith Pella coauthored her first book, *The Heather Hills of Stonewycke*, with friend Michael Phillips. They wrote six more books in the Scottish series plus several others before Judith struck out on her own. Since then she has authored ten historical novels and partnered with Tracie Peterson to write others.

Growing up, where others saw history, Judith saw stories. With dreams of becoming an author, she wrote a Civil War spy story at age eleven. But nursing seemed a more noble profession. For a time Judith even turned her back on reading, thinking it too frivolous for a good Christian girl.

A rocky period in her marriage motivated Judith to write as therapy. Then a friend, author Michael Phillips, recognized her gift and invited her to collaborate with him on a novel. The two passed a manuscript back and forth as they researched, wrote, and revised. Finally, a seamless manuscript emerged.

Unhappy in nursing, Judith turned to teaching but quit in 1991 when one of her children needed attention. As she contemplated returning to work, her husband encouraged her to do what she was good at—writing. Judith now does just that—along with quilting, collecting for her dollhouse, and sailing Oregon's Columbia River.

MY RESPONSE: Whom might I encourage to use her talents for God?

Put on the full armor of God so that you can take your stand against the devil's schemes.
Ephesians 6:11

HER SERVICE: Writing and speaking

HER MESSAGE: Where God blesses, Satan presses.

HER STORY: Through her writings, Jessie Penn-Lewis became one of the first women to be considered an authority on Christian doctrine. *War on the Saints*, which addresses spiritual warfare, became a Christian classic and received recognition in *100 Christian Books That Changed the Century.*

Jessie grew up in England, married an accountant, and, at the age of twenty-one, accepted Christ. In spite of poor health caused by a lung ailment, she organized Bible classes across England as part of her job with the YMCA. Her first publication, a booklet titled "The Pathway to Life in God," sold 32,000 copies in five years. She was the only woman to have an essay included in *The Fundamentals*, a compilation of ninety essays that addressed the modernist threat in America. As her name became known, Jessie received invitations to speak in Scandinavia, Switzerland, South Africa, and Russia. God blessed Jessie's efforts. She wrote *Conflict in the Heavenlies* to call attention to the spiritual warfare she had sensed while traveling in Russia.

MY RESPONSE: How might I better prepare myself to engage in spiritual warfare?

I want to know Christ and the power of his resurrection and the fellowship of sharing in his sufferings, becoming like him in his death.
Philippians 3:10

THEIR SERVICE: Martyrdom

THEIR MESSAGE: Godly servants may suffer rejection, pain, and persecution.

THEIR STORY: Two young mothers, Vibia Perpetua and her slave, Felicitas, faced persecution and certain death by going against an edict by Roman Emperor Septimius Severus that forbade Christians to share their faith.

Felicitas feared she would be denied martyrdom since she was eight months pregnant when imprisoned. She and Perpetua prayed the baby would come early, and it did. Though Perpetua's aging father begged her to recant her faith, she refused. Even when she had to surrender her nursing son, she stood firm. Rather than the elaborate last meal offered to prisoners before execution, these believers celebrated a love feast, a meal symbolizing Christian love and kindness. Perpetua then led the group into the arena singing a psalm.

Perpetua tried to protect Felicitas as a mad cow was placed before them to attack them. Even then, Perpetua called out to her brother to hold fast to his faith. As a gladiator tried to behead Perpetua, she guided his sword to her throat. In spite of rejection, pain, and persecution, Perpetua determined to serve God rather than submit to the ungodly edicts of the state.

MY RESPONSE: How might I strengthen my faith to withstand persecution?

We are the clay, you are the potter; we are all the work of your hand.
Isaiah 64:8

HER SERVICE: Hymnwriting and teaching

HER MESSAGE: Rather than clinging to rigid plans, cling to God and let Him shape your ministry.

HER STORY: Adelaide Addison Pollard wrote the words of the popular hymn "Have Thine Own Way, Lord." Although she wrote other lyrics, this is the only hymn still commonly sung.

Adelaide was born in Iowa but moved to Chicago as a young woman. She taught in girls' schools and established a good reputation as an itinerant Bible teacher. She also became involved in the healing and evangelistic ministries of two preachers and testified to being healed of diabetes.

Adelaide wrote "Have Thine Own Way, Lord" after hearing an elderly woman cry out, yielding her will to God's, during a prayer meeting. The words ministered to her own soul, for at the time Adelaide was disappointed that she could not raise funds to serve as a missionary to Africa.

Subsequently Adelaide taught at the Missionary Training School at Nyack-on-the-Hudson. She eventually served in Africa for a brief time, then in Scotland. After World War I, Adelaide ministered throughout New England. As she yielded to God's way rather than clinging to her own rigid plans, God molded and shaped her ministry into something He could use for His glory.

MY RESPONSE: How might God be asking me to yield to His way instead of my own?

Get rid of all bitterness, rage and anger, brawling and slander, along with every form of malice.
Ephesians 4:31

HER SERVICE: Writing poetry

HER MESSAGE: Like ugly scratches on a mirror, bitterness mars a Christian woman's beauty.

HER STORY: In 1987 Margaret Powers received the official copyright for the poem "Footprints." Hallmark Cards bought the poem, and eventually Margaret wrote a book telling the poem's story. She and her husband, Paul, travel with The Little People's Ministry.

As Margaret Fishback and fiancé Paul Powers stopped by a beach on their way to a camp where Paul would be speaking, they pondered their future. Paul saw the single set of footprints left after waves washed over their trail as symbolic that God would carry them through tough times. Margaret later jotted down a poem she called "I Had a Dream," and Paul read it at his speaking engagement. Margaret placed the poem in her wedding album.

Paul's work as an illusionist soon led to performances at amusement parks around the country, and Margaret quit her teaching job to travel with him. Then, in a Washington bookstore, they noticed a poem titled "Footprints." Margaret felt plagiarized. For the next seven years, anger and bitterness marred the beauty of her Christian life. But her daughter finally confronted Margaret scripturally regarding her attitude. She released her bitterness and found God's peace.

MY RESPONSE: How might I rid my life of bitterness from past injustices?

Put your hope in God, for I will yet praise him, my Savior and my God.
Psalm 42:5–6

HER SERVICE: Writing

HER MESSAGE: The right and the wrong, the comfort and the misery, the soothing and the unsettling—God uses all to lead us to Christian perfection.

HER STORY: Elizabeth Prentiss wrote many children's books and novels. She is best known for her poem, which became a hymn, "More Love to Thee, O Christ." Her novel *Stepping Heavenward* sold more than 200,000 copies in the United States and abroad.

Elizabeth grew up in Maine. The daughter of a Congregational pastor, she committed her life to Christ in 1831. She married George Lewis Prentiss, and the couple had six children. The deaths of two children within one year deeply grieved Elizabeth.

In 1853 Elizabeth published her first children's book. Thanks to her household full of kids, her children's stories rang true. Each summer she took her children to a Vermont cottage, where she wrote yet another book. Elizabeth struggled with poor health but counted her suffering as part of God's plan. Her writings indicate she believed that God uses every experience of life, both the good and the bad, to lead Christians down the path to Christian perfection.

MY RESPONSE: What experiences may God be using to mold me into the image of Christ?

Ann Preston, 1810–1906 September 10

Call to me and I will answer you and tell you great and unsearchable things you do not know.
Jeremiah 33:3

HER SERVICE: Praying

HER MESSAGE: Forget formulas, lists, and patterns. Just pray!

HER STORY: Ann Preston lived in constant communion with God. When she died at age ninety-six, ministers from six denominations paid her tribute.

Ann was born in a shanty in the county of Armagh, Ireland, the third of six children. When she was no longer needed to care for younger siblings, she worked as a nursemaid. Ann had less than a week's formal education, because a teacher had declared her unfit for learning. For a time Ann herded cattle; then a Christian woman hired her. Ann reluctantly accompanied her new employer to Methodist meetings, and a sermon on prayer brought Ann to repentance.

Eventually Ann moved to Canada. She couldn't read books, yet she had the ability to read the Scriptures. Hard as she tried, she couldn't memorize other things, yet she easily quoted from the Bible. Ann spent two hours daily at a prayer house in the woods. Once, when a doctor prescribed eggs to improve her health but the chickens were not laying, in answer to Ann's prayer, a hen visited her home daily for three weeks—each time leaving behind an egg. Some derisively dubbed her "Holy Ann." Throughout her life—although she boasted of no lists, formulas, or patterns of prayer—people called on Ann to pray.

MY RESPONSE: How much time will I spend praying today?

In him was life, and that life was the light of men.
John 1:4

HER SERVICE: Writing

HER MESSAGE: As the sun dispels shadows at its zenith, so Christ dispels darkness as we exalt Him.

HER STORY: Eugenia Price, the grande dame of Southern romantic fiction, wrote thirty-nine novels; many made the *New York Times* bestseller list. Her spiritual autobiography, *The Burden Is Light*, announced her conversion and is listed in *100 Christian Books That Changed the Century*.

Eugenia grew up in Charleston, West Virginia, and enrolled in dental school before switching to journalism. After college she wrote scripts for radio and television, but her private life fell apart. On a visit to New York, a friend invited Eugenia to hear Episcopal pastor Samuel Shoemaker. Then, through reading the Scriptures, Eugenia found the light for which she had been searching. As she began to exalt her savior, Jesus Christ dispelled the darkness of her soul.

After giving up her Chicago production company, Eugenia wrote for *Unshackled*, a Christian radio program that told stories of dramatic conversions. Light had been a common theme in her teenage poetry, so when, in 1961, she visited St. Simon's Island in Georgia, Eugenia was attracted to the light, airy atmosphere. She settled there, and it became the birthplace of future books such as *The Beloved Invader*, a novel based on the history of Christ Church in Frederica, located on the island.

MY RESPONSE: How is Christ's light evident in my life?

Leave your country, your people and your father's household and go to the land I will show you.
Genesis 12:1

HER SERVICE: Mission work

HER MESSAGE: Those who leave their families to serve God find new families waiting.

HER STORY: Lydia Christensen Prince mothered dozens of Arab and Jewish children in Jerusalem.

Lydia Christensen grew up in a wealthy Danish family and worked as a teacher; yet she felt unfulfilled. After being baptized in the Lutheran church, Lydia began reading her Bible during the 1926 Christmas season. When she cried out to God, she had a vision of Jesus. With that Lydia devoted herself to prayer and Bible study and was delivered from smoking cigarettes. As the result of two more visions, Lydia felt drawn to Israel. Missionary agencies refused to sponsor her because she, by then, was attending a Pentecostal church; so in 1928 she moved to Jerusalem independently.

One night a man visited Lydia's basement room, insisting she take in his sick baby daughter. Under Lydia's care, the child recovered, and Lydia began her ministry of caring for homeless children. She met Derek Prince in 1945, and he married into her "family," which by then included eight girls. The family stayed in Jerusalem until 1948, then pastored churches in Derek's native England. They also ministered in Kenya, where they adopted an ill African girl, and finally settled in the United States.

MY RESPONSE: Where has God asked me to minister?

Watch your life and doctrine closely. Persevere in them, because if you do, you will save both yourself and your hearers.
1 Timothy 4:16

HER SERVICE: Ruling

HER MESSAGE: Statements of faith clarify our beliefs.

HER STORY: Pulcheria served as empress in Constantinople. She is credited for preserving the orthodox faith after Nestorian and Eutychian heresies threatened to divide the early church. In 451, along with six hundred bishops, she attended the Council of Chalcedon—possibly the only woman to attend. That council drew up a historic statement of faith, the Nicene Creed, which preserved the doctrine of one Christ in two natures.

Pulcheria was only fifteen years old when she took over as regent to groom her brother Theodosius, two years her junior, for the throne. She studied Latin, Greek, medicine, and natural science. After Theodosius took over, she ruled with him for ten years and arranged his marriage to Athenias, who accepted Christianity under Pulcheria's influence.

After her brother's death in 450, Pulcheria continued to rule and took Marcian, a general, as her husband in name only, since she had taken a vow of virginity. She is remembered for building churches, hospitals, and a home for pilgrims. But her greatest legacy may be that of preserving a statement of faith that even today clarifies Christian beliefs and helps believers articulate their faith to others.

MY RESPONSE: Which creed might I memorize and use to share my faith?

Speak up for those who cannot speak for themselves, for the rights of all who are destitute.
Proverbs 31:8

HER SERVICE: Mission work and social advocacy

HER MESSAGE: One woman can't do everything, but she can do something.

HER STORY: In her crusade against the depravity she found within Hong Kong's Walled City, Jackie Pullinger developed St. Stephen's Society and Hang Fook Camp, groups that help drug addicts, prostitutes, and other urban youths.

Jackie's childhood desire to become a missionary was rekindled when she accepted Christ as a college student. Unable to find a missionary society to sponsor her, Jackie boarded a ship in 1966 and asked God where she should get off. She disembarked in Hong Kong and began working as a music teacher. Jackie felt burdened for the street gangs that roamed free, but they rebuffed her attempts to share the gospel. Undeterred, she started a youth club and became an advocate for the poor. Jackie became so accepted that a gang leader asked her to help get members off drugs. She developed a drug rehabilitation program and a church.

The ministries closed when the Walled City was turned into a park, but Jackie's coworkers took their work to the streets, and Jackie continues to speak for the destitute. She may not be able to do everything necessary to transform society, but Jackie has found that by doing something, one woman can make a huge difference.

MY RESPONSE: What might I do to help someone with no voice?

Come to me, all you who are weary and burdened, and I will give you rest.
Matthew 11:28

HER SERVICE: Social reform and Bible translation

HER MESSAGE: Where there is abuse, Christ affirms worth; where there is disgust, Christ imparts dignity.

HER STORY: Pandita Ramabai founded Mukti Mission in India. She translated the Bible into Marathi and is perhaps the only woman to have translated the entire Bible into another language.

The daughter of a Brahmin priest who believed in educating women, Pandita memorized eighteen thousand Sanskrit verses by age twelve. When her father lost land holdings, the family traveled to visit shrines and temples. Pandita felt pity for girls married and widowed in youth and outrage at women burned alive on their husbands' funeral pyres. When her parents and two siblings died of starvation, Pandita's faith in idols was shaken. At a meeting in Calcutta, she accepted Christ. Pandita then realized that where there is abuse, Christ affirms worth; where there is disgust, Christ imparts dignity.

Pandita married and had a daughter. After her husband died of cholera, Pandita began working for the betterment of women. She spent time in England, then went to America and wrote about life in India. The Ramabai Association was formed in Boston to support the education of child widows. Upon her return to Bombay, Pandita opened a widows' home and the Mukti Mission. During famines, she relied on prayer to feed hundreds of people and saw great revivals.

MY RESPONSE: How might I lift a woman's sagging self-esteem?

Faith comes from hearing the message, and the message is heard through the word of Christ.
Romans 10:17

HER SERVICE: Teaching and mission work

HER MESSAGE: Courage, humility, and hard work mark a life useful to God.

HER STORY: Melinda Rankin opened the first Protestant mission in Monterey, Mexico.

Melinda, a New Englander, moved to Kentucky in 1840 to open schools for Roman Catholic families who had settled there. After the war between Mexico and the United States, she learned of the spiritual needs of Mexicans from traveling soldiers. Melinda appealed to churches for help through newspaper articles, and when none responded, she moved to Texas herself.

While operating a school for Mexican girls in Brownsville, Texas, Melinda served as a pipeline for smuggling Bibles and tracts into Mexico. But during the Civil War, the school was confiscated because of her pro-Union sentiments, and Melinda fled to Mexico. There she established a mission in Monterey, an important population center. She repeatedly had to flee rented quarters as priests discovered that she was teaching the Bible. Converts from Monterey, however, carried the gospel to surrounding towns. Tumult in the region and failing health finally forced Melinda to turn the work over to others. But by courageously stepping forth, humbly enduring uncomfortable circumstances, and working hard for twenty years, Melinda introduced many to Christ.

MY RESPONSE: What do I wish someone would do for Christ that I could do myself?

If we died with him, we will also live with him.

2 Timothy 2:11

HER SERVICE: Mission work

HER MESSAGE: To live for Christ, die to self.

HER STORY: Mary Reed served as a missionary to lepers in India for more than half a century.

Mary was born in Ohio and taught public school before going to India in 1884 under the auspices of the Methodist Episcopal Church. Soon after, while recuperating from an illness in the Himalayan Mountains, Mary visited a leper colony. When she again fell ill in 1890, she returned to Ohio for treatment. A spot on her cheek and a tingling finger gave Mary advance warning of the diagnosis: leprosy. She reacted in horror when she heard the word, but on the way home from the doctor's office, Mary decided what would be her course of action. Rather than seek her own comfort, she would live for Christ: she would spend her remaining years reaching out to others who had contracted that dreaded disease. She returned to the Himalayas.

At first Mary's condition worsened as she ministered among the villages that housed lepers, who were rejected by society. Then, in spite her refusal of treatment, Mary's condition improved—and her health was restored. As superintendent of leper homes, Mary acquired additional land and had special houses built for about ninety lepers. She supervised the finances and ministered to patients both physically and spiritually.

MY RESPONSE: What expectation or plan may God be asking me to surrender to Him?

The authorities that exist have been established by God.
Romans 13:1

Her Service: National service

Her Message: Those in high positions need God's counsel.

Her Story: In January 2005 Dr. Condoleezza Rice was sworn in as America's first black woman secretary of state. She had previously served as National Security Adviser under President George W. Bush.

When Condoleezza was growing up in Birmingham, Alabama, her mother, a music teacher, took her shopping for fashionable clothes—regardless of the negative reactions from segregationist clerks. Condoleezza may have been banned from restaurants, but her father, a pastor, assured her that no child of God was second class. She earned a doctorate in international studies by combining three areas of interest: music, politics, and the Soviet Union. Described as a woman with a razor-sharp mind, Condoleezza was the first woman, the first nonwhite, and the youngest person to serve as provost at Stanford University.

Condoleezza held tight to her deeply rooted faith and played the piano at a Baptist church near Stanford University. In speeches she has encouraged listeners not to let circumstances defeat them. Those who work with Condoleezza affirm that her faith is fundamental to her identity. She once hosted an impromptu prayer meeting in her hotel room after a New Year's Eve dinner. With a worldview based on Christian ethics, Condoleezza approaches problems, ranging from personal challenges to national crises, by seeking God's counsel.

My Response: For which government leaders might I pray today?

My heart is stirred by a noble theme as I recite my verses for the king; my tongue is the pen of a skillful writer.
Psalm 45:1

HER SERVICE: Writing poetry

HER MESSAGE: Poems that comfort or chide draw readers closer to God's side.

HER STORY: The poetry of Helen Steiner Rice is found in books, on greeting cards, and on bookmarks. She established a foundation so the proceeds from her writing would benefit charities.

Personable, articulate, and a fashionable dresser, Helen did well working for a public service company. She also opened her own speakers' bureau to address matters such as women's rights. As Helen once faced an audience, unsure of what to say, she found peace through prayer. From then on she relied more on God and less on herself. Helen married a banker, but the Depression soon hit, and they lost their Ohio home. Her husband unexpectedly committed suicide.

Helen then poured all her energy into working for Gibson Art Company of Cincinnati and eventually became an editor. Her poems became popular during World War II, and when someone read one of her Christmas-card verses on a television show, her career took off. Helen trusted God and reveled in His goodness, and her attitude was contagious. Her poems remind readers of the blessings and joys of daily life. As they comfort or stimulate, they draw readers to God.

MY RESPONSE: Whom might I comfort or stimulate with godly counsel?

Rejoice in the Lord always. I will say it again: Rejoice!
Philippians 4:4

HER SERVICE: Founding a ministry

HER MESSAGE: God delights in those who delight in Him in spite of difficult circumstances.

HER STORY: Joy Ridderhof founded Gospel Recordings. The ministry now has a home office in Los Angeles and thirty distribution centers around the world.

While attending Columbia Bible College, Joy's contagious smile and attitude inspired many. She served as a missionary in Honduras, but in 1936 she returned home ill and without financial support. Rather than despair, Joy took to heart God's instruction to rejoice. She used her time of recuperation to delight in God in spite of her difficult circumstances and to pray for those who had responded to the gospel. But she yearned to be more involved. Then, as Joy remembered how the Hondurans had enjoyed playing gramophone records, she developed a plan. She would record the gospel message and songs in Spanish to reach people where she was physically unable to go.

God supplied workers who raised their own money to help run Gospel Recordings, and churches supported the effort. By the time of Joy's death, God had blessed the ministry by enabling workers to make recordings to minister to unreached people in more than four thousand languages.

MY RESPONSE: How might I delight in the Lord by singing, by praying—or by changing the focus of my ministry?

Live a life worthy of the calling you have received.
Ephesians 4:1

HER SERVICE: Preaching

HER MESSAGE: We may need to be uprooted to respond to God's call.

HER STORY: In 1983 Marchiene Rienstra became the first woman to serve as a senior pastor in a Reformed church in America. She helped found the Association for Interfaith Dialogue.

Born in Burma to missionary parents, Marchiene expressed a desire to become a minister at an early age. She moved to Grand Rapids, Michigan, at fourteen and enrolled at Calvin College in 1958. The sponsoring denomination, Christian Reformed Church (CRC), did not ordain women as pastors, and after two years of study, Marchiene struggled to identify her calling. Missionaries of both genders ministered freely, so she questioned the restrictions she faced in the stateside church. She left college to serve for a year as a missionary in Nigeria.

After preaching on a layman's Sunday, Marchiene received high praise and more invitations to speak. Eventually she graduated from Calvin Seminary, but her request for ordination was denied in 1978. She then faced a difficult decision: should she continue to advocate ordination for women within the CRC, or should she minister in a different denomination? After much prayer and family counsel, Marchiene changed denominations in order to follow God's call. Later, after the CRC changed its position on women, she served one of its churches as an interim pastor.

MY RESPONSE: Where can I best fulfill God's call on my life?

Jesus healed many who had various diseases.
Mark 1:34

HER SERVICE: Advocating for the mentally challenged

HER MESSAGE: Society sometimes neglects mentally challenged people—but God loves them.

HER STORY: In 1910 Jacoba Beuker Robbert was a driving force behind opening the Christian Psychopathic Hospital near Grand Rapids, Michigan, now known as Pine Rest Christian Hospital. The facility draws patients from across the United States and Canada.

Jacoba was born in the Netherlands, into a pastor's family. She also married a pastor, and the couple had ten children. The family moved to Chicago in 1893 to lead a Christian Reformed church. They later moved to Kalamazoo, where Jacoba ministered to women at a state mental hospital twice a week. In 1906 she wrote an article for the denomination's weekly magazine, addressing the need for Christian facilities for people with mental and emotional instability. Seeing a connection between body and soul, Jacoba pondered whether true healing could happen without assuring patients of God's love and forgiveness. She knew God loved mentally challenged individuals as much as anyone else, but she noticed that they were too often neglected by society.

With the support of a Kalamazoo pastor, Jacoba formed an association that purchased property to build a hospital to correct this oversight and minister to the physical and spiritual needs of the mentally challenged and troubled.

MY RESPONSE: How might I support someone who needs spiritual or mental healing?

Ellen Stowe Roberts, 1825–1908

It is better, if it is God's will, to suffer for doing good than for doing evil.
1 Peter 3:17

HER SERVICE: Supporting and teaching

HER MESSAGE: Jesus is Lord of the sweet and of the bitter.

HER STORY: Ellen Roberts encouraged her husband, Rev. Benjamin Titus (B. T.) Roberts, during forty years of ministry. He was expelled from the Methodist denomination for criticizing pew rentals and became a founder of the Free Methodist Church. Ellen led an evening class meeting, a group that met for study and prayer, at Chili Seminary, now Roberts Wesleyan College, in New York.

Ellen's religious influence came from an uncle with whom she lived from age fourteen. Watching him pray led her to consecrate herself to God. In 1848, while visiting a cousin, she met B. T. At his request, they communicated only by letters until their wedding day the following year.

As B. T. served in various New York churches, Ellen supported him in prayer. They had seven children, but their firstborn died before his first birthday. As Ellen prayed for power to reach souls, she felt God asking if she could accept such power with suffering, such as the loss of another child. She agreed—and soon received the sad news that her only daughter was dying. Remembered for her pithy sayings, Ellen was a great encourager of others.

MY RESPONSE: How might God use the suffering in my life to make me a more effective Christian?

In all things God works for the good of those who love him.
Romans 8:28

HER SERVICE: Singing and acting

HER MESSAGE: Life's losses leave battle scars, but God turns them into badges of courage.

HER STORY: Dale Evans Rogers played the heroine in twenty-seven films starring her husband, Roy Rogers. Her book *Rainbow on a Hard Trail* is a tribute to Roy, who died in 1998.

As a vocalist with big bands, Dale attracted talent scouts. Eventually she performed with Roy in a Hollywood western, and the two became friends. After Roy was widowed, he and Dale married. Dale, who had a daughter, also became mother to Roy's three children. As she took her new family—which came to include adopted and foster children—to Sunday school, her faith grew.

Dale's books tell how God helped her deal with losses. *Angel Unaware* tells of daughter Robin's death from Down syndrome. From that time on, Dale and Roy offered vibrant personal testimonies of God's faithfulness. Despite pressure to drop religious numbers, they continued singing gospel songs. Dale wrote *Dearest Debbie* to tell how faith sustained her following a daughter's death in a church bus accident, and she wrote *Salute to Sandy* after a son's death. By grace, God transformed Dale's battle scars into badges of courage that brought glory to Him.

MY RESPONSE: With whom might I share a testimony of God's help in overcoming a loss?

I am not ashamed of the gospel, because it is the power of God for the salvation of everyone who believes: first for the Jew, then for the Gentile.
Romans 1:16

HER SERVICE: Practicing law

HER MESSAGE: Many times we need not go to a mission field: it comes to us.

HER STORY: In 1979 Goldie Rotenberg became the first female attorney for Goldstick Weinberger et al. Firm. When she left ten years later, she was the first female partner in the firm that by then also included her name. Since 1984 the Manhattan attorney has served on the board of directors of Chosen People Ministries, an evangelistic organization.

Goldie's Polish Jewish parents came to the United States from Germany a few weeks before her birth, and she grew up in a South Bronx Yiddish-speaking community. Her father teased Goldie about her constant chatter, so she put her communication skills to work and went to law school.

When Goldie accepted Christ, for a time no one in her family except a sister would speak to her. But Goldie stood firm, and her Christian principles and profession of faith became evident at work. Though Jewish colleagues and clients may challenge her explanations of Christianity, she leaves things in God's hands. After all, rather than sending Goldie to a mission field, God brought a mission field to Goldie.

MY RESPONSE: How might I better witness to coworkers, friends, and neighbors?

If we hope for what we do not yet have, we wait for it patiently.
Romans 8:25

HER SERVICE: Writing, teaching, speaking, and singing

HER MESSAGE: Work for God—whether you see God at work or not.

HER STORY: Leola Rundall wrote many poems expressing how God's love and grace surpasses the doubts and disappointments of life. She also wrote a book, *Love Without Measure.*

Leola had a cheerful childhood in Nebraska, singing with four sisters around an old pump organ until it had to be chopped up for firewood one cold winter. Leola's father died when she was young. After high school Leola worked as a secretary, then earned a teaching certificate and taught school. She also studied voice.

Leola married in 1933, and the couple had three daughters. Her husband struggled with alcoholism, however, and Leola returned to teaching, a career she enjoyed for twenty-seven years. Late in life, in answer to Leola's faithful prayers, her husband turned to Christ. As a teacher, and later principal, of an elementary school, Leola lived by God's principles. She served on the first board of the Association of Christian Schools International. She taught Sunday school, sang in church, and frequently ministered in rescue missions. She also wrote seasonal plays for church groups. Leola faithfully served God, even when she couldn't see God at work in her life.

MY RESPONSE: How does my service to God depend upon God's "service" to me?

Lori E. Salierno, 1960–

I have come that they may have life, and have it to the full.
John 10:10

HER SERVICE: Founding a service organization

HER MESSAGE: Life is a gift from God: celebrate it!

HER STORY: In 1996 Dr. Lori Salierno founded Celebrate Life International. She serves as president and CEO of the nonprofit organization, which aims to keep at-risk youths from going astray. Lori has written four books and cocreated Teach One to Lead One, a program that trains young people to impact those in their spheres of influence.

A pastor's daughter, Lori accepted Christ at age nine and, while in high school, felt called to youth ministry. She met Kurt Salierno when he whistled at her in a college library, and she impulsively asked him to a girl-takes-guy event. Kurt was living on the streets to reach the homeless and shared Lori's passion to help people find fulfillment in Christ. They married in 1981. Kurt continues to minister through Church on the Street.

For twenty years Lori has challenged tens of thousands of young people to see life as a gift from God and to celebrate life by living responsibly and successfully. She memorizes her messages and relevant scriptures so she can speak from her heart without notes. Lori also earned a doctorate at Asbury Theological Seminary in Kentucky, and she encourages women to partner through mentoring so they, too, can celebrate life as they develop self-confidence and step out for God.

MY RESPONSE: How might I encourage someone to celebrate life?

"Neither do I condemn you," Jesus declared.
"Go now and leave your life of sin."
John 8:11

HER SERVICE: Pastoring and ministering to the homeless

HER MESSAGE: Christ frees us from sin's chains so we can help free others.

HER STORY: Lavonne Savage serves as church planting and missions director at Phoenix Inner City Church. She formerly served as a senior pastor in Los Angeles.

Molested by two relatives before she was old enough for school, Lavonne turned to prostitution by age seventeen. In 1996 a drug dealer dumped her at a Teen Challenge center, hoping freedom from drugs might make her a more valuable prostitute. Her rehabilitation went smoothly; Lavonne slept her way through withdrawal symptoms. In her dreams God fought the enemy, and Lavonne credits God with protecting her from contracting AIDS.

A drama team's ministry brought Lavonne to commit her life to Christ, and she returned to the streets—this time to share her faith with the homeless. Other Teen Challenge residents walked beside her. If no one answered her knock on cardboard boxes, Lavonne simply crawled in beside the inhabitants.

Taking classes through Global University, Lavonne is working toward ordination. Knowing that Christ frees us from sin's chains so that we can free others, she is developing "Jewels of the Night," a program designed to minister to women on the streets through evangelism, Bible studies, and church planting.

MY RESPONSE: What addiction or weakness might I help someone overcome?

How can they believe in the one of whom they have not heard?
Romans 10:14

HER SERVICE: Christian apology, scholarship, and writing

HER MESSAGE: Do we rule our traditions, or do our traditions rule us?

HER STORY: Dorothy Sayers established a reputation as a novelist, playwright, biblical scholar, and Christian apologist. She broke with tradition by presenting Christ as speaking modern English in a series of radio plays.

Born in Oxford, England, Dorothy grew up in a world of books supplied by her father, an Anglican minister, to his only child. She studied modern languages and taught school before becoming an advertising copywriter. Dorothy was a member of the Christian writers' group that included C. S. Lewis, where she was known for thought-provoking comments. Credited with the slogan "It pays to advertise," she also created "Lord Peter Wimsey," the amateur detective hero of her novels and short stories. She wrote *The Zeal of Thy House*, a verse play, and as an apologist for orthodox Christianity, *The Mind of the Maker*.

Dorothy's most controversial work was *The Man Born to Be King*, a series of plays performed on BBC in the 1940s. Rather than being ruled by tradition, she presented Christ as speaking modern English. Her innovative boldness changed the form of religious playwriting, and the firestorm that erupted stimulated, rather than silenced, Dorothy's voice.

MY RESPONSE: In what innovative way might I step out for God?

Practice hospitality.
Romans 12:13

HER SERVICE: Hospitality, writing, and speaking

HER MESSAGE: To open hearts to God, maintain an open hearth.

HER STORY: As wife of renowned evangelical scholar and philosopher Francis Schaeffer, Edith Schaeffer fully participated in maintaining L'Abri Fellowship, their home in the Swiss Alps. People came from around the world to explore questions of life and faith. An author in her own right, Edith Schaeffer has written sixteen books, including *The Tapestry*, the story of the Schaeffer family.

Born to missionary parents in China, Edith met Francis at First Presbyterian Church of Germantown, Pennsylvania, in 1932. They married three years later. To earn money while Francis attended seminary, Edith was a seamstress. After serving American parishes, the Schaeffers felt called to Europe to counteract the influence of humanist theologians. They settled in Switzerland, where they raised their four children. There, around the hearth and surrounded by the Schaeffer family, many visitors opened their hearts to God and grew in the Christian faith.

A gracious hostess, Edith decorated her Swiss chalet, participated in discussions, and sometimes cooked dinner for as many as seventy-five guests. She also kept in touch with visitors from many religious backgrounds. Francis died in 1984, and Edith moved to Rochester, Minnesota. She continues to support the work of L'Abri, which has six branches around the world, as well as the Francis Schaeffer Foundation.

MY RESPONSE: Whom might I invite into my home to encourage them in their faith?

October

I am sending you to them to open their eyes
and turn them from darkness to light.
Acts 26:17–18

HER SERVICE: Mission work

HER MESSAGE: Ministering to the least-reached requires the greatest commitment.

HER STORY: For more than twenty years Cindy Schmickle has served as a church-planting missionary to Muslims, first in the Philippines and now in Lyon, France, where she also serves as a language coach. She spent four years as assistant to the president of Christar in Reading, Pennsylvania.

Born and raised in Minneapolis, Cindy knelt by her bed to commit her life to Christ when she was sixteen. Five years later she learned that 4 percent of the missionary force was attempting to reach 96 percent of the world's population. Cindy immediately volunteered to go to the least-reached Muslim world.

Ministering to the least-reached has required great commitment from Cindy. She has never faltered from pursuing her call to ministry, although at times it meant breaking off relationships. A single woman, she credits God for meeting her needs so she can meet the needs of others.

Since the Muslim society views a woman living apart from family as immoral, Cindy has had to meticulously guard her reputation and assure neighbors of her family's long-distance relationship. Her North African Muslim community has grown to respect her.

MY RESPONSE: Will I pray for, give to, or go as a missionary to the least-reached?

Whoever follows me will never walk in darkness, but will have the light of life.
John 8:12

HER SERVICE: Mission work

HER MESSAGE: Use the tools at hand to win people to Christ—so they can win others.

HER STORY: Mary Fletcher Scranton founded Ewha School for girls in Korea. The first female missionary to Korea appointed by the Woman's Foreign Missionary Society, Mary befriended many Korean women and trained converts for outreach.

When Mary's son, a physician, was appointed as a missionary to Korea, the Woman's Foreign Missionary Society persuaded Mary, a widow, to go with him. The Society purchased a plot of ground with nineteen straw huts, and Mary opened a school for girls. It was a huge accomplishment: in that day girls of the upper class were educated at home, and Korean women and girls were discouraged from associating with strangers. Not to be deterred, Mary advertised her school as training to develop better Korean girls who would mature into better women. Under Mary's direction, missionaries taught the Lord's Prayer and hymns in English, and an interpreter translated. Mary's goal was to convert Korean girls to Christianity using the tool at hand—education—then train them to reach others.

After five years, Mary left Ewha to work among women from large Methodist Episcopal churches. A beloved figure to villagers, Mary took dangerous month-long trips into the country to evangelize, even after she turned seventy.

MY RESPONSE: What tool might I use to introduce women to Christ?

Speak, for your servant is listening.
1 Samuel 3:10

HER SERVICE: Medical mission work

HER MESSAGE: God calls us to Christian service through experiences and encouragement from others.

HER STORY: Dr. Ida Scudder ministered healing to the women of India, whose culture did not allow them to receive medical treatment from men. One of the first women to graduate from Cornell Medical College in New York, Ida raised funds to build a hospital in Vellore, South India, which eventually became the greatest medical center in Asia.

Ida came from a family of missionaries. Her grandfather was the first medical missionary from America. Her parents left Ida and five siblings while they served in India. Fifteen additional Scudders followed their ancestors' lead. But Ida let it be known that she would *not* walk in their footsteps. Then Ida's mother became ill, and Ida consented to go to India as a short-term missionary to care for her. Ida oversaw the household, taught at one school, and managed another.

Then, in one night, three young men knocked on her door, each begging help for a wife dying in childbirth. They refused to accept assistance from a male doctor. All three wives died. Through that experience and the encouragement of a friend who envied her opportunity to serve Christ, Ida felt God calling her to missionary service and returned home for training.

MY RESPONSE: How may God be using experiences or encouragement from others to speak to me about Christian service?

Blessed is he who has regard for the weak;
the Lord delivers him in times of trouble.
Psalm 41:1

HER SERVICE: Education and philanthropy

HER MESSAGE: God channels love to every segment of society through us.

HER STORY: Elizabeth Ann Seton was the first native-born American declared a saint by the Roman Catholic Church. In 1810 Mother Seton founded the American Sisters of Charity.

Perhaps Elizabeth's dedication to channeling God's love to every segment of society sprang from an early interest in reading Psalms. She married William Seton, a merchant, and with her sister-in-law, Rebecca Seton, founded the Society for Relief of Poor Widows with Small Children, which became known as the Protestant Sisters of Charity. In 1803 Elizabeth, William, and the oldest of their five children traveled to Italy for William's health. He died there, and his young widow returned to face financial trouble.

Influenced by her stay in Italy, Elizabeth converted to Roman Catholicism. In 1808 she opened a school for girls in Baltimore, Maryland. A year later she established a school for poor children near Emmitsburg. Her Sisters of Charity also founded orphans' homes and a school in Philadelphia, considered by some to be the first parochial school in America. Mother Seton's legacy continues through the work of the Sisters of Charity Federation, thirteen women's religious groups with thousands of nuns serving in North and Latin America.

MY RESPONSE: How might I serve as a channel of God's love to a needy segment of society?

I know that through your prayers and the help given by the Spirit of Jesus Christ, what has happened to me will turn out for my deliverance.

Philippians 1:19

HER SERVICE: Preaching

HER MESSAGE: Women may face obstacles, but God offers options.

HER STORY: In 1851 Lydia Sexton became the first woman licensed to preach by the United Brethren (UB), now part of the United Methodist (UM) denomination.

Lydia's father, a Baptist preacher, believed women should be silent in the church. After coming to Christ, Lydia joined a UB church. Upon hearing her speak at a church function, an elder offered Lydia a preaching license. Remembering her father's position, she twice declined before finally accepting. A small group with whom she met weekly for study and prayer presented her name to church officials, and the UB Illinois Conference granted Lydia a preaching license that needed quarterly renewals. When she requested annual licensing from the General Conference, her request was denied. Conference members feared that by granting Lydia's request, women might next desire positions as elders or bishops. Noting her giftedness, however, they did approve her for pulpit speaking.

At age seventy, Lydia became the first woman chaplain at Kansas State Prison. Although male preachers at times opposed her ministry, Lydia encouraged women to find options when they faced obstacles and to gain victory over fear of what men thought, as she had.

MY RESPONSE: What options for ministry has God offered to me?

Don't let anyone look down on you because you are young, but set an example for the believers.
1 Timothy 4:12

HER SERVICE: Evangelism

HER MESSAGE: God sets no age limits—or term limits—on effective Christian service.

HER STORY: With her mother and one hundred donated songbooks, Eliza Shirley sailed from England to start the work of the Salvation Army in America. In an old Philadelphia factory building with a sawdust floor, the Salvation Army opened in 1879.

Born to a Primitive Methodist pastor and his wife, Eliza accepted Christ at age fifteen. A year later William Booth, the founder of the Salvation Army, named her an assistant evangelist to a northern England coal-mining region. At seventeen Eliza asked Booth for permission to expand the work in America, where her father ran a silk mill. Booth declined to back her but gave her permission to use the Army's name.

At first no one showed up at Eliza's meetings. But one night someone lit a tar barrel, and people gathered. A well-known drunk became the first convert, then meetings attracted crowds—and funding. Eliza opened a second branch in West Philadelphia. In spite of being pelted with rotten eggs, Eliza preached salvation. She retired from the group's Chicago headquarters in 1921 as a commandant. Eliza's forty-three years of ministry show that God sets no age limits—or term limits—on Christian service.

MY RESPONSE: What can I accomplish for Christ at my particular age?

Whatever you do, work at it with all your heart, as working for the Lord, not for men.
Colossians 3:23

HER SERVICE: Writing, speaking, and teaching

HER MESSAGE: We dedicate and God deploys.

HER STORY: Margie Sims has written articles for many magazines, including *Brio*, *Breakaway*, *Focus on Your Child*, *Today's Christian Woman*, and *Marriage Partnership*. She also teaches creative-writing classes for homeschoolers and Bible studies for women.

When Margie was nine years old, her best friend invited her to church. Margie accepted Christ the first time she heard the gospel. Growing up, Margie dreamed of getting married, going to the mission field, and having lots of children. In college she majored in social work. Then, during her senior year, she discovered her gift of writing. The first two stories she submitted to magazines were accepted. Margie was hooked.

As she dedicated herself to Christian writing, God deployed Margie in an area of her expertise: family life. Her ministry centers on encouraging women through the hard seasons of marriage and mothering. Her eight children, born over a period of seventeen years, have given her plenty of anecdotes to share. For speaking engagements on family issues, such as those she offers as a New England Mothers of Preschoolers (MOPS) speaker, Margie blends biblical truths with humor. She also serves as the preteen columnist for *TeachKids!* magazine.

MY RESPONSE: How have I shown God that I'm willing to serve—wherever He needs me?

Although they knew God . . . their foolish hearts were darkened.
Romans 1:21

HER SERVICE: Mission work

HER MESSAGE: Life may be hard, progress slow, evil rampant—yet God works through us.

HER STORY: Mary Slessor served as a Scots Presbyterian missionary to Calabar, a region of Nigeria, for thirty-eight years.

Mary grew up the daughter of a shoemaker whose drunken tirades sometimes forced her into the streets. At age eleven she joined her mother in factory work and, once she learned to weave, supported the family. At church Mary was captivated by missionary stories she heard of Calabar. With faith that Christ was with her, Mary went to Calabar. There she taught women to sew, dispensed medicine, preached, and set up churches and schools. At that time the people of Calabar abandoned twins, believing one was evil, so Mary took them in. She trusted that God would see her and her charges through danger and difficulty.

After twelve years Mary moved inland, to a place of guns and rum. But experiences with her father had prepared her to deal with drunken men. Although Mary suffered from chronic malaria, she ignored her pain. Time between furloughs lengthened, and Mary served even farther inland, until her death from swamp fever. Her hands often bled from hard work, but Mary recorded God's faithfulness to her even though her progress had been slow in places where evil was rampant.

MY RESPONSE: How might I minister to a non-Christian whose sin is destroying his or her life?

Surely I am with you always, to the very end of the age.
Matthew 28:20

HER SERVICE: Mission work

HER MESSAGE: Abandonment to God means we need fear no earthly abandonment or loss.

HER STORY: Known as the spiritual great-grandmother of many Tzeltal Indians in Mexico, Marianna Slocum translated the New Testament in two dialects and also wrote primers and a bilingual dictionary over a period of twenty-three years.

During college Marianna felt called to translate Scripture for an unreached tribe. She had a heart defect from a childhood illness, so her parents asked her to wait a year. After taking courses at Philadelphia School of the Bible, Marianna joined Wycliffe Bible Translators in 1940 and began work among the Chol tribe in southern Mexico. Bill Bentley already worked in the region among the Tzeltal Indians, and Marianna eventually served with him.

The two planned to marry on August 30, 1941. While staying at Marianna's home in Philadelphia prior to the wedding, Bill died in his sleep, evidently from a heart problem. Abandoned to God and resting in the knowledge that God had called her and would not abandon her, Marianna returned to her work. With a new colleague, Florence Gerdel, she spent twenty years translating the Bible into the language of the Paez Indians of the Andes Mountains.

MY RESPONSE: What verse will I memorize to remind myself that God won't abandon me?

You did not choose me, but I chose you and appointed you to go and bear fruit—fruit that will last.
John 15:16

HER SERVICE: Preaching and evangelism

HER MESSAGE: God's vision for us turns into reality as we step out to claim it.

HER STORY: Amanda Smith preached her way from north to south in the United States, then took off for England, Scotland, India, Burma, and Africa.

Amanda's father purchased freedom from slavery for his family. At age thirteen, following her mother's death, Amanda worked as a domestic servant. A sermon on holiness prompted her to surrender her heart to God.

Amanda had a beautiful voice and a way with words, and she felt that God had given her a vision to preach. A widow whose children had died, she had no family ties. But she also had no reason to think she could ever attain God's call. She had little education, and few churches accepted women preachers. Still, after attending a conference held by a black denomination in Tennessee, Amanda packed her belongings in a carpetbag and went to Washington DC. Although at times restaurants closed their doors to her, churches opened theirs. Success at preaching in America brought an invitation to preach in England and led to a twelve-year evangelistic ministry abroad. As Amanda stepped out in faith, her vision turned into reality.

MY RESPONSE: What step of faith may God be asking me to take?

Confess your sins to each other and pray for each other so that you may be healed.

James 5:16

HER SERVICE: Mission work

HER MESSAGE: God calls us first to personal holiness, then to Christian service.

HER STORY: Bertha Smith served as a missionary to China for more than four decades. After Communists forced missionaries to leave, she became the first Southern Baptist missionary to Formosa, now Taiwan, where she served for ten years.

Bertha surrendered to Christ as a teenager and sailed for China at age twenty-eight. She didn't believe women should preach, but while serving as the only Baptist missionary in a Shantung province town, she had no choice but to speak.

In 1935 Bertha asked a visiting pastor to pray for a buzzing in her ears, which she had been told would lead to deafness. The pastor put her off. As he preached on personal holiness, Bertha realized that by expecting people to praise her, she had used her ears to sin. Convinced that God calls Christians first to personal holiness, then to service, Bertha confessed and committed her healing to God. After the pastor prayed for Bertha, her ears not only buzzed but hurt. During the next six weeks, however, all symptoms vanished. Bertha retired from missionary service in 1958 and spoke throughout the United States until she died at almost one hundred years of age. The Peniel Prayer Center near her childhood home in South Carolina commemorates her legacy.

MY RESPONSE: How pure are my ears? My eyes? My tongue?

Preach the Word; be prepared in season and out of season.
2 Timothy 4:2

HER SERVICE: Speaking

HER MESSAGE: Our ministry may include dormant seasons.

HER STORY: A deaconess who gained a reputation as a captivating speaker, Daisy Billings Smith laid aside her ministry to marry evangelist Oswald J. Smith.

After Bible college Daisy served in West Virginia's Appalachia, where she preached in an old schoolhouse with an ash-can podium. Next she trained as a deaconess and worked at a Presbyterian church in Toronto. There Daisy enjoyed preaching once a month, counseling, and ministering in the slums.

When Oswald joined the church staff and proposed to Daisy, she struggled before giving up her professional ministry, which was expected of married women in those days. Oswald's evangelical bent, however, clashed with parishioners, and the couple soon turned to mission work among lumberjacks. In 1920 Oswald started a church and began traveling as an evangelist. Daisy, who stayed behind with their three children, felt left out. Oswald later founded the People's Church, but his travel continued. Later in life Daisy joined him and at last found her niche of service—speaking to women's groups about the needs of women in the world. She also hosted a month-long series of radio and television programs. The years when Daisy's ministry seemed dormant were not wasted. Her son Paul succeeded his father as pastor.

MY RESPONSE: What kind of ministry is right for this season of my life?

Trust in the Lord with all your heart and
lean not on your own understanding.
Proverbs 3:5

HER SERVICE: Writing, preaching, and teaching

HER MESSAGE: The Christian's secret of a happy life lies not in ideal circumstances but in trusting Christ in spite of circumstances.

HER STORY: Hannah Whitall Smith's classic book, *The Christian's Secret of a Happy Life,* is still in print.

Hannah grew up a fun-loving child in a Philadelphia Quaker family and daydreamed of becoming more pious. At age nineteen she married Robert Pearsall Smith, a successful publisher, and they settled in Germantown. The couple's first tragedy struck when their oldest child died at age five of a bronchial infection. Four of the couple's seven children died, and at one point Robert's business went bankrupt. He suffered periodic nervous breakdowns. While meditating on Scripture, Hannah was reassured that her salvation did not depend on her circumstances but on God's grace.

Robert established a preaching reputation abroad, and Hannah, too, became known for Bible teaching and preaching. At the peak of his career, Robert was accused of inappropriate conduct toward a woman he counseled, a scandal that ruined his ministry. Through it all, Hannah's life showed she lived by one of the principles about which she wrote: the secret of a happy life lies not in ideal circumstances but in trusting Christ in spite of circumstances.

MY RESPONSE: Have I learned the secret of a happy life?

Anyone who loves his son or daughter more than me is not worthy of me.
Matthew 10:37

HER SERVICE: Mission work

HER MESSAGE: Our most precious possessions—our children—are secure in God's hands.

HER STORY: Nelle Breen Smith was a missionary in Nigeria.

After growing up in Holland, Michigan, Nelle taught school. Missionary speakers were frequent guests in her home, and at a Bible conference she met Johanna Veenstra, a missionary from Nigeria. The two corresponded, and soon Nelle heard God's call. A heart murmur threatened to derail her application for missionary service, but during a year of study at Moody Bible Institute, the murmur disappeared. Friends at her church supported her, and Nelle went out under the auspices of Sudan United Missions, London.

Once settled, Nelle established a school. The women wore boots for protection from snakes as they evangelized villages. During Nelle's first furlough in 1934, she married fellow missionary Edgar Smith, who also was dedicated to reaching the people of Nigeria. Within a few years they had two children. The family returned home for a furlough when the children were toddlers, and Nelle considered staying behind to raise their family. Edgar, however, felt they were both needed on the field. Reluctantly, the Smiths left the children with grandparents. The Smiths' most precious possessions, their children, remained in the United States, safe and secure in God's hands.

MY RESPONSE: How might I show that I trust God to care for my most precious possessions?

Go and proclaim the kingdom of God.
Luke 9:60

HER SERVICE: Evangelism

HER MESSAGE: We are never too old to start something new for God.

HER STORY: At the age of sixty-one, Sarah Sauer Smith began itinerant evangelistic work. For four years she traveled throughout ten states and Canada.

In 1842 a violent windstorm left Sarah shaken, and when a brother accepted Christ on his deathbed, she also repented. Her parents forbade her to attend prayer meetings, so she withdrew to the woods to pray. In 1859 Sarah relinquished all to Christ and later testified of being filled with boldness. Once, when ruffians from a bar repeatedly disturbed a revival service, Sarah publicly prayed that God would convert or remove the bar owner. He died a few days later, and sixty-five people came to Christ.

For a time, a Holiness association met four times each week in Sarah's Ohio home. Then, though Sarah had only received a few months of schooling as a child, she formed a traveling evangelistic team. She left her husband and farm in the care of her oldest son. Two men wrote songs, which Sarah's team sang from a wagon as they arrived in towns. Sarah sometimes preached, and she encouraged other preachers with hearty amens. In these meetings, people were miraculously healed. Although mobs sometimes attacked the evangelists, God protected them, supplied their needs, and planted congregations in their wake.

MY RESPONSE: What may God be calling me to do for Him?

Do not despise these small beginnings, for
the Lord rejoices to see the work begin.
Zechariah 4:10 NLT

HER SERVICE: Ministry and speaking

HER MESSAGE: To do great things, first do small things in a great way.

HER STORY: As chairperson of women's ministries of the Eastern District of the Evangelical Free Church (EFC), Ruth Solberg frequently speaks at conferences and retreats. For four years she and her husband, Dr. W. Richard "Brooke" Solberg, also served as part of the pastoral care team of EFC personnel.

At age fifteen Ruth dedicated her life to Christian service. She attended nursing school and Bible college before marrying. As a young mother of four and a pastor's wife, Ruth organized the Sunday school, served in the nursery, and typed church bulletins. Once parenting demands eased, Ruth, a people person, had more time to lead women's Bible studies and develop relationships. In 1986 Brooke became pastor of a large Allentown, Pennsylvania, church, and Ruth was asked to help reorganize the denomination's district women's ministry. Her great work there led to an invitation to serve as chairperson. That position landed Ruth a spot on the national EFC Women's Ministry Networking Team, where she links local churches to ministry resources and equips women for church leadership through workshops.

Now officially retired, Brooke maintains an active ministry and Ruth frequently speaks. Her dedication to doing small things well has led to steady growth of her ministry.

MY RESPONSE: What small things might I do in a great way?

Very early in the morning . . . Jesus got up, left the house and went off to a solitary place, where he prayed.
Mark 1:35

HER SERVICE: Praying and mothering

HER MESSAGE: Make communing with God a priority—whether or not you see results, feel blessed, or have time.

HER STORY: Kwei-tseng Soong is best known for molding her children's lives through prayer. Chinese statesman Chiang Kai-shek married one of her daughters, and two other daughters married important government officials. A son became a statesman in international finance.

An ancestor of Ni Kwei-tseng was converted by a Jesuit missionary, bringing the family to Christ and the Chinese Episcopal church. At age seventeen she married Charles Jones Soong, a Methodist pastor educated in America. The couple had six children.

Often likened to the biblical Dorcas, Kwei-tseng encouraged women with gifts and Bible stories. She prayed with mothers who brought sick children to her. She met with her family regularly for devotions, and the children knew not to disturb her as she prayed—she frequently rose at dawn and stayed in her prayer room for hours at a time. Her children relied on her prayers, and through her influence, son-in-law Chiang Kai-shek was baptized a year before her death. Kwei-tseng continued to pray—whether or not she saw results, felt blessed, or had time to spare.

MY RESPONSE: How might I develop a stronger prayer life?

When you come, bring . . . my scrolls, especially the parchments.
2 Timothy 4:13

Her Service: Providing reference books for pastors

Her Message: Men and women of God need tools for study.

Her Story: Susannah Spurgeon, wife of well-known preacher Charles Haddon Spurgeon, created a fund to supply reference books to pastors.

Born in the suburbs of London, Susannah grew up in a Christian home. Although she was unimpressed when she first heard Charles H. Spurgeon preach, Susannah was favorably impressed by the interest he showed in her spiritual growth. In 1856 they married. Though she suffered from frail health throughout her lifetime, that didn't keep her from supporting her husband in ministry.

Charles once asked Susannah's opinion of a book he wrote. When she expressed a wish that every preacher in England have a copy, he asked how much she might contribute toward such a project. Susannah responded by placing before him money she had been saving, enough to purchase one hundred copies. When Charles publicized her offer, two hundred Baptist pastors requested copies.

In his next book Charles noted Susannah's creation of a book fund, and money from contributors poured in. Susannah, an author in her own right, will always be remembered for providing tools for study to pastors during an era in which they barely earned enough to feed their families.

My Response: What useful study tool might I provide for a pastor?

October 19 *Elisabeth "Betty" Alden Scott Stam*, 1906–1934

Whether I am in chains or defending and confirming the gospel, all of you share in God's grace with me.
Philippians 1:7

HER SERVICE: Mission work and martyrdom

HER MESSAGE: We can count on God's grace when we need it—in life and in death.

HER STORY: Betty Stam and her husband, John, died at the hands of Communists while serving with China Inland Mission. Betty's poems reveal the soul of a woman totally devoted to God, relying on God's grace both in life and in death.

Betty's parents left Michigan as missionaries to China soon after her birth. She met John while attending Moody Bible Institute. Both put the Lord's will above their own. Betty left for China in 1931, and John followed the next year. They married in 1933. Baby Helen arrived September 11, 1934, and by December the family had settled in Tsingteh. Rife with political unrest, the region was nonetheless deemed safe for missionaries. But on December 6 Communist forces attacked. Although Betty served her captors tea and cakes, they led the family away. The baby's life was spared when an old farmer offered his life for hers. On December 8 the Stams faced the executioner's sword with calmness and courage. Two days later baby Helen was found by local Christians, snugly wrapped in a sleeping bag, hungry but safe. The Stams' courageous martyrdom inspired greater missionary efforts in China.

MY RESPONSE: For what do I need God's grace today?

You are worried and upset about many things.
Luke 10:41

HER SERVICE: Speaking and writing

HER MESSAGE: Busyness for God is no barometer of devotion to God.

HER STORY: For thirty-seven years Wilma Stanchfield has given her testimony at Christian Women's Clubs. She shares her story in *Struck by Lightning, Then by Love.*

In 1956, while on a camping trip, Wilma and her husband, Roald, were struck by lightning while watching a thunderstorm from the door of a tent. Only the quick action of a passerby saved their lives. Wanting to pay God back for sparing her life, Wilma threw herself into church work. She served on the religious education board and advised young people. She sat on charity boards. When church members hosted minority children, Wilma took two, all the while counting the points she must be earning in God's eyes.

Wilma and Roald adopted a baby girl and appeared to be the happy family. But inside, Wilma harbored a fear of dying. In 1966 she attended her first Christian Women's Club; there, struck by the love of God, Wilma accepted Christ. Before the year ended, Roald, his three grown children, and their spouses also came to Christ. As Wilma realized that her busyness for God had nothing to do with her devotion to God, she dropped her frenzied activity and concentrated on obeying God, which led her to public speaking and writing.

MY RESPONSE: How does my life show my devotion to God?

What Zelophehad's daughters are saying is right. You must certainly give them property as an inheritance.
Numbers 27:7

HER SERVICE: Education, writing, and ministering

HER MESSAGE: Women are called by God to both lay and professional leadership positions.

HER STORY: In 1991 Dr. Susie C. Stanley founded Wesleyan/Holiness Women Clergy, International, and continues to serve as executive director. The organization's biannual conferences, popularly known as "Come to the Water," draw hundreds of women from various denominations and several countries. Susie authored two books that focus on Wesleyan/Holiness women preachers.

From the time she made a commitment to Christ in her childhood, Susie intended to become a missionary. She studied Spanish, anticipating serving in Latin America. But while serving as youth director, Susie met John Stanley, and they married in 1970. Both became college professors, and since 1995 Susie has taught historical theology at Messiah College in Grantham, Pennsylvania. Ordained to ecumenical ministry, much of Susie's work has crossed denominational lines.

Affirming women in ministry has been an important part of Susie's calling. Some have disagreed with her interpretation of Scripture, which supports women in lay and professional ministry leadership positions. Some have challenged her right to preach, so she understands the obstacles her female students may face. But one of her greatest joys is speaking at women's ordinations and preaching at weddings in which she affirms equality in marriage and in ministry.

MY RESPONSE: How have I embraced my calling?

Whether you turn to the right or to the left, your ears will hear a voice behind you, saying, "This is the way; walk in it."
Isaiah 30:21

HER SERVICE: Writing and medical mission work

HER MESSAGE: Nurture childlike faith.

HER STORY: Best remembered for her children's books, Patricia St. John also wrote nonfiction and novels. *An Ordinary Woman's Extraordinary Faith: The Autobiography of Patricia St. John* tells her life story, including twenty-seven years as a missionary nurse in Morocco.

Patricia's mother raised her five children in England while Patricia's father served as a missionary in South America. Patricia's childlike love of life blossomed during her father's visits home, when the family romped and hiked together. She later trained as a nurse at a military hospital during World War II, and following the war Patricia worked as a boarding-school housemother, entertaining homesick children with stories she wrote. She turned her writing into a ministry by incorporating Christian themes. *Treasures of the Snow* taught postwar children about forgiveness. Through her stories, Patricia has nurtured a childlike faith in generations of readers.

In 1949 Patricia moved to Tangier, Morocco, to assist her brother, the medical director of a mission hospital. She eventually settled in a mountain village, where women and children needed medical care. The childlike faith of new converts amazed Patricia. They insisted she pray about everything and were not at all surprised when prayers were answered.

MY RESPONSE: In what area of life do I need childlike faith?

[Barnabas] encouraged the believers to stay true to the Lord.
Acts 11:23 NLT

HER SERVICE: Pastoring

HER MESSAGE: Accept who you are, and trust God for who you can become.

HER STORY: Sunny Stock was the first woman to pastor First Congregational Church in Minersville, Pennsylvania. Attendance has risen from fifteen to one hundred during her ministry.

Sunny married her husband, John, when she was nineteen, just three months after they met. When the first of two sons was born ten years later, Sunny wanted to be the perfect parent and took him to church. There she accepted Christ and promised God she would do anything—except pastor a church. Sunny was firmly convinced that women should not be pastors.

After retiring from cardiovascular pharmacology, Sunny sought God's direction for a second career, and John, knowing her spirituality, urged her to attend seminary. Even after she enrolled, she agonized over her calling. But a church in her community soon called Sunny as pastor. When a woman confided to Sunny that she would not have felt comfortable talking about her mastectomy with a male minister, Sunny felt her decision to become a pastor was confirmed. She urges women to accept who they are and to trust God for who they can become. Since Sunny graduated from the Evangelical School of Theology in 1994, at least one woman has always been enrolled at that seminary as a result of her encouragement.

MY RESPONSE: To what role has God called me?

Perhaps the reason he was separated from you for a little while was that you might have him back for good —no longer as a slave, but . . . as a dear brother.
Philemon 15–16

HER SERVICE: Social reform and writing

HER MESSAGE: The written word can illuminate scriptural truths and transform society.

HER STORY: Harriet Beecher Stowe wrote stories that opened people's eyes to injustice. Her novel *Uncle Tom's Cabin* contributed to the start of the Civil War.

Lyman Beecher, a minister, taught Harriet and her eight brothers to right any wrongs they could. Her brothers became pastors, and Harriet taught school when she was barely sixteen. The family moved to Ohio, where Harriet heard abolitionists' stories of rescuing runaway slaves.

After marrying Calvin E. Stowe, a seminary professor, Harriet smuggled her servant girl, a runaway slave, along the Underground Railroad. Harriet began writing for magazines to earn money, and being inspired by a sermon she heard, she wrote a series about slave life for the *National Era*. That eventually led to the publication of her famous novel. Harriet's writing illuminated scriptural truths and helped to transform society. In 1862 she visited the White House to urge President Lincoln to sign an emancipation decree.

MY RESPONSE: What scriptural truth might I address by writing a story or writing a letter to an editor, congressperson, or senator?

We are God's workmanship, created in Christ Jesus to do good works.
Ephesians 2:10

HER SERVICE: Mission work

HER MESSAGE: If we sit at Christ's feet, He invites us to take new steps with Him.

HER STORY: Susan Strachan and her husband, Harry, founded what is now known as Latin America Mission.

Susan grew up Episcopalian but converted to evangelical Christianity at a Methodist chapel. At Harley College in London, the petite, outgoing coed met Harry, a tall, serious Scot. Both accepted mission assignments in Argentina, and they married in 1903. During a 1918 furlough, Susan observed women supporting the war effort and mobilized a League of Evangelical Women in Argentina to support an evangelism effort.

In 1919 the couple established a Latin America Evangelization Campaign. As Harry conducted evangelistic crusades across the Spanish-speaking continent, Susan directed the hub of the ministry while also raising their three children in Costa Rica. When Susan saw a need, she sprang into action. Her legacy to Costa Rica includes Clica Biblica (Bible Hospital), Templo Biblico, Latin American Biblical Seminary, and Roblealto Children's Home. After Harry's death in 1945, their oldest son, Kenneth, became the ministry's codirector with Susan, and they established a radio station and publishing house. Susan's writings reveal the secret of her success—an ongoing, intimate relationship with her Lord. As she sat at Christ's feet, He led her to take new steps through new ministries.

MY RESPONSE: What new step may Christ be inviting me to take?

Everything should be done in a fitting and orderly way.
1 Corinthians 14:40

HER SERVICE: Writing

HER MESSAGE: You can serve God by equipping others to serve Him.

HER STORY: Since 1986 Sally Stuart has published an annual *Christian Writers' Market Guide*, which has become an indispensable aid to Christian writers. She has also authored thirty books and more than a thousand articles and columns. Her expertise puts her in demand as a writers' conference speaker.

Sally started writing in 1967, when the youngest of her three children was about a year old. After writing about Christian education, Sally published a children's picture book and a secular western novel, then branched into Christian-living magazine articles.

When Sally contacted publishers looking for materials on marketing, one publisher offered to print a marketing guide—if she wrote it. As a person who thinks logically and appreciates order, Sally recognized the value of such a book to writers and accepted the challenge. She now serves God by equipping others to serve God through writing. Sally and her husband, Norman, live in Oregon, where Sally spends her days in her home office, converted from two bedrooms, updating the annual reference and developing other resources. The *Market Guide* has helped Christian writers adapt to the ever-changing face of technology in the publishing industry. Her latest edition includes resources on blogging.

MY RESPONSE: How might I equip someone to minister?

Don't copy the behavior and customs of this world, but let God transform you into a new person by changing the way you think.
Romans 12:2 NLT

HER SERVICE: Singing

HER MESSAGE: God's "repairs" leave us stronger—and transform us into the image of Christ.

HER STORY: Diane Susek's concerts have blessed audiences in the United States, Canada, and abroad. A graduate of Peabody Conservatory of Music, Diane has recorded eleven sacred music albums. The soprano has sung with The Friends of Israel, in Billy Graham Crusades, and for many other ministries and conferences. She also ministers with her husband, Ron Susek, a crusade evangelist.

The daughter of career Christian musicians, Diane sang as a child with her family, practiced the piano an hour before breakfast, and appeared with her brother on a school television show. Just before she was to sing at her high-school graduation, Diane accidentally punctured an eardrum. Scar tissue formed, but Diane's hearing was perfectly restored. Her doctor assured her that such scar tissue is often stronger than the original. Diane treasures that experience as a reminder that God's "repairs" can leave us stronger and can transform us into Christ's image as we trust God in the face of life's injuries.

As a college freshman Diane looked forward to a career, possibly on Broadway, but then she felt God's calling. At that time she also met Ron, and they joined in marriage and ministry.

MY RESPONSE: How have the scars of life strengthened and transformed me?

I endure everything for the sake of the elect, that they too may obtain the salvation that is in Christ Jesus.
2 Timothy 2:10

HER SERVICE: Medical mission work

HER MESSAGE: By stepping into untested waters, we may relay God's blessings to many lives.

HER STORY: Dr. Clara Swain went to India as the world's first woman missionary doctor. She established the Clara Swain Hospital on land donated by a local prince.

Born and raised in New York, Clara was self-educated. As a young woman she taught school and then became a doctor—a career women were not encouraged to pursue. She volunteered at an orphanage in India, and upon her arrival in 1870, Clara set up a dispensary and trained fourteen medical students. Her hospital, the first to serve women of the Orient, opened in 1874. Patients received Bible verse cards along with their treatments, and the hospital became so popular that healthy women sometimes asked to stay.

In 1883 Clara treated more than eight thousand patients. A few years later she became a palace physician. With a Christian teacher in tow, she treated palace women, opened a regional dispensary, and started a girls' school. The Indians readily sang the catchy Bible songs the women taught them. By stepping into untested waters, Clara served as a channel to direct God's blessings into many lives.

MY RESPONSE: What's holding me back from stepping out for God?

This is the day the Lord has made;
I will rejoice and find adventure in it.
Psalm 118:24 (Luci Swindoll's paraphrase)

HER SERVICE: Speaking, writing, and photography

HER MESSAGE: Life is a blessed adventure from God too exciting to be squelched by fear of the unknown.

HER STORY: A Women of Faith conference speaker since 1995, Luci Swindoll previously enjoyed a thirty-year career as an oil-company executive and for five years worked at Insight for Living, the ministry of her brother Charles Swindoll. Luci tells her story in *I Married Adventure.*

Sandwiched between two brothers, Luci grew up in a devout Texas family and accepted Christ as a preteen. After high school she got engaged, then decided she wasn't cut out for matrimony. In college Luci majored in music, then switched to commercial art. For fourteen years she sang with the Dallas Civic Opera Company. Bible studies at her church, five times a week for two years, laid a firm foundation for Luci's faith.

Luci got hooked on travel during a 1966 trip to Europe. She has photographed leopards in Africa and a roadrunner in the California desert. She has also photographed friends against the stark backdrop of Antarctica—a trip taken after her seventieth birthday. Luci's enthusiasm has inspired women of all ages to view life as a blessed adventure, too exciting to be squelched by fear of the unknown.

MY RESPONSE: What have I put off doing because of fear? Where would I like to travel?

Let nothing move you. Always give yourselves fully to the work of the Lord.
1 Corinthians 15:58

HER SERVICE: Ministry founder, singer, and writer

HER MESSAGE: I want to be God's best audio-visual aid of how His power shows up best through weakness (2 Corinthians 12:9).

HER STORY: As a seventeen-year-old, Joni Eareckson dove into the Chesapeake Bay and broke her neck, which resulted in quadriplegia. Nearly forty years later, she leads Joni and Friends, an organization that reaches out to thousands of people around the world with disabilities. She has authored more than forty books, including *Joni*, her autobiography.

Joni, pronounced "Johnny," grew up in Maryland, a fun-loving girl who enjoyed painting and horseback riding. After the accident an occupational therapist coaxed Joni to paint holding a brush in her mouth. She sometimes spit the brush on the floor in frustration, but her therapist patiently picked it up for her. Joni's spirit revived as she realized her talent was unspoiled. Through friends she came to accept her condition as permitted by God's sovereignty. Her disability forces her to focus on God's ability as she daily treasures God's presence, senses God's power in her ministry, and waits for God's ultimate healing in heaven. Joni served on the National Council on Disability at the time the Americans for Disabilities Act was passed. In 1982 Joni married Ken Tada, a former schoolteacher, who now joins her in the work of Joni and Friends.

MY RESPONSE: In what way do I need to depend on God's ability instead of my own?

In our hearts we felt the sentence of death. But this happened that we might not rely on ourselves but on God.
2 Corinthians 1:9

HER SERVICE: Mission work

HER MESSAGE: Our prison experiences better equip us to carry God's Word to those imprisoned by culture, corruption, or circumstances.

HER STORY: Carol Terry Talbot served for twenty years at the Ramabai Mukti Mission in India and rose to be superintendent. Her journey to the mission field took more than four years. *Escape at Dawn* tells her story.

A materialistic college girl, Carol dedicated her life to God after hearing a church speaker. She entered Biola College for missions training and on December 8, 1941, was on her way to India when her ship docked in Manila. The world plunged into World War II, and Carol and her fellow travelers were incarcerated at a Japanese internment camp. There she languished for three and a half years, suffering from impetigo, beriberi, and sometimes extreme hunger.

After being freed by American paratroopers and recuperating in the United States, Carol completed her journey to India in 1946. Upon returning home she met and married one of her former professors, Dr. Louis Talbot, a widower. He encouraged Carol to speak and write to those who were hurting, and she found that her prison experience and mission work had better equipped her to carry God's Word to others imprisoned by culture, corruption, or even circumstances.

MY RESPONSE: How have my circumstances prepared me to minister?

November

Jelske TenHove Talstra, ca. 1888–1979

Each one should use whatever gift he has received to serve others, faithfully administering God's grace in its various forms.
1 Peter 4:10

HER SERVICE: Prairie pioneering and mentoring

HER MESSAGE: The highest service we give may be the most humble.

HER STORY: As a newlywed Jelske Talstra emigrated from Holland to Canada. For decades afterward she served as a mentor to those who followed in her footsteps.

Jelske worked as head nurse of a Christian mental hospital in Holland. She married Harm Jan TenHove in 1929, just before boarding a ship for Canada. Although the Great Depression threatened, the couple bought land and raised a family that came to include six children.

Jelske missed her professional work, but believing that wives should be submissive, she stayed by the hearth while her husband served the community and the Christian Reformed Church. She cleared land and harvested grain. She fed and housed families that Harm brought home in his role as a "fieldman" who helped Dutch immigrants acclimate. Jelske used her nurse's training to treat emergencies and deliver babies for families living in the rough territory of Alberta. While she never had an "official" role in building God's kingdom, Jelske's humble service and deep faith in a loving God inspired all who knew her. During the latter half of her life, she amazed doctors by surviving and recovering from a malignancy, multiple myeloma, and a stroke.

MY RESPONSE: How might I serve God by serving others?

Many live as enemies of the cross of Christ.
Philippians 3:18

HER SERVICE: Mission work

HER MESSAGE: As we align ourselves with Christ, enemies attack.

HER STORY: Ruth Marstaller Taylor and her husband, Clyde, served as Christian and Missionary Alliance (C&MA) missionaries to Colombia from 1932 to 1941.

Ruth was born in Texas to a Christian family of German descent. The family later moved to Maine, and Ruth graduated from the C&MA Missionary Training Institute, now Nyack College, in New York. Her brother, who served as a missionary in Peru, introduced her to Clyde Taylor. The two married in 1930 and answered God's call to minister in Latin America.

The Taylors settled in Colombia in 1932, in a time of strong opposition to Protestants. Ruth taught classes of women and directed kitchen operations at the Bible Institute they founded. As people noticed the missionaries' strong alignment with Christ, enemies attacked. A Roman Catholic priest once offered three hundred dollars for Clyde's murder. On another occasion a man pulled the hair of the Taylors' young daughter and stuck a lit cigar into her ear. Through the years Ruth suffered from typhoid, malaria, and an overdose of arsenic as treatment. Serious medical problems finally forced the Taylors out of Columbia, but they had laid the foundation for a thriving congregation, a seminary, and a school.

MY RESPONSE: How might I better prepare myself to face the enemies of the Cross?

Forgive, and you will be forgiven.
Luke 6:37

HER SERVICE: Speaking and writing

HER MESSAGE: From our enemies we learn to forgive, and God's healing love flows through us—to them.

HER STORY: Corrie ten Boom spoke in more than sixty countries following her release from Ravensbruck, a German concentration camp. Her books tell the story of her imprisonment and the death of her beloved sister Betsy at the camp.

During World War II Corrie's father offered protection to persecuted Jews. Corrie was in her early fifties when thirty-five members of the family and their friends were arrested. Corrie spent time in a German concentration camp and later was herded into a boxcar for a three-day trip to Ravensbruck prison. Rancid bedding straw was infested with fleas, young guards taunted and struck old women, food was sparse, and workdays were long. Seven months later, through an administrative error, Corrie was released.

A compulsion to come to the United States laid the groundwork for a worldwide ministry to tell others of the faithfulness of God in the midst of misery. Following a speaking engagement in Munich, Germany, Corrie recognized the man walking toward her as a former Ravensbruck guard. He reached out to shake her hand, but she recoiled at the thought. Breathing a prayer, she finally took his hand and felt God's love and forgiveness flow through her—to him. From her enemy, Corrie learned to forgive.

MY RESPONSE: To whom might I extend a gesture of forgiveness?

I will meditate on all your works and consider all your mighty deeds.
Psalm 77:12

HER SERVICE: Founding monasteries and convents and writing

HER MESSAGE: We may accomplish more for heaven by placing less emphasis on earthly things.

HER STORY: Teresa of Avila was named the patron saint of Spain for founding monasteries and nunneries and for her practical and meditative ministry.

Her mother died when Teresa was twelve, and Teresa turned to God in her loneliness. But when the pretty, vivacious girl developed teenage interests, her father sent her to a convent. During an illness Teresa read the Epistles of St. Jerome and dedicated her life to the church. She joined the Order of the Carmelites and developed what she called mental prayer, a way of relating to God in frequent conversation. As she identified with Christ, Teresa served the poor and needy, calling herself Teresa of Jesus rather than Teresa of Cepeda, her family name.

A supporter of the Counter Reformation, a movement to reform the church from within, Teresa expanded and reformed the Carmelites. She also opened a convent of a more austere nature, where nuns' lives revolved around prayer. These nuns became known as Barefoot Carmelites; they wore coarse brown serge and sandals, clipped their hair, and slept on straw. Teresa stressed prayer, silence, and penance in the religious communities she founded. By placing less emphasis on earthly things, Teresa accomplished more for heaven.

MY RESPONSE: How might I place less emphasis on earthly things to accomplish more for heaven?

Whatever you did for one of the least of these brothers of mine, you did for me.
Matthew 25:40

HER SERVICE: Mission work

HER MESSAGE: Instead of analyzing, patronizing, and politicizing the poor, break bread with them.

HER STORY: In 1979 Mother Teresa was awarded the Nobel Peace Prize for her ministry to the destitute and dying.

Mother Teresa was born Agnes Gonxht Bojaxhiu to a family that lived in Skopje, Albania. After her father's death when Agnes was nine, her mother supported the family by selling cloth and embroidery. Agnes was active in parish youth activities and, through a Jesuit priest, developed an interest in missionaries.

At eighteen Agnes joined the Sisters of Loreto and, a year later, began teaching at St. Mary's High School in Calcutta. In 1931 she took vows of poverty, obedience, and service and chose to be called Teresa in memory of St. Therese of Lisieux. On a train ride to the Himalayas to recuperate from tuberculosis, Mother Teresa received a directive from God to give up all she had to serve the poorest of the poor. When she recovered, she left the security of the convent to minister on the streets of Calcutta. Instead of analyzing, patronizing, or politicizing the poor, Mother Teresa simply broke bread with them. Teams of nuns have carried the work of the Order of the Missionaries of Charity, which she founded, to countries around the world.

MY RESPONSE: How might I minister to someone living in poverty?

A little here, a little there.
Isaiah 28:10

HER SERVICE: Mission work

HER MESSAGE: Small steps of faith lead to achieving large goals.

HER STORY: In 1870 Isabella Thoburn became the first missionary sent out by the fledgling Woman's Foreign Missionary Society of the Methodist Episcopal Woman's Board of Boston. In India Isabella opened a mission school for girls, which grew into Isabella Thoburn College, affiliated with Calcutta University. For thirty-one years she educated Hindu women and girls.

Isabella graduated from Ohio's Wheeling Female Seminary and from art school. A brother, who was a missionary, invited her to India to educate oppressed Hindu women. In spite of apathy and antagonism from others, Isabella opened a school and taught seven girls the first year.

By the time the second term began, Isabella had purchased a house on a beautiful seven-acre garden plot. She lacked reference books and equipment for an institution of higher education, yet Isabella's Ruby Garden for Girls grew into a college. A Christian mother gave five hundred rupees so her daughter could continue her education in a Christian environment. Isabella and a student, Lilavati Singh, raised twenty thousand dollars toward a building and equipment by traveling and making their needs known. By taking small steps of faith, the women achieved their goal. When Isabella died of cholera, Lilavati succeeded her as president of the college.

MY RESPONSE: What goal might I set for my ministry?

Make every effort to add to your faith . . . perseverance.
2 Peter 1:5–6

HER SERVICE: Writing

HER MESSAGE: We may need to persevere and step out in faith before God steps in to use us.

HER STORY: A pioneer in Christian fiction, Bodie Thoene has written more than twenty novels. She has won eight Gold Medallion Awards from the Evangelical Christian Publishing Association for historical fiction.

Bodie's father was Jewish, and family discussions often centered on world politics. Her mother read to her regularly, but much as Bodie loved listening, she struggled with reading. Not until college did she learn that she was dyslexic. Bodie grew fascinated with the rebirth of Israel during college and intellectually accepted Christ as Savior. She married a childhood friend, Brock Thoene, who became her writing partner and researcher. Once Bodie became a mother, she was impressed with God's love for His children and wholeheartedly opened her heart to Christ.

For a time Bodie and Brock wrote for Batjac Productions, run by John Wayne. The actor challenged Bodie to fulfill her dream to write about Israel. The couple stepped out in faith and resigned from their jobs to write *The Gates of Zion*, the first book of The Zion Chronicles series. Brock reads to Bodie, everything from fan mail to first drafts of novels. By persevering and stepping out in faith, the Nevada couple has found that God uses their books to educate believers and to persuade unbelievers to trust Christ.

MY RESPONSE: What ministry project might I revive through perseverance?

I glory in Christ Jesus in my service to God.
Romans 15:17

HER SERVICE: Ministering, writing, speaking, and consulting

HER MESSAGE: Examine the world through Christ's eyes, ease a need, and equip others to join you.

HER STORY: In 1968 Donna S. Thomas and her husband, Chuck, established Project Partner With Christ (PPWP), an Ohio-based missions agency that has taken more than six thousand people around the world to build churches, schools, and hospitals. During terms as president and CEO, Donna, who was ordained by the Church of God, trained pastors in eighteen countries, developed relationships with Christian leaders in seventy-four, and developed partnerships between many overseas and American churches.

Donna accepted Christ at age eleven. She married Chuck in 1947, and a few years later the couple planted Pawnee Avenue Church in Wichita, Kansas. After a short-term mission trip to Mexico, Donna and Chuck began recruiting others to go there and bought a forty-passenger airplane to provide transportation. Since Chuck's death in 1992, Donna has launched Christian Vision Ministries to write, speak, and serve as a missions consultant to churches and international leaders from her home in Carmel, Indiana. By examining the world through Christ's eyes, easing needs, and equipping others to join her, Donna has developed relationships with families and has become an "American grandmother" to children in India, China, Mexico, and Nicaragua. She wrote *Climb Another Mountain* and *Becoming a World Changing Family.*

MY RESPONSE: What world need might I and fellow believers help to relieve?

The Lord himself goes before you and will be with you; he will never leave you nor forsake you. Do not be afraid; do not be discouraged.

Deuteronomy 31:8

HER SERVICE: Mission work

HER MESSAGE: God supplies strength for the journey.

HER STORY: Called the mother of American missions in Hawaii, Lucy Thurston served there for forty-eight years.

The daughter of a prosperous Massachusetts farmer, Lucy graduated from Bradford Academy before marrying Asa, a seminary graduate. The two soon sailed for Hawaii with fifteen others. There they found a village of thatched huts built on lava beds. Lucy likened the islanders to volcanoes with wickedness smoldering within.

The Thurstons lived in a one-room thatched hut until supporters shipped them a wooden house. They had six children, and Lucy struggled to protect them from pagan influences. The missionaries built houses, schools, and churches and taught locals to read and write. Lucy taught women to sew. She had to undergo surgery for breast cancer with no anesthetic because of partial paralysis she had suffered in earlier years, possibly from illness related to the climate or insects. But she clung to her Bible and a hymnbook, and God, as always, provided strength for her journey. A month later she was back to her routine. At age seventy-five Lucy spoke at a Honolulu church, the first woman allowed to speak from that pulpit. She outlived all of the missionaries who had gone to Hawaii with her.

MY RESPONSE: For what do I need God's strength today?

If God has given you leadership ability,
take the responsibility seriously.
Romans 12:8 NLT

HER SERVICE: Education

HER MESSAGE: Good leadership stems from stepping out in God's will instead of always sticking to time-honored ways.

HER STORY: Johanna Timmer became the first dean of women at Calvin College in Michigan. In 1940 she became acting president and the first dean of Reformed Bible Institute (RBI), now Reformed Bible College.

During her time at Calvin, Johanna wrestled with keeping young women from the worldliness of theater, card playing, and dancing, yet she was not legalistic. When a woman's application as a schoolteacher was rejected because she had attended movies in her youth, Johanna appealed and won her the job. Always looking to step out in God's will as revealed by an accurate interpretation of Scripture, Johanna supported a controversial plan to form a college, separate from Calvin, to teach Bible and evangelism from a Reformed perspective. Her involvement led to her leadership positions at RBI.

Johanna urged the creation of societies for young women, and they later joined male groups to become the Young Calvinists of the Christian Reformed Church. After leaving RBI in 1943, Johanna served as a principal and later founded a Christian high school in Philadelphia. She had devoted her life to teaching and governance.

MY RESPONSE: How am I clinging to the way we've always done things instead of clinging to God?

They entered into a covenant to seek the Lord, the God of their fathers, with all their heart and soul.
2 Chronicles 15:12

HER SERVICE: Entrepreneurial endeavors

HER MESSAGE: As we pray about choosing plan A or plan B, God may show us plan C.

HER STORY: Jeanette Towne runs Towne Communications from her California home. In her first six years of business, annual sales at the computer networks company mushroomed to seven million dollars.

Jeanette wanted to stay home with her eighteen-month-old twins, so she asked her congregation to pray about how she should juggle her career and family. One believer counseled her to quit her job. Jeanette took the advice—even though her husband's business was floundering. A month later she was offered consulting work, which led to the creation of her business. Instead of forcing Jeanette to choose between plan A and plan B, God showed her plan C, an option that creatively met her needs.

As the owner, Jeanette is free to run her business on Christian principles. She prays with groups and individuals as appropriate, follows scriptural guidelines on finances, and insists on integrity in the workplace. And she adjusts her schedule to accommodate the schedules of her family, which also includes two adopted children.

MY RESPONSE: How may I be limiting God by my own expectations and how I pray?

Jesus said, "Let the little children come to me, and do not hinder them."

Matthew 19:14

HER SERVICE: Founding an orphanage

HER MESSAGE: Jesus loves little children.

HER STORY: Called "Mother of the Nile," Lillian Trasher spent fifty years ministering to children in Egypt.

Through a missionary speaker, Lillian felt God calling her to Africa—just two weeks before her wedding day. She cancelled the wedding and stepped out in faith. In Egypt Lillian at first stayed with a missionary family, but she left when they balked at housing an orphaned baby she'd brought home.

Jesus's love for children flowed through Lillian. By the time five years had passed, she had cared for fifty neglected children. She built an orphanage with donations from supporters, and in 1919 Lillian was accepted under the auspices of a young denomination, the Assemblies of God. Lillian wrote textbooks and taught children, but her ministry had many ups and downs. Muslim authorities once took the Islamic children from her. However, after years of little spiritual impact, at last revival struck, and dozens of children were converted. Lillian sometimes had to ride a donkey to town, begging for donations. But once a ship bound for Greece unexpectedly dropped a Red Cross shipment of supplies.

By the time Lillian died, more than fourteen hundred children and widows lived at her orphanage, and she had ministered to more than eight thousand children.

MY RESPONSE: To what child might I show the love of Jesus?

God does speak—now one way, now another.
Job 33:14

HER SERVICE: Mission work

HER MESSAGE: God speaks—through the colors on a canvas, the verse of a poem, or the words of a song.

HER STORY: Lilias Trotter served as a missionary to the Muslims of Algeria for forty years. She organized the Algiers Mission Band, now part of Arab World Ministries.

An educated Victorian woman who enjoyed the life of a socialite, Lilias Trotter was considered one of the best artists of the nineteenth century. During a religious awakening that swept London, she met such notable Christians as Hannah Whitall Smith, who became her role model. Evangelist Dwight L. Moody trained Lilias to counsel at religious crusades, and she began work with the Young Women's Christian Association.

Once, noticing the pierced hands of Christ depicted on the bottom of an offering plate, Lilias gave all the money she had in her purse. And when she felt those hands beckoning her to North Africa, she went, even though a medical condition caused one mission to reject her. In 1888 she and two friends arrived on the field independently. Knowing that God speaks through the colors of a canvas, the verses of a poem, or the words of a song, Lilias used her passion for art and literature to reach a people who proved difficult to reach by the usual methods of evangelism.

MY RESPONSE: What medium might I use to illustrate God's truth?

Forgive us our debts, as we also have forgiven our debtors.
Matthew 6:12

HER SERVICE: Preaching and reform

HER MESSAGE: The glory of God's love dispels the darkness of negative attitudes.

HER STORY: Sojourner Truth traveled as an itinerant preacher. At times she shared the platform with orator Frederick Douglass.

As a child slave, Sojourner created a hideaway under willow branches to commune with God. But God must have seemed far away during the years in which she was bought and sold, beaten, and separated from her husband. For a time Sojourner harbored deep bitterness against whites. But amazingly, God changed that bitterness to love for those who had mistreated her.

After Sojourner joined the African Methodist Episcopal Church, an evangelist noticed her speaking ability and invited her to preach. Given the name Isabella at birth, Sojourner changed her name in response to God's call to itinerant ministry. Beginning in 1843 she traveled through New York, Connecticut, and Massachusetts and also took a trip west. When a group of rowdy men carrying clubs once disrupted a Massachusetts camp meeting, Sojourner at first hid in a corner. Then she courageously climbed a nearby hill and sang a gospel song. The men surrounded her—wanting to hear more singing. In time Sojourner advocated abolition and women's suffrage. The glory of God's love that shone through Sojourner dispelled the darkness of negative attitudes of those around her.

MY RESPONSE: How might God's love shine through me to dispel a negative attitude?

The fruit of the Spirit is love, joy, peace, patience, kindness, goodness, faithfulness, gentleness and self-control.
Galatians 5:22–23

HER SERVICE: Evangelism

HER MESSAGE: When we display the fruit of the Spirit, relatives may reach out to pick some for themselves.

HER STORY: Christiana Tsai led fifty-five relatives to Christ. *Queen of the Dark Chamber: The Story of Christiana Tsai* tells her story.

Called Sister Seven, Christiana opened her heart to the gospel as she listened to a visiting American preacher. Her mother wept in disappointment. Sixth Brother ripped up Christiana's Bible and hymnbook. One of the first Chinese girls to graduate from high school, Christiana turned down prestigious positions so that she might live at her family's apartment complex and witness to her twenty-four siblings and half-siblings and their families.

While teaching at a girls' school, Christiana led seventy-two of her two hundred students to Christ. From 1914 to 1920 she traversed China, translating and speaking with an evangelism team sponsored by an American millionaire. From 1930 to 1937 Christiana assisted her godmother, Mary Leaman, who developed a simplified system of writing Chinese. Then a debilitating illness struck. Christiana was later diagnosed with a combination of pellagra, dysentery, and malignant malaria. After observing the fruit of the Spirit in Christiana's life—peace in the midst of intense suffering—Sixth Brother finally announced that he, too, believed.

MY RESPONSE: How might I demonstrate the fruit of the Spirit to my extended family?

It is more blessed to give than to receive.
Acts 20:35

HER SERVICE: Philanthropy and emancipation

HER MESSAGE: When we exercise wise stewardship, we show that we affirm God's ownership.

HER STORY: Through the generosity of Emily H. Tubman, churches were built and slaves freed. She entertained statesmen and supported the nation's faltering economy by encouraging manufacturing in the South during the Reconstruction period.

Emily's father, Edmund Pendleton Thomas, was Kentucky's first land registrar. By the time of his death, when Emily was nine, he had acquired more than seventeen thousand acres of land. Orator Henry Clay became Emily's legal guardian. Emily married Englishman Richard C. Tubman, and they settled in Augusta, Georgia, because of his business as a planter and exporter.

Richard died in Emily's arms in 1836, and in his will he encouraged her to work for the emancipation of his slaves. She studied law before administrating his estate. When Emily offered freedom to Richard's slaves, she provided passage to Liberia to the sixty-nine who chose to go. A community there, Tubmantown, bears tribute. For the slaves who chose to stay, Emily provided land and financial support. She supported the founders of Disciples of Christ and provided money to build, and later rebuild, First Christian Church in Augusta. Other churches, colleges, and even industries benefited from her generosity. By exercising wise stewardship, Emily showed that she affirmed God's ownership of all she had and appreciated the trust God placed in her.

MY RESPONSE: How might I practice better stewardship?

If I have denied justice . . . what will I do when God confronts me?
Job 31:13–14

HER SERVICE: Activism and reform

HER MESSAGE: To set others free, we may have to risk ourselves.

HER STORY: Harriet Tubman is credited with leading more than three hundred African American slaves to freedom. In 1896 she opened the John Brown Home for indigents in New York.

Araminta Greene, who later took her mother's name, Harriet, was born in Maryland. From the age of seven she was hired out and often beaten, but her father, Ben Ross, encouraged Harriet to trust God for the future. When Harriet tried to warn an escaping slave of an approaching overseer, she was struck by an iron weight thrown at the slave. The injury caused her to fall asleep unexpectedly at times for the rest of her life.

At age twenty-four Harriet married John Tubman. Five years later, fearing she would be sold to a Southern plantation, she escaped to Pennsylvania via the Underground Railroad. By the time Harriet returned to her husband, he had remarried. She continued to assist slaves, and a forty-thousand-dollar reward was posted for her capture—dead or alive. Harriet resolutely risked her own freedom in order to free others from slavery. She served in various capacities in the Union Army, then returned to New York and was active in the African Methodist Episcopal Zion Church.

MY RESPONSE: What risks might I have to face to set someone free in Christ?

Greet Mary, who worked very hard for you.
Romans 16:6

HER SERVICE: Mission work and writing

HER MESSAGE: Talent plus passion add up to service.

HER STORY: Charlotte Maria Tucker published eight religious storybooks in England and forty more in India. Probably the first to offer religious literature in various Indian dialects, Charlotte wrote under the pen name A.L.O.E., which stood for A Lady of England. She also edited *The Christian Juvenile Instructor.*

From childhood Charlotte expressed interest in missionary work in India. A gifted writer who employed metaphor and allegory, she faithfully wrote Christian literature even as she grieved family members' deaths and took in a deceased brother's children. Charlotte studied the language of Punjab, and at age fifty-four she finally set out for India, paying her own way, under the auspices of the Church of England Zenana Missionary Society. During her eighteen years on the field, she never returned home.

Charlotte could never predict how the women of India would react to her visits to their *zenanas*, or living quarters. Some welcomed her; others spit or threw pieces of pottery at her. But Charlotte never gave up. Along with her missionary outreach, she continued to write books, tracts, and pamphlets that proved popular with Indian Christians. Her talent of writing plus her passion for ministry added up to many years of fruitful Christian service.

MY RESPONSE: To what kind of Christian service do my talents and passion lead me?

Now that you know these things, you will be blessed if you do them.
John 13:17

HER SERVICE: Business and volunteering

HER MESSAGE: Freedom from work frees us to serve God.

HER STORY: Doris Tuinstra has served on the Christian Reformed Synodical Committee on Race Relations and on the Christian Reformed World Relief Committee (CRWRC). She has been active in the Cottage Industries program, a ministry that teaches people how to support themselves through small businesses.

Doris served in the U.S. Navy's Women Accepted for Volunteer Emergency Service (WAVES) during World War II. Life after the war led to a horticultural business partnership with her brother Bob. Doris opened a second store in 1973 and held a public service to celebrate God's goodness. Besides supporting the education of nieces and nephews, Doris created a scholarship fund for women in business. She took time off from business to represent the CRWRC in Sri Lanka and Indonesia, seeking to establish self-support programs there.

Doris views the freedom of retirement as an opportunity to use more of her strength, experience, and time to serve God. As part of her work for the CRWRC, she has offered advocacy and needs-assessment assistance in places hit by catastrophes, including Mississippi, Missouri, West Virginia, and California. She has ministered to the homeless through a downtown Grand Rapids, Michigan, ministry. She continues to look for new assignments that allow her to use her resources and talents for God.

MY RESPONSE: How might I serve God in my leisure time?

The lips of the righteous nourish many.
Proverbs 10:21

HER SERVICE: Writing and teaching

HER MESSAGE: By reading to children, we introduce them to truths, literary styles, and maybe even their own talents.

HER STORY: Jamie Langston Turner has written novels, plays, poems, and short stories. Her first novel, *The Suncatchers*, was published in 1995.

By reading poetry during recess, Jamie's fifth-grade teacher whetted an appetite in the young girl that was only satisfied when Jamie curled up in her bedroom and wrote poetry of her own. Then, when her teacher liked and asked for copies of her poems, she realized that her writings were special. In time Jamie became an elementary teacher and wrote plays for students to perform. A few scripts were published. As her husband, Daniel, studied for a doctorate, Jamie began freelance writing in earnest. She saved rejection slips as fodder to encourage future writing students.

Now a creative writing teacher at Bob Jones University in South Carolina, Jamie strives to overcome stereotypes by showing that Christians can appreciate art and express themselves intelligently. The characters in her novels show the impact ordinary Christians can have upon others. Her own life offers ample evidence of that. By introducing Jamie to life's truths through the literary style of poetry, her teacher uncovered a young girl's talents—and enabled Jamie to bless future readers.

MY RESPONSE: What story or poem might I read to a child today?

A woman named Martha opened her home to him [Jesus]. She had a sister called Mary, who sat at the Lord's feet.
Luke 10:38–39

HER SERVICE: Writing, speaking, and scholarship

HER MESSAGE: Prayer and service balance the scales of the Christian's life.

HER STORY: A British religious writer, Evelyn Underhill's first book of importance, *Mysticism*, was published in 1911.

The daughter of an English barrister, Evelyn studied history and botany. She came to appreciate art and literature during summers spent in France and Italy. A bookbinder as an adult, Evelyn experienced a religious conversion and from then on emulated the mystics. She prayed for an hour daily and practiced living in the presence of Christ. Striving to balance her life with prayer and service in the spirit of the meditative Mary and working Martha, Evelyn spent mornings writing and afternoons serving the poor.

In 1924 Evelyn began offering retreat conferences to help others develop their spiritual lives. Although she had worked in the department of naval intelligence during World War I, she wrote *The Church and War* as a member of the Anglican Pacifist Fellowship. Evelyn wrote three novels and published other writings, including lectures on religion she gave at Manchester College in Oxford. She was the first woman appointed as an outside lecturer at Oxford University.

MY RESPONSE: How might I evaluate whether my life is balanced with prayer and service?

The kingdom of heaven is like treasure hidden in a field. When a man found it, he . . . sold all he had and bought that field.
Matthew 13:44

HER SERVICE: Mission work

HER MESSAGE: The greater the treasure, the higher the cost.

HER STORY: Dr. Lillias Underwood served as a missionary in Korea for twenty-eight years.

Trained in nursing and medicine in the United States, Lillias joined Presbyterian missionaries in Korea in 1888. The next year she married fellow missionary Horace Underwood, and they took a two-month honeymoon to the interior, a dangerous region with robbers and wild animals. Most villagers welcomed the first white woman they had ever seen. On their journey of a thousand miles, she treated more than six hundred patients while Horace shared the gospel.

Lillias also served as physician to the royal family. After Japanese invaders killed the queen, Lillias and her friends took the king food locked in a box to ensure that he would not be poisoned.

In the mornings Lillias treated patients for ailments ranging from sore throats to smallpox and cholera. During the afternoon she taught the Bible to women and children.

The Underwoods were persecuted for refusing to worship the Japanese emperor. But convinced that the greater the treasure, the higher the cost, Lillias continued to fulfill what she considered a high calling.

MY RESPONSE: What might God be asking me to give for the privilege of serving Him?

Bless those who persecute you; bless and do not curse.
Romans 12:14

HER SERVICE: Mission work

HER MESSAGE: By God's grace, we can embrace those who hurt us.

HER STORY: Marj Saint was thrust into the role of single parent in 1956, when her husband, Nate Saint, was among five men martyred by the Auca Indians of Ecuador. *End of the Spear*, a movie released in 2006, tells the story.

After Nate's death, Marj and her three young children, Kathy, Steve, and Phil, moved from the Mission Aviation Fellowship base to Quito, Ecuador. She traveled, telling the world Nate's story as well as the experiences of his sister, Rachel, who moved into an Auca village in 1958. Marj not only showcased the need for missionary work, but her continued support of missionary outreach after the tragedy offered hope and an example to others who had experienced heartbreak.

In 1965 the family visited the spot where Nate had been killed. There Kathy and Steve were baptized, along with two Aucas. One of the killers prayed. By going back, Marj signaled to the world that by God's grace, we can embrace those who hurt us. She continues to support missionary work and her son Steve's Indigenous People's Technology and Education Center in Florida.

MY RESPONSE: What gesture of kindness might I make toward someone who has hurt me?

God created people in his own image; God patterned them after himself; male and female he created them.
Genesis 1:27 NLT

HER SERVICE: Scholarship and psychology

HER MESSAGE: Dialogue about gender roles should be embraced rather than feared.

HER STORY: Now a professor at Eastern University in St. Davids, Pennsylvania, Dr. Mary Van Leeuwen has written several books about gender roles. *Gender and Grace: Love, Work, and Parenting in a Changing World* was published in 1990.

Mary Stewart grew up in Ontario. In college she studied psychology, then joined the Canadian University Service Overseas and taught at a Salvation Army high school in Zambia from 1965 to 1967. Doctoral research led her back to Zambia in 1970, and there she accepted Christ. As a new Christian she studied to reconcile her faith with psychology and feminism.

After marriage, Mary and her husband, Ray Van Leeuwen, shared equally in parenting their two sons. Mary was the family's primary breadwinner while Ray completed his doctoral work. Eventually Ray taught at Calvin Theological Seminary, and Mary carried a reduced teaching load at the college. Believing that dialogue about gender roles should be embraced rather than feared, Mary organized a team to study gender roles for the Calvin Center for Christian Scholarship in 1989. A year later she agreed to coedit *Partnership*, a publication of the Committee for Women in the Christian Reformed Church.

MY RESPONSE: Have I identified my role in reaching the world for Christ?

Well done, good and faithful servant!
Matthew 25:21

HER SERVICE: Volunteering and public service

HER MESSAGE: Rather than focus on closed doors, focus on God and look for windows of opportunity.

HER STORY: In 1983 Shirley Van Zanten became the first woman elected as a county executive in the state of Washington. She got involved in government during the 1970s and helped draft a new county charter that reorganized local government.

After high school Shirley enrolled at Calvin College in Grand Rapids, Michigan, the first of her parents' families to pursue higher education. Nineteen years and three daughters later, she graduated from Western Washington University. For a time she worked as a teacher and as a librarian.

Born with natural leadership abilities, Shirley became frustrated with limitations placed on women's ability to minister in her denomination. But never one to focus on closed doors, Shirley instead focused on God—and a window of opportunity opened for her to serve in the public sector. She continued to serve her church in minor roles as a volunteer. Shirley's analytical mind serves her well in evaluating situations and articulating concerns, both inside and outside the church.

MY RESPONSE: Where can I best use my God-given talents and spiritual gifts?

The steps of the godly are directed by the Lord.
Psalm 37:23 NLT

HER SERVICE: Education

HER MESSAGE: Instead of giving in to pressure to conform or giving up because of lack of opportunity, give your plans to God and look for His direction.

HER STORY: Nelle VanderArk has devoted her life to education. In 1964 she became the first curriculum coordinator for the National Union of Christian Schools. Nelle taught at Reformed Bible College (RBC) in Grand Rapids, Michigan.

Nelle and her four brothers and three sisters were treated equitably growing up on a Montana farm. When she was eleven, she helped a brother-in-law by plowing with six horses. Nelle longed to attend seminary, but at that time few women did, so she became a teacher.

At RBC Nelle grieved as she prepared women for largely nonexistent ministry jobs—but rejoiced as many chose missionary service. Nelle was appointed by the Christian Reformed Church in 1988 to examine the meaning of "headship" as relevant to women in the church. In 1990 she addressed synod delegates, an unusual opportunity for a woman, and the group decided to permit churches to use discretion in appointing women as elders or ministers. Nelle credits her family background for keeping her from becoming embittered over women's roles. Instead of giving in to pressure to conform or giving up because of lack of opportunity, Nelle encourages women to give their plans to God and to look for His direction.

MY RESPONSE: For what plans do I need God's direction?

Katherine M. Vander Ziel Vandergrift, 1947–

He is the Rock, his works are perfect, and all his ways are just.
Deuteronomy 32:4

HER SERVICE: Public service and environmental activism

HER MESSAGE: Acknowledge the earth as a wonderful gift from God—and accept responsibility for its care.

HER STORY: Katherine Vandergrift works as senior policy analyst in the advocacy department of World Vision Canada. She has devoted her life to supporting issues of personal and public justice.

Katherine was the seventh of nine children born to farming parents in southwest Minnesota. The family's Dutch Christian Reformed community, with its emphasis on home, school, and church, felt confining to Katherine. Her father discussed world news with her, and she wanted to witness to a wider society. With scholarships and hard work, Katherine put herself through Calvin College.

After marrying in 1969, Katherine and her husband, a Canadian, moved to Edmonton in Alberta, Canada. Since setting up a library at Edmonton Christian High School, Katherine has been involved in the community. As part of a Citizens for Public Justice chapter, Katherine spoke out against ruining Canada's virgin North to accommodate a pipeline. She was named Edmonton's Outstanding Citizen of 1988. Soon afterward, she became the mayor's personal assistant. Katherine promoted building a park and bicycle path in the community. Acknowledging the earth as a wonderful gift from God and accepting responsibility for its care at the local level has led to Katherine's involvement in the world community.

MY RESPONSE: How might I help care for the natural world around me?

It was by faith that Rahab the prostitute did not die with all the others in her city who refused to obey God. For she had given a friendly welcome to the spies.

Hebrews 11:31 NLT

HER SERVICE: Pro-life advocacy, writing, and ministering as a pastor's wife

HER MESSAGE: Don't just tell—show society how to change.

HER STORY: A staunch pro-life advocate, Eunice and her husband, Rev. Jim Vanderlaan, had three children, then adopted four African American children. She has served on various committees of the Christian Reformed Synod and written articles for Christian publications.

The granddaughter of German immigrants attended a Minnesota Christian school. Eunice and her brother won high-school oratorical contests sponsored by their denomination—after their father coached them to practice speaking to a row of straw bales in the family's hog pen.

Eunice first used her gift for speaking as a teacher, then began speaking out for the unborn. But Eunice doesn't just tell people what to do; she shows them—by adopting children of mothers who reject abortion as an option for unwanted pregnancies. As she and her husband have served various congregations, their open hearts have inspired others, resulting in still more adoptions. The couple's approach to tackling the challenges of Jim's blindness with humor has also helped members of their congregations better relate to people with special needs.

MY RESPONSE: How might I show a right course of action I've only told about?

Greet Tryphena and Tryphosa, those women who work hard in the Lord. Greet my dear friend Persis, another woman who has worked very hard in the Lord.

Romans 16:12

HER SERVICE: Letter writing

HER MESSAGE: Affirm others to show that you appreciate their using their abilities for God.

HER STORY: Argula von Grumbach wrote letters to protest the persecution of believers who supported Reformer Martin Luther.

The wife of a nobleman, Argula corresponded with Martin Luther. And when officials of the University of Ingolstadt fired an instructor because he supported Luther's doctrine, she penned a stern letter of protest. Argula insisted that Luther and other Reformers taught only the Word of God, and she challenged officials to refute them from that same Word. Her writings show a familiarity with Scripture, upon which she based her opinions of the Reformers. She also wrote to governing officials to remind them of dire consequences if they took upon themselves authority that belonged to God. In addition, her letters denounced the fiscal irresponsibility and lack of morality of some clergy.

Argula's letters circulated as a pamphlet. Although her missives were ignored by university officials and magistrates, they triggered responses in others. Clergy called her names. A student ridiculed her in verse. Her husband was deposed from his office of prefect, and some historians believed he abused her. Yet the letters that have been preserved show that Argula refused to be intimidated.

MY RESPONSE: To whom or about whom might I write a note of affirmation?

The good soil represents honest, good-hearted people who hear God's message, cling to it, and steadily produce a huge harvest.
Luke 8:15 NLT

HER SERVICE: Singing, speaking, and writing

HER MESSAGE: By sharing how we overcome struggles by God's grace, we help other struggling women.

HER STORY: Sheila Walsh speaks of overcoming her struggle with depression at Women of Faith conferences. The talented musical artist has also written and contributed to several books.

Sheila grew up in Scotland, where her father died of a brain thrombosis when she was four. At age eleven she accepted Christ. After studying theology at London Bible College, Sheila worked as a musical evangelist with Youth for Christ, then hosted a show at the British Broadcasting Corporation. In 1986, with her career blossoming, she and her husband moved to Los Angeles. Her marriage ended six years later, the same year she was named cohost of The 700 Club, a Christian television show.

As Sheila worked thirteen-hour days and traveled to weekend engagements, she grew increasingly tired and dejected. Realizing she needed help, Sheila committed herself to the psychiatric ward of a hospital. She was diagnosed with clinical depression, the result of deep feelings of anger and shame, some stemming from the early loss of her father. In her book *Honestly*, Sheila shares how she had buried her feelings, hiding behind the persona of a successful woman. Now committed to living honestly before God and others, Sheila encourages other women to live honestly as well.

MY RESPONSE: Whom might I encourage by sharing a life story?

December

The word of God is full of living power. It is sharper than the sharpest knife, cutting deep into our innermost thoughts and desires. It exposes us for what we really are.
Hebrews 4:12 NLT

HER SERVICE: Martyrdom

HER MESSAGE: Scripture guards our hearts when we lose our dignity, meet disaster, or face death.

HER STORY: Joan Waste, a blind twenty-two-year-old, called on the name of Jesus as she was burned at the stake.

The daughter of an English rope maker, Joan helped by knitting stockings. As the Protestant church took root, Joan attended services regularly and saved her money to buy a New Testament. A man in debtors' prison and a parish clerk read to her. If they were not available, she paid others. As they read, she memorized. That knowledge of Scripture guarded her heart throughout her life—even as she faced death.

When Queen Mary came to the throne, officials arrested Joan for heresy. Her detractors accused her of denying the real presence of Christ in the Eucharist. Although she pleaded to be excused since she was poor, blind, and uneducated, Joan proclaimed she was ready to die for her faith. She was sentenced to death. A chancellor stood Joan before the pulpit and condemned her in a sermon. He forbade the people to pray for her. Joan's brother held her hand as she was led to the stake.

MY RESPONSE: What scripture might I memorize to sustain me during a time of need?

Are not two sparrows sold for a penny? Yet not one of them will fall to the ground apart from the will of your Father.
Matthew 10:29

HER SERVICE: Singing

HER MESSAGE: With God's help, a woman of noble character rises above life's ignoble circumstances.

HER STORY: Ethel Waters will long be remembered for her rendition of "His Eye Is on the Sparrow" during Billy Graham crusades. When she first appeared with the group in 1957, she was already an Academy-Award nominee with a well-established reputation as a singer.

Ethel grew up as a poor African American girl in Chester, Pennsylvania. She started singing in church at age five and had a spiritual awakening when she was twelve. She dropped out of school a year later and supported herself as a domestic. At a Madison Square Garden crusade, Ethel's faith deepened, and she joined the crusade choir. When invited to sing a solo, she chose what became her signature song. Ethel then sang at crusades regularly and continued occasionally up to the time of her death.

When antiwar protesters disrupted a crusade at which President Richard Nixon spoke, Ethel reprimanded them in such a loving way that some were converted. During her lifetime many doors remained closed to women of her heritage; but the noble woman rose above ignoble circumstances to attain success on stage and in music.

MY RESPONSE: How might I respond graciously to someone who treats me poorly?

December 3 *Marie Vander Weide*, birth date unknown–1982

Hatred stirs up dissension, but love covers over all wrongs.
Proverbs 10:12

HER SERVICE: Ministering as a dorm mother

HER MESSAGE: Deliver retorts and offer solutions with doses of love and humor.

HER STORY: For thirty-three school years, Marie Vander Weide served as a dorm mother at Rehoboth Christian Boarding School in New Mexico. On duty twenty-four hours a day, seven days a week, she cared for more than sixty Navajo boys each year.

Born in Chicago, Marie began work at Rehoboth in 1920. Colleagues appreciated her keen sense of humor and her gift for storytelling. When a visitor once seemed surprised that Marie wore a lovely dress rather than dowdy missionary clothes, she proudly explained that she and the other women were King's daughters—who dressed well.

Marie not only delivered retorts with doses of love and humor, but while others worried, she found creative solutions in the same positive spirit. She once gave a boy a freshly laundered, warm, dry mop head to sooth an earache. It worked. After retiring in 1953, Marie conducted visitors' tours of the school until 1974. She spent her final years at Artesia Christian Home for the Aged.

MY RESPONSE: What humor do I see even in life's difficult situations?

In this world you will have trouble. But take heart! I have overcome the world.
John 16:33

Her Service: Speaking, teaching, writing, and singing

Her Message: Limitations can kindle determination to reach goals.

Her Story: Since 1996 Thelma Wells has spoken at more than three hundred Women of Faith conferences across the United States and Canada. A professor at Master's Divinity School and Graduate School in Evansville, Indiana, Thelma is founder and president of A Woman of God Ministries, based in Dallas, Texas, where she lives. She has written five books.

For the first two years of her life, Thelma and her mother lived in servants' quarters in a Dallas home. When her mother became ill and lost her job, Thelma moved in with great-grandparents. Her grandfather assured her that someday she would not have to enter through side doors and taught her how to handle prejudice respectfully. But even with relatives, life had hard moments. A light-skinned grandmother locked Thelma in a closet because she was dark skinned.

At St. John Missionary Baptist Church in Dallas, Thelma learned to sing, pray, and hope. She went to college, married George Wells, and earned a degree in education. The mother of three became a leader in the banking industry and gives motivational talks worldwide. Her life demonstrates that limitations can kindle determination. She wears a bumblebee pin to illustrate that women can soar to new heights—in spite of limitations.

My Response: What goal might I set for myself—in spite of limitations?

The one whom God has sent speaks the words of God.
John 3:34

HER SERVICE: Social reform and journalism

HER MESSAGE: To change society we must act rather than acquiesce, speak up rather than keep silent, and continue in God's strength rather than quit.

HER STORY: Ida B. Wells-Barnett was an articulate speaker and candid journalist whose pen name was Iola. She sought social justice in England and helped establish the British Anti-Lynching Committee. Ida also organized Illinois' first black woman's suffrage association.

A slave for her first three years of life, Ida began teaching at age sixteen to support her family after her parents died. Writing about inequities in black schools cost Ida her teaching job, so she purchased an interest in a newspaper. Understanding the impact young men could have motivated Ida to organize a Sunday-school class for them.

Ida was once physically ejected from a train for refusing to move to a smoking car where African Americans were seated. She won a lawsuit against the railway but lost on appeal. Ida vehemently protested the lynching of a friend in 1892, and vandals destroyed her newspaper office. She moved to Chicago and married an attorney in 1895. For a time Ida stayed home, raising their five children; but reform organizations coaxed her into action again. She helped change society by acting rather than acquiescing, speaking up rather than keeping silent, and continuing in God's strength rather than quitting.

MY RESPONSE: How can I help to right an injustice?

As she stood behind him at his feet weeping, she began to wet his feet with her tears. Then she wiped them with her hair, kissed them and poured perfume on them.
Luke 7:38

HER SERVICE: Mothering and preaching

HER MESSAGE: A woman is never too busy to spend time with God.

HER STORY: Susanna Wesley's "method" of training her children won her the title "Mother of Methodism," the movement founded by her son John Wesley. She wrote three religious textbooks.

The daughter of a pastor, Susanna married Samuel Wesley, who became a curate in the Church of England in London. Susanna gave birth to nineteen children, but only ten lived to adulthood. Susanna homeschooled her children six hours a day for twenty years. On Sunday evenings she read sermons borrowed from a library to her family and neighbors' children gathered in her kitchen. Soon word-of-mouth drew so many listeners of all ages that she had to hold her meetings in the barn. Her husband was criticized for allowing her to "preach," but he didn't ask her to stop.

With all that, Susanna still found two hours for prayer and Bible reading and an hour a week to be alone with each child. Although Susanna was never too busy to spend time alone with God, she lamented that she didn't have more time to pull away from the cares and responsibilities of the world.

MY RESPONSE: When might I schedule a time to commune with God?

Let the little children come to me, and do not hinder them, for the kingdom of God belongs to such as these.
Luke 18:16

HER SERVICE: Teaching

HER MESSAGE: To change society, teach children.

HER STORY: Mary Louisa Whately built a mission house and schools near Cairo, Egypt, where she ministered for thirty years.

The daughter of famous logician Archbishop Whately of the Church of England, Mary Louisa, her mother, and sisters ministered in Irish mission schools following the Irish famine. That experience proved valuable to Mary Louisa's later work in Egypt. She toured Cairo with friends in 1858 and returned two years later when a doctor suggested her health might improve in a warmer climate.

Mary Louisa's heart was touched when she observed uneducated, neglected Muslim girls. To change a society that placed no value on educating women, she taught the children. Mary Louisa hired a Syrian woman to translate and opened a girls' school in her rented home. Later, with the help of two male missionaries, she added a boys' school. Through a donation of land, funding supplied by friends in England, and her own resources, Mary Louisa built the educational facility.

By 1879 Mary Louisa's school drew more than six hundred children, and she opened a medical mission. She became known as "the Lady of the Book" to Nile villagers, who looked forward to visits when she read to them.

MY RESPONSE: How can I help meet physical, academic, or spiritual needs of children in my community?

Who knows but that you have come to royal position for such a time as this?
Esther 4:14

HER SERVICE: Acting, writing, ministering to moms

HER MESSAGE: God uses our past to build new ministries.

HER STORY: In 2002 Lisa Whelchel founded MomTime Get-A-Ways, weekend conferences for mothers. Television viewers remember her as a teenaged Mouseketeer in Disney's *New Mickey Mouse Club* and as Blair Warner in *The Facts of Life*.

A native of Texas, Lisa accepted Christ at age ten. Steve Cauble walked into her life at a prayer group; they married in 1988 and had three children. Lisa chose to stay home, and while her children were young, she invited her mother and two other women to a weekly lunch and game time. She used the same approach when she was invited to participate in a women's church retreat.

That concept led to her current MomTime ministry, which focuses on fun, food, faith, and friendships. Many moms got to know Lisa through the Internet journal she posted in 2001, when the family took a yearlong educational tour of America. Her book *Creative Correction*, inspired by her personal experience with her son's Attention Deficit Disorder, has sold more than eighty thousand copies. Lisa has also written about homeschooling her children. Through her roles as parent, friend, educator, and wife, and even through her fame as an actress, God used Lisa's past to prepare her for new ministries.

MY RESPONSE: How might God want to use my past to build a ministry?

*Grow in the grace and knowledge of our
Lord and Savior Jesus Christ.*
2 Peter 3:18

HER SERVICE: Ministering to working women through radio and writing

HER MESSAGE: Women from all walks of life need to learn how to love Jesus and grow in faith.

HER STORY: Mary Whelchel serves as director of women's ministries at Moody Church in Chicago, Illinois. She established *The Christian Working Woman* radio program in 1984 as an outgrowth of her church's ministry to working women. The program airs on more than five hundred stations in the United States and abroad.

Mary became a career woman and single mom with an eight-year-old daughter. Her years as a working woman gave her a burden to teach women biblical principles that they could apply in their workplaces and gave the impetus for founding The Christian Working Woman, an independent, nonprofit organization supported by friends and listeners. Mary has written ten books, including *If You Only Knew* and *How to Thrive from 9 to 5.*

While her mother was a traditional stay-at-home mother, Mary's life has taken a far different track. She is a trendsetter, comfortable in corporate boardrooms and hosting live radio call-in shows. She now speaks to women from all walks of life about how to love Jesus and grow in the faith.

MY RESPONSE: What group of women has my background prepared me to reach for Christ?

Am I now trying to win the approval of men, or of God? Or am I trying to please men? If I were still trying to please men, I would not be a servant of Christ.

Galatians 1:10

HER SERVICE: Evangelism and preaching

HER MESSAGE: God offers ministry opportunities.

HER STORY: Alma White founded her own church, the Pentecostal Union, which later became known as the Pillar of Fire.

Young Alma felt overgrown, the unattractive one of eleven children. She joined the Methodist Episcopal Church when she was twelve and, after a teenage conversion experience, decided to be a preacher. Women preachers were not accepted in that denomination, however, so Alma prepared for a teaching career. She married a pastor, Kent White, who invited her to speak from his pulpit. Soon Alma became a popular evangelistic preacher. But Kent felt snubbed for denominational appointments because Alma's ministry was not accepted.

Lack of recognition from the denomination motivated Alma to establish her own church. Kent's mother disliked Alma, however, and soon he, too, began to criticize her sermons. Embracing the Pentecostal movement, Kent left Alma's church—and then left Alma. Several times they tried unsuccessfully to reconcile their marriage and their beliefs. Their two sons became leaders in Alma's movement. Rejected by a denomination not ready to embrace women preachers, Alma found that God offered opportunities to those He called.

MY RESPONSE: How might God be leading me to a place of ministry?

I can do everything through him who gives me strength.
Philippians 4:13

HER SERVICE: Performing music and singing

HER MESSAGE: "Survivors" remind those experiencing loss not to lose heart.

HER STORY: Judy Cave Whitman has toured North America and Europe as a classical pianist. She has recorded five albums. Although she has lived in blind darkness since infancy, Judy has brought light to hospitals, nursing homes, prisons, and churches.

Judy knelt at the altar of a country church to dedicate her life to Christ at age nine. In 1969 she married a composer and pianist and began touring with him. Daughter Melody was born a year later, but the marriage fell apart after seven years, and Judy settled near relatives in the Midwest. Melody died at age seventeen after developing the same type of cancer that had robbed Judy of her sight.

Having drifted from her spiritual moorings, Judy cried out to the Lord for direction. And God answered. For concert appearances, Judy needed transportation, and God supplied a friend to chauffeur her. Then Judy met Paul Whitman, a visual artist. They married in 1995 and settled in Lebanon, Pennsylvania. Paul, a baritone, now joins Judy in concerts. In a style most influenced by Canadian artist Gordon Lightfoot and the folk tunes of Appalachia, Judy sings of God's grace as she accompanies herself on harp, dulcimer, psaltery, and guitar. A survivor, Judy reminds those experiencing loss not to lose heart.

MY RESPONSE: What have I survived? Whom might my story inspire?

Whoever finds his life will lose it, and whoever loses his life for my sake will find it.
Matthew 10:39

HER SERVICE: Pioneering mission work

HER MESSAGE: To be Christlike means we endure rejection and heartache and even suffer death for the cause of the gospel.

HER STORY: In 1836 Narcissa Whitman and her husband, Marcus, established the Presbyterian Mission, one of the first mission homes in the Pacific Northwest. Narcissa was killed in a massacre by Cayuse Indians, a tribe the Whitmans tried to evangelize.

Born in New York, Narcissa professed Christ at age eleven and dedicated her life to Christian service. For a few years she taught school. When Dr. Marcus Whitman applied for missionary service, he was urged to marry so he would have a helpmate. He married Narcissa in February 1836 and headed west, arriving in Washington on September 1.

Narcissa taught Indian children in her kitchen. A daughter drowned at age two, but Narcissa cared for three Indian children and adopted seven whose parents had died on the Oregon Trail. She assisted her husband in conducting Indian camp meetings and copied and printed a book in the Indian language. The Indians blamed Dr. Whitman for diseases introduced by white settlers and attacked the family on November 29, 1847. Narcissa, the doctor, and several of their adopted children died in the assault. Narcissa had not only bravely endured rejection and heartache but also died for the cause of the gospel.

MY RESPONSE: How can I become more committed to spreading the gospel?

Let your unfailing love surround us, Lord,
for our hope is in you alone.
Psalm 33:22 NLT

HER SERVICE: Founding a ministry to women

HER MESSAGE: The lowliest women can be lifted up.

HER STORY: Emma Whittemore founded Door of Hope, a ministry to offer food, shelter, medical help, and spiritual outreach to prostitutes and other women with no hope.

At the invitation of a friend, Emma, a New York City socialite, visited a YMCA to hear an evangelist speak. Unbeknownst to Emma, her husband also attended the meeting. Both were convicted of the futility of their indulgent lifestyles and vowed to do better. After Emma experienced healing from a serious back injury, she sought direction for her life. She thought of the women she had seen on the streets of the city, but being a timid woman, she recoiled at the thought of reaching out. Determined to please God, however, Emma walked the streets that very night, searching for downtrodden women to lift up physically and spiritually.

In 1890 Emma opened the first Door of Hope, determined to depend on God alone to meet the ministry's needs. During the first four years she rescued 325 girls from destructive lives. God supplied unsolicited donations, and by the time of Emma's death, ninety-seven ministry homes were operating in the United States, Canada, Great Britain, Germany, Africa, Japan, and China.

MY RESPONSE: How might I develop compassion for those less fortunate than me?

Gray hair is a crown of splendor; it is attained by a righteous life.
Proverbs 16:31.

HER SERVICE: Writing

HER MESSAGE: Senior years bring experience, time, and self-confidence through which we can be used by God.

HER STORY: Laura Ingalls Wilder wrote ten books depicting life on the American frontier—but not until after she turned sixty-three. The popular television series *Little House on the Prairie* was based on her books.

Frequent moves during Laura's childhood—from Wisconsin to Kansas, Minnesota, Iowa, and finally South Dakota—provided rich fodder for the stories that would later flow from her pen. At age twelve, while attending a sick neighbor, Laura sensed God's presence in prayer and believed He would always guide her. She read the Bible and memorized many verses.

Laura began teaching school at age fifteen, then married Almanzo Wilder a few years later. Like Laura's parents, the Wilders became farmers and moved frequently, finally settling in the Ozark Mountains, where Laura raised Leghorn hens. Once asked to speak about poultry, she sent a written article instead and was invited to write a weekly newspaper column. By then her daughter, Rose Wilder Lane, was a journalist.

Laura tried writing. Her first book, *Little House in the Big Woods*, took a year to market; but her stories inspired readers during the Great Depression and World War II. In her senior years, Laura found the wealth of experience, the time, and the self-confidence she needed to be used by God.

MY RESPONSE: How might I serve God in my senior years?

December 15 *Ann Wilkins*, 1806–1857

I desire to do your will, O my God; your law is within my heart.

Psalm 40:8

HER SERVICE: Mission work

HER MESSAGE: The greatest offering we can give is our lives.

HER STORY: With little money to put in the offering plate, Ann Wilkins dropped in a note saying she cheerfully offered her life. Beginning in 1837 Ann spent twenty years as a missionary in Liberia, Africa.

Ann grew up in New York, the daughter of Methodists who taught her to love God and His work. She gave her life to Christ when she was fourteen. Ann taught Sunday school at Bedford Street Methodist Episcopal Church in New York City. It was there that a pastor who had visited Liberia spoke on the need for missionaries and evoked Ann's sincere desire to go as a teacher. She volunteered for missionary service. The following June she brought light to a dark continent when she brought her Christian values to a school in Millsburg, Liberia. The students loved her.

Poor health forced Ann to return to the United States three times, but she always returned to the field as soon as she had recuperated from the effects of the severe African climate.

MY RESPONSE: How have I offered my life for Christian service?

Be persistent in your prayers for all Christians everywhere.
Ephesians 6:18 NLT

HER SERVICE: Education and social reform

HER MESSAGE: Don't get discouraged if others fail to embrace your vision. Persist!

HER STORY: Although she died before the passage of the Nineteenth Amendment, Frances Willard blazed a trail that led to women's right to vote. A leader of the Women's Christian Temperance Union (WCTU), Frances saw women's right to vote as a logical step leading to prohibition.

Frances graduated from Northwestern Female College in Illinois. Under Phoebe Palmer's evangelistic ministry, Frances experienced what was called Christian perfection, something friends advised her not to speak of when she joined the staff of Genesee Wesleyan Seminary in New York. She later became president of Evanston College for Ladies, perhaps the first woman college president to hand out degrees.

In her book *Woman in the Pulpit*, Frances urged women to seek ordination. She served Methodism well, helping to raise thirty thousand dollars to build Garrett Seminary hall; but as was customary, a man read the speech she wrote for its dedication. Frances's request to greet the 1880 Methodist General Conference on behalf of the WCTU sparked two hours of debate before it was finally approved. She withdrew—leaving a note to be read by a man. In 1888 Frances was one of five women elected to that conference, but they were denied seats. Never one to be discouraged if others failed to embrace her vision, Frances simply persisted.

MY RESPONSE: How might I rekindle a vision and persist until it's realized?

I am going to do something in your days that you would not believe, even if you were told.
Habakkuk 1:5

HER SERVICE: Writing, speaking, and ministering to other ministers

HER MESSAGE: Our service to God may be delayed but need not be defeated.

HER STORY: Joyce Williams and her husband, Gene, are founding directors of Shepherds' Fold Ministries, an organization dedicated to encouraging pastors and church staff members. She has written three books.

With a desire to serve God, Joyce enrolled at a Tennessee college. She married, had two daughters, and appeared to have the perfect family. But after twenty-six years of marriage, her husband walked out. As Joyce cried out to God, He renewed her call to Christian service.

Joyce was the first woman elected to a District Advisory Board in the Church of the Nazarene. After working in marketing and management, she moved to Florida and served for two years as minister of Christian education and outreach at a Clearwater church. A couple there introduced her to Gene Williams, a Kansas pastor, by telephone. Following a long-distance courtship, they married in 1992, and Joyce moved west. When Gene retired in 1998, the couple founded Shepherds' Fold Ministries to offer retreats, personal contact, and safe havens to weary ministerial staff. Joyce's service to God was delayed by circumstances beyond her control, but not defeated.

MY RESPONSE: How might I seek refreshment so I can fulfill a commitment to Christian service?

All the days ordained for me were written in your book before one of them came to be.
Psalm 139:16

HER SERVICE: Mission work

HER MESSAGE: Our lives and times are in God's hands.

HER STORY: Mary Chauner Williams served as a missionary on the South Sea Islands from 1817 until her husband, John, died at the hands of cannibalistic tribesmen in 1840.

After a yearlong voyage from England, the Williamses landed on the island of Eimeo. Two months later Mary gave birth and worried about her new son's welfare in a land of pagan rites and fetishes. The family settled on Raiatea, about one hundred miles from Tahiti, where the people had practiced infanticide and human sacrifice before converting to Christianity two years earlier. Each morning Mary and John taught people of all ages. Soon hundreds of children expressed gratitude that the gospel had spared their lives, and they demonstrated a knowledge of Scripture.

Mary suffered ill health, and seven of her ten children died prematurely or in infancy. Yet she ministered to neglected elder islanders, teaching them to make bonnets from bark cloth and coconut fiber, which they proudly wore to church services. As John traveled more than one hundred thousand miles establishing mission outposts, Mary released him into God's hands, praying for his protection but also accepting that all of their lives were ultimately in God's hands.

MY RESPONSE: How can I better release my loved ones into God's hands to do His work?

December 19 — *Jennie Fowler Willing*, 1834–1916

I have been crucified with Christ and I no longer live, but Christ lives in me.
Galatians 2:20

HER SERVICE: Social reform, writing, and speaking

HER MESSAGE: We demonstrate devotion to God by our devotion to His children.

HER STORY: As corresponding secretary of the Woman's Foreign Missionary Society of the Methodist Episcopal Church, Jennie organized societies from Ohio westward. As president of a local temperance league, she was instrumental in forming a national society. As a widow Jennie financed and opened the New York Training School and Settlement Home in Hell's Kitchen.

Born in what is now Ontario, Jenny moved with her family to Illinois. She was largely self-educated because of her poor health. In 1853 Jennie married Methodist Episcopal preacher William Crossgrove Willing and moved to New York. Controversy over sanctification, a doctrine both supported, prompted their move back to Illinois in 1860. There Jennie taught college English and became involved in the temperance movement. She edited the National Women's Christian Temperance Union's first publication and left the organization half of her estate.

Devotion to God motivated Jennie to devote her life to helping God's children. She worked untiringly for causes that protected women from poverty and abuse. She viewed alcohol as a major contributor to society's ills. She saw potential in every woman, and she encouraged women to band together to achieve social reform.

MY RESPONSE: How might I discover the needs of women in my community?

Let us leave the elementary teachings about
Christ and go on to maturity.
Hebrews 6:1

HER SERVICE: Education and training

HER MESSAGE: The church fails to utilize half its resources if it fails to equip half its members.

HER STORY: Through Biblical Education by Extension (BEE) International, Wendy trains women to use their spiritual gifts. Her goals are to see women better cared for, practically and spiritually, and to help them find places of service in the kingdom of God.

Wendy trusted Christ as her savior at age eleven. When a Vacation Bible School teacher told of Russian Christians who had made huge sacrifices out of love for God, it changed Wendy's life. She realized that she had a new purpose to live out. In college she majored in accounting, but her dream to become a corporate leader was forgotten as she participated in the college ministry of a local church. Wendy earned a degree at Dallas Theological Seminary with an eye on a career in missions.

Since 1984 Wendy has served with BEE International to reach women in Eastern Europe and the former Soviet Union. Believing that if the church fails to equip women, it fails to utilize half its resources, Wendy has developed a curriculum that provides comprehensive training through study and mentoring.

MY RESPONSE: How might I help women in my congregation better discover and use their spiritual gifts?

Praise the Lord, O my soul; all my
inmost being, praise his holy name.
Psalm 103:1

HER SERVICE: Singing and songwriting

HER MESSAGE: Don't be ashamed to worship.

HER STORY: The first black woman to receive a Dove Award as female vocalist of the year, recording artist CeCe Winans has also won many Grammy and Stellar Awards and has numerous gold albums. She appears at Women of Faith conferences and coauthored *Throne Room: Ushered into the Presence of God.*

Born in Detroit, Michigan, the eighth of ten children, Priscilla, called CeCe, sang in church as a child. Her parents frowned upon any music but gospel. CeCe and her brother Benjamin, called BeBe, began singing as the PTL Singers in 1982. They broke into the recording world in 1987 with *BeBe and CeCe*. In 1995 CeCe recorded her first solo album. Her worshipful music has touched the hearts of millions. A suicidal caller once told a church secretary that hearing CeCe's music on the hold line brought her such peace that she would be all right.

CeCe and husband, Alvin L. Love II, live in Nashville, Tennessee, where they homeschool their two children. The kids sing in the choir of Born Again Church, and CeCe sings with the church's praise and worship team. She serves as a spokesperson for Teen Save, a teen suicide-prevention organization. At conferences CeCe claps her hands, waves her handkerchief, and teaches women to do what she does best—worship God unashamedly.

MY RESPONSE: How might I unashamedly worship God?

They will still bear fruit in old age, they will stay fresh and green.
Psalm 92:14

HER SERVICE: Volunteering

HER MESSAGE: God offers no retirement plan. Missed opportunities for service mean missed opportunities for joy.

HER STORY: Jean Henninger Witmer served God through every stage of life. She founded a crisis hotline, organized social-needs programs at two churches, and played a role in founding a crisis-pregnancy ministry.

Raised in a Christian family in rural Pennsylvania, Jean began teaching Sunday school at age sixteen and taught on and off throughout her lifetime. She married her high-school sweetheart, John Witmer. While their daughters were still young, Jean earned a master's degree in education.

For five years the Witmers lived in Arizona, where Jean founded and directed The Listening Post crisis hotline. After returning to Pennsylvania, Jean organized and directed a Good Samaritan ministry at her church. In time the outreach evolved into a dozen subministries, including baby-sitting, meals, and a job bank. Jean also hosted a monthly women's Bible study for more than twenty years. She served as an ambulance dispatcher, and even while vacationing, Jean prayed with people who expressed needs. She and a telemarketer became pen pals after Jean once offered to pray for her. Rather than retire from ministry, Jean viewed any missed opportunity for service as a missed opportunity for joy.

MY RESPONSE: What opportunities to serve God might I be missing that could enrich my life and the lives of others?

Though you do not see him, you trust him.
1 Peter 1:8 NLT

HER SERVICE: Mission work and teaching

HER MESSAGE: Worry erodes our trust; trust erodes our worry.

HER STORY: Pauline Woerner served beside her husband, Gustave, as a missionary in China and Indonesia for almost twenty years. The couple taught at Bible schools in both countries, and after World War II forced their return to America, they taught at what is now Toccoa Falls College in Georgia.

While working in New York City, Pauline attended the Gospel Tabernacle, accepted Christ, and felt called to missions. She met Gustave, who had already served as a missionary in Peru, at what is now Nyack Bible Institute. Always practical, Pauline refused an engagement ring but did accept a much-needed engagement watch. The Christian and Missionary Alliance mission board required the couple to serve on the field for two years before marriage, so they traveled to China separately and married in 1925. As newlyweds they shared a home with nearly thirty others, women sleeping in one room and men in another.

Pauline taught at a girls' school and visited homes with "Bible women." Knowing that worry erodes our trust but that trust erodes our worry, she released her husband to God's care as Gustave traveled to distribute Bibles, a venture made dangerous by political instability and armed bandits. She also released their three children as they went off to boarding school.

MY RESPONSE: What person or situation do I need to turn over to God?

Even on my servants, both men and women,
I will pour out my Spirit in those days.
Joel 2:29

HER SERVICE: Evangelism

HER MESSAGE: Neither denomination nor gender limits God's Spirit.

HER STORY: Although she had little education, Maria Woodworth-Etter preached in tent meetings across the United States.

The daughter of an alcoholic father, Maria came to know Christ as a teenager. She felt called to the pulpit, but her church did not recognize women in public ministry. So Maria married John Woodworth, hoping to partner with him in ministry. John, however, did not share her calling. By the time Maria was thirty-five, five of her six children had died, and she was frequently ill herself.

Maria began preaching locally and was soon in great demand as an evangelist. After she and John joined the United Brethren Church, which accepted women preachers, Maria divorced John, charging him with adultery. He died the next year.

Maria faced some opposition because of her emphasis on charismatic gifts. But she found that neither denomination nor gender limited the work of God's Spirit. She was widely accepted across denominational lines. In 1902 Maria married S. P. Etter, who supported her ministry in many practical ways. Besides conducting services, Maria planted churches and baptized believers. As she approached seventy years of age, she held meetings in Indiana that were estimated to have drawn twenty-five thousand people.

MY RESPONSE: What boundaries may God be calling me to cross for Him?

Beulah Woolston, 1828–1886
Sarah Woolston, ca. 1831–1910

Be faithful, even to the point of death, and
I will give you the crown of life.
Revelation 2:10

THEIR SERVICE: Mission work

THEIR MESSAGE: Faithful Christian servants change lives, communities, and cultures.

THEIR STORY: Beulah Woolston and her sister Sarah organized and for twenty-five years operated a girls' boarding school in China. The women also opened day schools at other locations. They translated textbooks and edited the *Child's Illustrated Paper* in Chinese.

Born in New Jersey, Beulah graduated from Wesleyan Female College in Wilmington, Delaware. She took a job teaching at the college, but when she heard an appeal for missionary teachers in China, Beulah and Sarah volunteered. They landed at Foo-Chow in March 1859. In spite of prejudice against the education of women and ill will created by foreign traders, the women persevered. Their work under the China Female Missionary Society of Baltimore won the respect of both Chinese and Americans. Girls at the school were trained academically as well as practically so they might become good wives and mothers. The influence of the missionaries changed those girls, their community, and even their culture, as graduates became known for excellent character.

What the sisters lacked in facilities and curriculum, they made up for in dedication and perseverance. Their work was later connected to the Woman's Foreign Missionary Society.

MY RESPONSE: How might I influence a person, my community, or my culture for Christ?

The one who calls you is faithful and he will do it.
1 Thessalonians 5:24

HER SERVICE: Child evangelism

HER MESSAGE: God uses our education, commitment, and service to bear spiritual sons and daughters.

HER STORY: Dr. Mable Ruth Wray served as a home missionary to children for fifty years, twenty-eight as state director of Child Evangelism Fellowship (CEF) of Eastern Pennsylvania, located in Harrisburg.

Born in Tennessee, Mable Ruth was dedicated to God before birth by loving parents. A pastor led her to Christ at age ten. After high school she graduated from a Memphis engineering school, then worked at a military base and a corporation for several years before responding to God's call.

Mable Ruth was once lost for words when a friend asked how to be saved. So she decided she would learn how to witness. After graduating from Moody Bible Institute in 1955, Mable Ruth settled in Pennsylvania as a CEF field worker, then served as a county director. In 1971 she graduated from CEF's Leadership Training Institute in Michigan and went on to establish similar institutes in Kenya, Ghana, Indonesia, and Pakistan. Mable Ruth laid aside an early goal of marriage to produce and nurture sons and daughters in the Lord. Bob Jones University, where Mable Ruth serves as an adjunct professor, awarded her an honorary doctorate for her devotion to the Lord and to reaching children.

MY RESPONSE: How might I bear a spiritual son or daughter?

Now that you have been set free from sin and have become slaves to God, the benefit you reap leads to holiness, and the result is eternal life.
Romans 6:22

HER SERVICE: Ministering to prisoners

HER MESSAGE: No one is chained who cannot be freed in Christ.

HER STORY: For forty years Mathilde Wrede ministered to men and women locked in prison cells.

Mathilde received the education and training due her as daughter of the provincial governor of Vasa, Finland, but as a child she was grieved when she observed prisoners being branded by hot irons. Mathilde came to Christ as a young adult and immediately realized that even those who are chained can be free in Christ. While others viewed inmates as hopelessly depraved, Mathilde recognized the potential of the gospel to transform these people's lives.

Responding to a vision of a prisoner calling to her, Mathilde began visiting Finland's prisons. The first time she preached in a prison chapel, she left hundreds of inmates in tears. Mathilde taught. She sympathized. And after prisoners were released, she wrote notes of encouragement and visited them. Many in need of counseling and encouragement, including families of inmates, sought help at her modest home, where she adopted the diet of prisoners so she could better relate to them. In gratitude, one prisoner carved a beautiful brooch for her from a soup bone, symbolizing Mathilde's capacity to see beauty and good in the most corrupt men and women.

MY RESPONSE: To whom and in what way might I offer freedom in Christ?

If they persecuted me, they will persecute you also.
John 15:20

HER SERVICE: Cofounded Voice of the Martyrs

HER MESSAGE: Speak out for those who have been silenced.

HER STORY: Sabina Wurmbrand and her husband, Richard, cofounded Voice of the Martyrs to speak out for persecuted Christians around the world.

Born into a Jewish family in Czernowitz, part of Romania, Sabina converted to Christianity in 1936, as did Richard. They married that same year. When their country was occupied during World War II, the couple worked to save Jewish children from the Nazis. Sabina's parents, two sisters, and a brother died in concentration camps, and the Wurmbrands were arrested for participating in Christian activities.

Under postwar communism Sabina organized Christian camps to minister to religious leaders of all denominations. Her street meetings drew thousands. In 1948 Richard was arrested. Left with a young son, Sabina continued her work of helping the persecuted church. In time she, too, was arrested and confined to a slave labor camp and prison for three years while her son fended for himself. Sabina refused to believe reports that her husband had died, and in 1964, after Richard had spent fourteen years in prison, the couple was reunited. Following his release, they went to the United States. For thirty-two years Sabina continued to speak out for those whose voices were silenced in places such as Vietnam, China, North Korea, Cuba, Laos, and the former Soviet Union.

MY RESPONSE: How might I support persecuted Christians?

You will receive an inheritance from the Lord as a reward.
Colossians 3:24

HER SERVICE: Business

HER MESSAGE: Do your earthly best as you wait for heavenly rewards.

HER STORY: Bonnie Wurzbacher has climbed the corporate ladder at The Coca-Cola Company, from regional account executive of the firm's Minute Maid division to Coke's vice president of customer strategy.

After growing up as a pastor's daughter, Bonnie ignored her bent for business that had surfaced in childhood ventures. Instead, she became a teacher. But after five years Bonnie felt unfulfilled and took a job that led to her present career. Married at thirty-seven to a senior executive in a related industry, Bonnie gave birth to premature twin daughters who lived only a few hours. Church training has equipped her to minister in crisis situations, and she now shares with others who are grieving her hope that she will see the girls in heaven.

Bonnie loves the challenge of corporate management and international business and strives to integrate her faith with her lifestyle. She looks to Jesus as a carpenter and to God as a creator to define her work ethic. She encourages all Christians, both men and women, to be leaders and to do their earthly best as they wait for heavenly rewards.

MY RESPONSE: What might I do to better integrate my lifestyle and my faith?

Finally, all of you, live in harmony with one another; be sympathetic, love as brothers, be compassionate and humble.
1 Peter 3:8

HER SERVICE: Actively supported the Reformation

HER MESSAGE: Hatred leads to persecution, but compassion leads to peace.

HER STORY: Katherine Zell, wife of German reformer Matthew Zell, debated theology with the best minds of the Reformation.

Reputed from her childhood to have been a student of sermons, Katherine published pamphlets of hymns and tracts. After marrying Matthew, she gave birth to two babies who died soon after birth. Katherine spoke her mind when her husband and other priests were suspended from duties because they married. She took in Protestants fleeing persecution and wrote letters based on Scripture to encourage the wives of men who were in hiding. Katherine supplied the needs of thousands when refugees deluged Strasbourg during the Peasants' War. Knowing that while hatred leads to persecution, compassion leads to peace, she traveled with her husband urging peace.

Criticized for helping those of various theological positions, Katherine insisted she only took in those who acknowledged Christ. She continued her humanitarian efforts after her husband's death. In her old age Katherine led a funeral service after a Lutheran minister threatened to renounce the deceased woman for denying the faith.

MY RESPONSE: How might I inspire compassion where there is hatred?

We who are strong ought to bear with the failings of the weak.
Romans 15:1

HER SERVICE: Social work

HER MESSAGE: Godly servants showcase God's sufficiency rather than self-sufficiency.

HER STORY: Elvinah Spoelstra Zwier directed the Christian Adoption Program of Korea, a program people said would never work in that country. Her organization became the first licensed as an in-country adoption agency.

Raised in South Dakota during the Depression, Elvinah worked in a candy factory to save money for business school. But sixteen years of secretarial work left her wanting to do more, so she earned a degree in social work. She continued work on a graduate degree during a three-year engagement to Les Swanson, and during that time the couple dedicated their lives to God. Then, just before their wedding date, Les died in a car crash. While Elvinah questioned God's will, she rededicated her life to His service. Her background and training made her well suited for the job she took with the Denver Welfare Department.

In 1965 Elvinah volunteered to serve in Korea with the Christian Reformed World Relief Committee. For six years she promoted adoption, a challenging mission in a country that had considered adoption taboo. After working with the Luke Society in Cary, Mississippi, Elvinah learned to view poverty as a symptom of deeper needs. Always showcasing God's sufficiency rather than her own, Elvinah and a colleague developed an advocacy ministry for individuals with disabilities.

MY RESPONSE: How might I help someone discover that God can meet a need?

Bibliography

Books

Anglin, Patty, with Joe Musser. *Acres of Hope.* Uhrichsville, OH: Promise Press, 1999.

Bainton, Roland H. *Women of the Reformation in Germany and Italy.* Minneapolis: Augsburg Publishing House, 1971.

Barnes, Emilie. *If Teacups Could Talk.* Eugene, OR: Harvest House, 1994.

Barnett, Tommy, Jill Briscoe, Nancie Carmichael, Gordon MacDonald, John C. Maxwell, J. I. Packer, Charles Stanley, John Trent, and Sheila Walsh. *The Desert Experience.* Nashville: Thomas Nelson Publishers, 2001.

Beamer, Lisa, with Ken Abraham. *Let's Roll: Ordinary People, Extraordinary Courage.* Wheaton, IL: Tyndale House, 2002.

Beaver, R. Pierce. *American Protestant Women in World Mission.* Grand Rapids: William B. Eerdmans, 1980.

Bell, Gloria J., ed. *Cloud of Witnesses: Portraits of Women Ministers in the Wesleyan/Holiness Movement.* Grantham, PA: Wesleyan/Holiness Women Clergy, Inc., Messiah College, 2000.

Bernall, Misty. *She Said Yes: The Unlikely Martyrdom of Cassie Bernall.* Farmington, PA: The Plough Publishing House, 1999.

Bingham, Helen E. *An Irish Saint: The Life Story of Ann Preston (Holy Ann).* Toronto: William Briggs, 1907.

Brabon, Margaret, with Ed Erny. *What Now, Lord?* Greenwood, IN: OMS International, 1993.

Brestin, Dee. *The Friendships of Women.* Colorado Springs: Cook, 2005.

Briscoe, Jill, Laurie Katz McIntyre, and Beth Seversen. *Designing Effective Women's Ministries.* Grand Rapids: Zondervan, 2000.

Brown, Earl Kent. *Women of Mr. Wesley's Methodism.* Lewiston, NY: The Edwin Mellen Press, 1983.

Bibliography

Burgess, Alan. *The Small Woman.* New York: E. P. Dutton and Co., 1957.

Burnham, Gracia, with Dean Merrill. *In the Presence of My Enemies.* Wheaton, IL: Tyndale House, 2003.

Caesar, Shirley. *Shirley Caesar: The Lady, the Melody, and the Word.* Nashville: Thomas Nelson, 1998.

Christenson, Evelyn. *What Happens When Women Pray.* Wheaton, IL: Victor Books, 1980.

Christie, Vance. *John and Betty Stam: Missionary Martyrs.* Uhrichsville, OH: Barbour, 2000.

Clairmont, Patsy. *Under His Wings: And Other Places of Refuge.* Colorado Springs: Focus on the Family, 1994.

Cornwell, Patricia Daniels. *A Time for Remembering: The Ruth Bell Graham Story.* San Francisco: Harper & Row, 1983.

Curry, Dayna, and Heather Mercer. *Prisoners of Hope.* Colorado Springs: Waterbrook Press, 2002.

Curtis, Carolyn. *A Man for All Nations: The Story of Clyde and Ruth Taylor.* Camp Hill, PA: Christian Publications, 1998.

Deen, Edith. *Great Women of the Christian Faith.* Westwood, NJ: Barbour and Co., 1959.

DeTellis, Jeanne, with Renee Meloche. *A Stubborn Hope without Disappointment.* Orlando, FL: NEW Missions, 1996.

Douglas, J. D., ed. *Twentieth-Century Dictionary of Christian Biography.* Grand Rapids: Baker Books, 1995.

Drummond, Ellen L. *Queen of the Dark Chamber: The Story of Christiana Tsai.* Chicago: Moody Press, 1963.

Eble, Diane. *Behind the Stories.* Minneapolis: Bethany House, 2002.

Edwards, Sue, and Kelley Mathews. *New Doors in Ministry to Women.* Grand Rapids: Kregel Publications, 2002.

Elliot, Elisabeth. *A Chance to Die.* Old Tappan, NJ: Fleming H. Revell, 1987.

Evans, Debra. *Women of Courage.* Grand Rapids: Zondervan, 1999.

Flowers, Lois. *Women, Faith, and Work.* Nashville: Word Publishing, 2001.

Goll, Michal Ann. *Women on the Front Lines: A Call to Courage.* Shippensburg, PA: Destiny Image® Publishers, Inc., 1999.

Gordon, Ernest. *A Book of Protestant Saints.* Chicago: Moody Press, 1946.

Gracey, Mrs. J. T. *Eminent Missionary Women.* New York: Eaton & Mains, 1898.

Grissen, Lillian V., ed. *For Such a Time as This: Twenty-Six Women of Vision and Faith Tell Their Stories.* Grand Rapids: William B. Eerdmans, 1991 (reprinted 1992).

———. *A Path through the Sea: One Woman's Journey from Depression to Wholeness.* Grand Rapids: William B. Eerdmans Publishing, 1993.

Hardesty, Nancy. *Great Women of Faith.* Grand Rapids: Baker Book House, 1980.

Henry, Marie. *Hannah Whitall Smith.* Minneapolis: Bethany House Publishers, 1984.

Hosier, Helen Kooiman. *100 Christian Women Who Changed the 20th Century.* Grand Rapids: Fleming H. Revell, 2000.

———. *Living Cameos.* Old Tappan, NJ: Fleming H. Revell, 1984.

Jacobson, S. Winifred. *The Pearl and the Dragon: The Story of Gerhard and Alma Jacobson.* Camp Hill, PA: Christian Publications, 1997.

Janney, Rebecca Price. *Great Women in American History.* Camp Hill, PA: Horizon Books, 1996.

Johnson, Barbara. *Fresh Elastic for Stretched Out Moms.* Old Tappan, NJ: Fleming H. Revell, 1986.

Keller, Rosemary Skinner, ed. *Spirituality and Social Responsibility: Vocational*

Vision of Women in The United Methodist Tradition. Nashville: Abingdon Press, 1993.

Koons, Carolyn A. *Beyond Betrayal.* San Francisco: Harper & Row, 1984.

Kurian, George Thomas, ed. *Nelson's New Christian Dictionary.* Nashville: Thomas Nelson Publishers, 2001.

Lawson, James Gilchrist, comp. *The Best-Loved Religious Poems.* Old Tappan, NJ: Fleming H. Revell Co., 1933.

Lewis, A. Rodger. *The Battle for Bali: The Story of Rodger and Lelia Lewis.* Camp Hill, PA: Christian Publications, 1999.

Martin, Lowell A., ed. director. *The American Peoples Encyclopedia.* New York: Grolier Inc., 1961.

Matthews, Winifred. *Dauntless Women: Stories of Pioneer Wives.* New York: Friendship Press, 1947.

McCasland, David. *Oswald Chambers: Abandoned to God.* Grand Rapids: Discovery House Publishers; Oswald Chambers Publications Association, Ltd., 1993 (distributed Nashville: Thomas Nelson Publishers).

McGuinness, Cheryl. *Beauty beyond the Ashes: Choosing Hope after Crisis.* West Monroe, LA: Howard Publishing, 2004.

McPherson, Anna Talbott. *Spiritual Secrets of Famous Christians.* Grand Rapids: Zondervan, 1964.

Moothart, Lorene. *Heartbeat for the World: The Story of Gustave and Pauline Woerner.* Camp Hill, PA: Christian Publications, 1999.

Morgan, Robert J. *On This Day.* Nashville: Thomas Nelson Publishers, 1997.

Neudorf, Eugene. *A Light to All Japan: The Story of Susan Dyck.* Camp Hill, PA: Christian Publications, Inc., 1998.

Osbeck, Kenneth W. *101 More Hymn Stories.* Grand Rapids: Kregel Publications, 1985.

Partner, Daniel. *Quicknotes™: Great Women of Faith.* Wheaton: Tyndale House Publishers, 2000.

Petersen, William J. *Martin Luther Had a Wife*. Wheaton: Living Books, 1988.

Petersen, William J., and Randy Petersen. *100 Christian Books That Changed the Century.* Grand Rapids: Fleming H. Revell, 2000.

Pitman, Emma Raymond. *Heroines of the Mission Field.* New York: Cassell, Petter, Galpin & Co., 1880.

Prince, Derek and Lydia. *Appointment in Jerusalem: A True Story of Faith, Love, and the Miraculous Power of Prayer.* 30th anniversary ed. New Kensington, PA: Whitaker House, 2005.

Reid, Daniel G., Robert D. Linder, Bruce L. Shelley, Harry S. Stout, and Craig A. Noll, eds. *Concise Dictionary of Christianity in America.* Downers Grove, IL: InterVarsity Press, 1995.

Roberts, W. Dayton. *One Step Ahead.* Miami: Latin America Mission, 1996.

Rohrick, Lisa M. *Both Feet on God's Path: The Story of Julie Fehr.* Camp Hill, PA: Christian Publications, 1996.

Senter, Ruth, and Jori Senter Stuart. *A Tribute to Moms*. Sisters, OR: Multnomah Books, 1997.

St. John, Patricia. *An Ordinary Woman's Extraordinary Faith: An Autobiography of Patricia St. John.* Wheaton: Harold Shaw Publishers, 1993.

Stanchfield, Wilma, with Helen Kooiman Hosier. *Struck by Lightning Then by Love.* Nashville: Thomas Nelson, 1979.

Stanley, Susie Cunningham. *Feminist Pillar of Fire: The Life of Alma White.* Cleveland, OH: The Pilgrim Press, 1993.

Stuart, Sally E. *Christian Writers' Market Guide 2003*. Colorado Springs: Shaw Books, 2003.

Swan, Laura. *The Forgotten Desert Mothers: Sayings, Lives, and Stories of Early Christian Women.* Mahwah, NJ: Paulist Press, 2001.

Swindoll, Luci. *I Married Adventure.* Nashville: W Publishing Group, 2002.

Tada, Joni Eareckson. *A Christmas Longing.* Portland: Multnomah Press, 1990.

Taylor, Mrs. Howard. *John and Betty Stam: A Story of Triumph.* Chicago: Moody Press, 1935.

Ten Boom, Corrie. *The Hiding Place.* New York: Bantam Books, 1974.

Ten Boom, Corrie, with Jamie Buckingham. *Tramp for the Lord.* Fort Washington, PA: Christian Literature Crusade, 1974.

Thompson, David. *Beyond the Mist: The Story of Donald and Dorothy Fairley.* Harrisburg, PA: Christian Publications, Inc., 1998.

Tucker, Ruth A. *Guardians of the Great Commission: The Story of Women in Modern Missions.* Grand Rapids: Academie Books, Zondervan, 1988.

Tucker, Ruth A. *Private Lives of Pastors' Wives.* Grand Rapids: Zondervan, 1988.

Tucker, Ruth A., and Walter Liefeld. *Daughters of the Church.* Grand Rapids: Zondervan, 1987.

Vardey, Lucinda, comp. *Mother Teresa: A Simple Path.* New York: Ballantine Books, 1995.

Walsh, Sheila. *Honestly.* Grand Rapids: Zondervan Publishing House, 1996.

Walsh, Walter. *The Women Martyrs of the Reformation.* London: Religious Tract Society, 1903.

Williams, Joyce, comp. *Unshakable Faith for Shaky Times.* Kansas City: Beacon Hill Press, 2002.

———. *My Faith Still Holds.* Kansas City: Beacon Hill Press, 2003.

Periodicals

Alford, Deann. "New Life in a Culture of Death." *Christianity Today*, February 2004, 48. Article on Jeannine Brabon.

Blunt, Sheryl Henderson. "The Unflappable Condi Rice." *Christianity Today,* September 2003, 42.

Brosseau, Jim. "George & Laura: How Faith Keeps Them Strong." *Women's Faith & Spirit*, Fall 2003, 28.

Christianity Today. Briefs. June 2003, 21. Obituary of Marj Van Der Puy's husband.

———. North America News Wrap. December 2003. On the death of Madame Chiang Kai-shek.

Courtney, Camerin. "The REAL Facts—and Fun!—of LIFE." *Today's Christian Woman*, May/June 2004, 38.

Duin, Julia. "GOP Keeps Faith, but Not in Prime Time." *Washington Times*, September 1, 2004. http://www.washingtontimes.com/national/20040901-123957-8334r.htm (accessed December 20, 2005).

Evenhouse, Neva. "A Call to Retirement." *Journey into Freedom.* http://www.journeyintofreedom.org/featurewriter.htm (accessed June 12, 2004).

Gaither, Gloria. "Liddy Did It." *Homecoming,* March/April 2003, 22.

Gearan, Anne. "From Segregated South to Cabinet." *Patriot-News*, January 29, 2005.

Guthrie, Stan, and Wendy Murray Zoba. "Double Jeopardy." *Christianity Today,* July 8, 2002, 26. Article on Dayna Curry and Heather Mercer.

History's Women. "Sabina Wurmbrand: Co-Founder of the Voice of the Martyrs." http://www.historyswomen.com/womenoffaith/sabina.htm (accessed January 20, 2006).

Lee, Joyce, and Glenn Gohr. "Women in the Pentecostal Movement." *Enrichment Journal* 4, Fall 1999. http://www.ag.org/enrichmentjournal/199904/060_women.cfm (accessed July 6, 2004). Article on Carrie Judd Montgomery.

Norment, Lynn. "At Home with CeCe Winans." *Ebony*, November 1998. http://www.findarticles.com/p/articles/mi_m1077/is_nl_v54/ai_21270365 (accessed July 21, 2004).

Sellers, Jeff M. "Dayna Curry Will Celebrate Her 30th Birthday in a Taliban

Prison." *Christianity Today*, November 2, 2001. http://www.christianitytoday.com/ct/2001/144/53.0.html (accessed January 26, 2006).

Storer, Dawn. "Profile: Millie Lace—The Truth Will Set You Free." *Woman's Touch*. http://www.womanstouch.ag.org/womanstouch/profiles/ (accessed December 9, 2003).

Struck, Jane Johnson. "Spirited Surrender." *Today's Christian Woman*, May/June 2001. http://www.christianitytoday.com/tcw/2001/003/2.36.html (accessed December 16, 2003). Article on Renee Bondi.

Vinely, Andrea. "CeCe Winans: Stuck on Faith." *Woman's Touch*. http://womanstouch.ag.org/womanstouch/profiles/cece-winans.cfm (accessed December 16, 2003).

Walden, Colette. "Supernatural Transformation." *Woman's Touch*. http://www.womanstouch.ag.org/womanstouch/profiles/lavonne-savage.cfm (accessed December 16, 2003). Article on Lavonne Savage.

Woman's Touch. "The Heart of a Champion: An Interview with Jean Driscoll." http://womanstouch.ag.org/womanstouch/profiles/jean-driscoll.cfm (accessed September 22, 2003).

———. "Only a Woman." http://www.womanstouch.ag.org/womanstouch/profiles/terri-mcfaddin.cfm (accessed December 3, 2003). Article on Terri McFaddin.

———. "Profile: Kristy Dykes." http://womanstouch.ag.org/womanstouch/profiles/kristy-dykes.cfm (accessed December 19, 2003).

———. "Touching the World Wide Web." http://womanstouch.ag.org/womanstouch/profiles/peggie-bohanon.cfm (accessed December 10, 2003). Article on Peggie Bohanon.

Web Sites

A. D. Players. http://www.adplayers.org/news/history.htm (accessed February 11, 2003). Information on Jeanette Clift George.

About, Inc. "This Day in Women's History: June 21." http://womenshistory

.about.com/library/cal/bl0621.htm (accessed April 1, 2006). Information on Lillias Horton Underwood.

Acres of Hope. http://www.acresofhope.com (accessed July 23, 2004). Information on Patty Anglin.

Afrocentric Voices. http://www.afrovoices.com/anderson.html (accessed May 4, 2004). Information on Marian Anderson.

American Christian Romance Writers. Interview of Kristy Dykes by Sandra D. Moore. http://www.acrw.net/interviews/inlh21.shtml (accessed December 19, 2003).

American Medical Association. Obituaries, July 2003. http://www.ama-assn.org/ama/pub/category/10950.html (accessed July 26, 2004). Information on Debra Dixon Deur.

Azusa Pacific University. http://www.apu.edu/iom/mexout/staff/ckoons/ (accessed January 22, 2004). Information on Carolyn Koons.

Back to the Bible. http://www.backtothebible.org/devotions/bio_elliot.htm (accessed March 27, 2003). Information on Elisabeth Elliot.

Blackwell, Lawana. http://www.lawanablackwell.com (accessed September 23, 2003).

Bly Books. http://www.blybooks.com/aboutus.htm (accessed April 14, 2004). Information on Janet Bly.

Bolton, Martha. http://www.marthabolton.com/html/bio.html (accessed April 4, 2003).

Bondi, Renee. http://www.reneebondi.com (accessed December 16, 2003).

Brestin, Dee. http://www.deebrestin.com/about.html (accessed March 27, 2003).

Calvin College. http://www.calvin.edu/publications/spark/fall02/60s.htm (accessed February 23, 2004). Information on Katherine M. Vander Ziel Vandergrift.

Campus Crusade for Christ. http://www.ccci.org (accessed June 18, 2003). Information on Vonette Bright.

Carlson, Melody. http://www.melodycarlson.com/myinfo.html (accessed January 7, 2004).

Catholic Encyclopedia. http://www.newadvent.org (accessed June 12, 2004). Information on Elizabeth of Hungary.

Catholic Information Network. http://www.cin.org/kc87-2.html (accessed July 14, 2003). Information on Frances Xavier Cabrini.

Catholic Online. http://www.catholic.org/saints/saint.php?saint_id=1714 (accessed September 16, 2003). Information on Bathildis.

Celebrate Life International. http://www.CelebrateLife.org (accessed August 11, 2003). Information on Lori Salierno.

Chadwick, Patricia. "Emeline Dryer." *History's Women*. http://www.historyswomen.com/womenoffaith/EmelineDryer.html (accessed March 24, 2006).

———. "Susannah Spurgeon." *History's Women*. http://www.historyswomen.com/womenoffaith/SusannahSpurgeon.html (accessed March 17, 2006).

Christian Book Distributors. http://www.christianbook.com/html/authors/501.html (accessed January 10, 2004). Information on Patsy Clairmont.

———. http://www.christianbook.com/html/authors/422.html/135516628 (accessed June 24, 2004). Information on Barbara Johnson.

———. http://www.christianbook.com/html/authors/101.html/135516628 (accessed July 8, 2004). Information on Janette Oke.

———. http://www.christianbook.com/html/authors/5153.html/135516628 (accessed July 8, 2004). Information on Catherine Palmer.

———. http://www.christianbook.com/html/authors/5300.html/127326999 (accessed January 10, 2004). Information on Lisa Whelchel.

Christian History Heroines. http://www.christianheroines.com/Bonnie.html (accessed April 13, 2004). Information on Bonnie L. Bachman.

Christian History Institute. "British Compelled 'Mother of the Nile' to Leave Egypt." http://chi.gospelcom.net/DAILYF/2002/03/daily-03-27-2002.shtml (accessed April 8, 2006). Information on Lillian Trasher.

Christian History Institute. "Diamond Dust Socialite Lands on Skid Row; Emma Whittemore and Door of Hope." http://chi.gospelcom.net/GLIMPSEF/Glimpses2/glimpses196.shtml (accessed April 7, 2006).

Christian Leaders, Authors, and Speakers Service. http://www.classervices.com/FlorenceLittauer.html (accessed January 21, 2003). Information on Florence Littauer.

Christian Medical College. http://cmch-vellore.edu/htm/scudder.htm (accessed July 13, 2004). Information on Ida Scudder.

Christian Schools International. http://community.gospelcom.net/Brix?pageID=2848 (accessed February 23, 2004). Information on Sheri Haan.

Christian Vision Ministries. http://cvministries.org/bio.ihtml (accessed July 27, 2004). Information on Donna S. Thomas.

Christian Working Woman. http://www.christianworkingwoman.org/ (accessed July 14, 2003). Information on Mary Whelchel.

Church in Westland. http://www.churchinwestland.org/id289_m.htm (accessed July 9, 2004). Information on Jessie Penn-Lewis.

Crouse, Janine Shaw. "A Modern Mother Teresa." Concerned Women for America. http://www.cwfa.org/articles/4607/BLI/dotcommentary/ (accessed March 6, 2004). Information on Jeannine Brabon.

Dallas Theological Seminary. http://www.dts.edu/profiles/default.aspx?id=10178 (accessed March 15, 2004). Information on Lucy Mabery-Foster.

Dorothy L. Sayers Society. http://www.sayers.org.uk/dorothy.html (accessed February 19, 2003).

Driscoll, Jean. http://www.jeandriscoll.com/ (accessed December 18, 2003).

Esther, Inc. http://www.heatherwhitestone.com (accessed February 18, 2003). Information on Heather Whitestone McCallum.

Evelyn Underhill Association. http://www.evelynunderhill.org/life.htm (accessed July 14, 2003).

Excellence in Media. http://www.angelawards.com (accessed June 10, 2004). Information on Mary Dorr.

Fordham University. http://www.fordham.edu/halsall/basis/macrina.html (accessed January 31, 2003). Information on Macrina.

Free Methodist Church. http://www.freemethodistchurch.org/~marston/historic.htm (accessed October 22, 2003). Information on Ellen Stowe Roberts.

Gospel Communications. http://www.gospelcom.net/chi/DAILYF/2003/06/daily-06-07-2003.shtml (accessed October 17, 2003). Information on Maria Zeller Gobat.

The Handbook of Texas Online. http://www.tsha.utexas.edu/handbook/online/articles/view/AA/fam6.html (accessed January 28, 2004). Information on Jessie Daniel Ames.

Hatcher, Robin Lee. www.robinleehatcher.com (accessed December 19, 2003).

Healthy Hearing. http://www.healthyhearing.com/healthyhearing/newroot/interview/displayarchives.asp?ID=86 (accessed February 18, 2003). Information on Heather Whitestone McCallum.

Higgs, Liz Curtis. http://www.lizcurtishiggs.com/whoisliz.htm (accessed April 4, 2003).

Holiness Conference North America. http://www.omsholiness.org/info/download/facts.pdf (accessed June 7, 2004). Information on Lettie Cowman.

Hunt, Angela Elwell. http://www.angelaelwellhunt.com (accessed January 5, 2004).

InterVarsity Press. http://www.gospelcom.net/cgi-ivpress/author.pl/author_id=217 (accessed February 4, 2004). Information on Mary Stewart Van Leeuwen.

InTouch Ministries. http://www.intouch.org/myintouch/mighty/portraits/fanny_crosby_213693.h5ml (accessed February 22, 2006). Information on Fanny J. Crosby.

———. http://www.intouch.org/myintouch/mighty/portraits/henrietta_mears_213642.html (accessed October 30, 2002). Information on Henrietta Mears.

Jewel among Jewels Adoption Network. http://www.adoptionjewels.org/pdfs/Spring95.pdf (accessed July 26, 2004). Information on Carolyn Koons.

Kiefer, James E. "Gladys Aylward, Missionary to China." Society of Archbishop Justus. http://justus.Anglican.org/resources/bio/73.html (accessed November 17, 2003).

Marilyn Hickey Ministries. http://www.mhmin.org/visitors/MhmHist.htm (accessed January 20, 2004). Information on Marilyn Hickey.

———. http://www.mhmin.org/FC/fc-0296MahaliaJ.htm (accessed January 20, 2004). Information on Mahalia Jackson.

———. http://www.mhmin.org/FC/fc-0496Maria%20WE.htm, (accessed January 22, 2004). Information on Maria Woodworth-Etter.

Marketplace Leaders. http://www.marketplaceleaders.org (accessed April 15, 2004). Information on Angie Hillman.

Mary Kay, Inc. http://www.marykay.com/Headquarters/MaryKayBiography/Biography2.asp (accessed May 5, 2004). Information on Mary Kay Ash.

Missions Frontiers. http://www.missionfrontiers.org/1999/08/slocum.html (accessed July 13, 2004). Information on Marianna Slocum.

Moody Bible Institute. "Beginnings." http://re.moody.edu/GenMoody/default.asp?SectionID=FD16FFDD8F144A9E8FF9696F36331E58 (accessed March 27, 2006). Information on Emeline Dryer.

Mt. Holyoke College. http://www.mtholyoke.edu/marylyon/opening.html (accessed March 14, 2003). Information on Mary Lyon.

Multnomah Books. http://www.letstalkfiction.com/DianeNoble.html (accessed January 26, 2004). Information on Diane Noble.

National Day of Prayer Task Force. http://www.nationaldayofprayer.org (accessed June 19, 2003). Information on Shirley Dobson.

Network for Strategic Missions. http://www.strategicnetwork.org/index.php?loc=kb&view=v&id=3465&fct=IND&. Information on Mary Reed.

Noble, Diane. http://www.dianenoble.com (accessed January 26, 2004).

Northwest Christian Speakers Bureau. www.nwspeakers.com (accessed April 22, 2004). Information on Christie Miller.

The Official Roy Rogers–Dale Evans Web site. http://www.royrogers.com/dale_evans_bio.html (accessed February 18, 2003).

Ohio History Central. http://www.ohiohistorycentral.org/entry.php?1767 (accessed January 26, 2006). Information on Marabel Morgan.

Overcomer Books. http://www.daveneta.com/about-us/About-us.htm (accessed April 7, 2003). Information on Neta Thiessen Jackson.

Papers of Petra Malena "Malla" Moe. Billy Graham Center Archives. http://www.wheaton.edu/bgc/archives/GUIDES/280.htm (accessed April 8, 2006).

Peggie's Place. http://www.peggiesplace.com (accessed June 15, 2004). Information on Peggie Bohanon.

Pella, Judith. http://www.judypella.com (accessed December 19, 2003).

Peter Reynolds Books. http://www.freenetpages.co.uk/hp/reynoldsp/aloeinindia.htm (accessed November 17, 2003). Information on Charlotte Maria Tucker.

PraiseGathering Music Group. http://www.praisegathering.com/billgloriagaither/ (accessed April 24, 2003). Information on Gloria Gaither.

Ramon Magsaysay Award for Public Service. http://www.rmaf.org.ph/

RMAFWeb/Documents/Awardee/Biography/hk_03bio.htm (accessed January 9, 2004). Information on Helen Kim.

Red and Proud. http://www.redandproud.com/famous%20redheads20media%20M-Z.htm. Information on Heather Mercer.

The Reformed Reader. http://www.reformedreader.org/armstrong.htm (accessed January 19, 2004). Information on Annie Walker Armstrong.

Roseville Church of Christ. http://www.rosevillechurchofchrist.org/articles/052503.htm (accessed January 9, 2004). Information on Lelia Naylor Morris.

SBurton Services. Black Achievers: A Year 2000 Project of The Timothy Smith Computer Learning Lab, The John A. Shelburne Community Center, Roxbury, MA. http://www.wntb.com/blackachievers/ethlwaters/ (accessed February 18, 2003). Information on Ethel Waters.

Sims, Margie. http://www.margiesims.com/ (accessed July 27, 2004).

The Susan B. Anthony House. www.susanbanthonyhouse.org/biography.html (accessed February 19, 2003).

Tameside MBC. http://www.tameside.gov.uk/leisure/new/bp_42.htm (accessed October 17, 2003). Information on Mary Smith Moffat.

Thoenebooks.com. Bodie and Brock Thoene official Web site. http://www.thoenebooks.com/m-bio.html (accessed July 16, 2004).

United States Senate. http://www.senate.gov/pagelayout/senators/one_item_and_teasers/dole.htm (accessed June 19, 2003); Information on Elizabeth Dole.

University of Manchester John Rylands University Library. Methodist Archives. http://rylibweb.man.ac.uk/data1/dg/methodist/bio/biom.html (accessed February 20, 2003). Information on Lady Darcy Maxwell.

Voyager Press Rare Books. http://www.polybiblio.com/milenium/21926.html. Information on Christina Colliard.

Wellesley College. http://www.wellesley.edu/Anniversary/appenzeller.html (accessed May 5, 2004). Information on Alice Rebecca Appenzeller.

West Virginia Wesleyan College. http://www.wvwc.edu/lib/wv_authors/authors/a_marshall.htm (accessed July 2, 2004). Information on Catherine Marshall.

Wheaton College. Billy Graham Center Archives, June 2004. http://www.wheaton.edu/bgc/archives/bulletin/bulletin.htm (accessed June 12, 2004). Information on Colleen Townsend Evans.

———. Billy Graham Center Archives. http://www.wheaton.edu/bcg/archives/GUIDES/280.htm (accessed April 8, 2006). Information on Malla Moe.

———. Billy Graham Center Archives. http://www.wheaton.edu/bgc/archives/GUIDES/435.htm#3 (accessed April 12, 2006). Information on Isobel Kuhn.

Whelchel, Lisa. http://www.lisawhelchel.com (accessed December 19, 2003).

The White House. http://www.whitehouse.org/firstlady/birthday03.asp (accessed July 26, 2004); http://www.whitehouse.gov/firstlady/flbio.html (accessed December 16, 2003). Information on Laura Bush.

Who2. http://www.who2.com/elizabethdole.html (accessed June 19, 2003). Information on Elizabeth Dole.

Wikipedia. http://en.wikipedia.org/wiki/Anita_Bryant (accessed May 21, 2004). Information on Anita Bryant.

———. http://en.wikipedia.org/wiki/Leoba (accessed February 20, 2006). Information on Lioba.

———. http://en.wikipedia.org/wiki/Mathilda_Wrede (accessed March 17, 2006). Information on Mathilde Wrede.

Wolf, Mur. "Madame Chiang Kai-shek." Wellesley College. http://www.wellesley.edu/Anniversary/chiang.html (accessed December 11, 2003).

A Woman of God Ministries with Thelma Wells. http://www.thelmawells.com/doca/biography.html (accessed March 24, 2004).

Women With a Mission. http://www.womenwam.com/founder/credentials.htm (accessed March 1, 2004). Information on Lana Heightley.

Zonderkidz. http://www.zonderkidz.com/profile.asp?BioID=DeJongeJ (accessed February 20, 2004). Information on Joanne Haan DeJonge.

Personal Contacts

Ambler, Sharon. E-mail interview, March 11, 2004.

Anglin, Patty. Telephone conversation, April 23, 2004.

Appleton, Kathy. E-mail interview, April 8, 2004.

Bachman, Bonnie L. E-mail interview, April 12, 2004.

Baer, Linda Smallback. E-mail interview, March 11, 2004.

Bagnull, Marlene. E-mail interview, July 1, 2004.

Bly, Janet Chester. E-mail correspondence, April 14, 2004.

Bohanon, Peggie. E-mail correspondence, June 15, 2004.

Bolton, Martha. E-mail correspondence, April 5, 2003.

Bondi, Renee. E-mail correspondence, December 22, 2003.

Bonkowski, Allyson Hodgins. E-mail correspondence, July 11, 2003.

Boyd, Veda. E-mail interview, March 1, 2004.

Brabon, Margaret. Prayer letter, May 2003.

Brestin, Dee. E-mail correspondence, March 27, 2003.

Carlson, Melody. E-mail correspondence, January 10, 2004.

Carmichael, Nancie. E-mail correspondence, April 8, 2004.

Case, Susie. E-mail correspondence, April 16, 2003.

Connelly, Laurette. E-mail interview, February 27, 2004.

Cox, Sara McBrayer. Telephone interview, March 1, 2004.

Deaconess Program Office. E-mail regarding Lucy Rider Meyer, January 5, 2006.

Dodds, Lois. Telephone interview with author, June 3, 2004.

Dorr, Mary. E-mail correspondence, July 10, 2004.

Driscoll, Jean. E-mail correspondence, December 19, 2003.

Dykes, Kristy. E-mail correspondence, January 6, 2004.

Gillikin, Jack. Son-in-law and caregiver of Ruth Marstaller Taylor. Telephone conversation regarding Ruth, January 16, 2006.

Hatcher, Robin. E-mail correspondence, January 6, 2004.

Heightley, Lana. Telephone interview, March 8, 2004.

Higgs, Liz Curtis. E-mail correspondence, April 9, 2003.

Hillman, Angie. E-mail interview, May 2, 2004.

Hosier, Helen Kooiman. Correspondence and telephone interview, June 21, 2004.

Huggins, Juanda. Telephone interview, December 16, 2003.

Hullinger, Dustee. E-mail interview, April 13, 2004.

Hunt, Angela Elwell. E-mail correspondence, January 6, 2004.

Huntzinger, Diane. E-mail interview, March 22, 2004.

Inrig, Elizabeth. E-mail correspondence, March 12, 2004.

Jackson, Neta Thiessen. E-mail correspondence, April 7, 2003.

Jacobs, Joy. Telephone interview, April 20, 2004.

Kallander, Marsha. E-mail interview, April 17, 2004. For more information, send e-mail to kallander@juno.com.

Kraft, Vickie. E-mail interview, March 31, 2004.

Lace, Millie. E-mail correspondence, December 11, 2003.

LeFever, Marlene. E-mail interview, July 2, 2004.

Lind, Marcie. E-mail interview, April 23, 2004.

Lobdell, Rita. E-mail interview, March 6, 2004.

Mavretic, Ella. Telephone interview, August 26, 2003.

McGuinness, Cheryl. E-mail correspondence, July 1, 2004.

Meson, Elizabeth. E-mail interview, April 20, 2004.

Miller, Christie. E-mail interview, April 20, 2004.

Miller, Dianne. E-mail interview, March 16, 2004.

Nordlund, Colleen. E-mail interview, April 25, 2004.

Pasch, Frances. E-mail interview, May 12, 2004.

Pattillo, Marion. E-mail interview, April 1, 2004.

Salierno, Lori. E-mail interview, April 28, 2004.

Saunier, Mike. U.S. Christian & Missionary Alliance Web Manager. E-mail correspondence regarding Susan Dyck, March 12, 2004.

Savage, Lavonne. Telephone conversation, January 7, 2004.

Schmickle, Cindy. E-mail interview, February 28, 2004.

Sims, Margie. E-mail interview, April 13, 2004.

Solberg, Ruth Houck. Interview, July 18, 2003.

Stanchfield, Wilma. Telephone conversation, June 10, 2004.

Stanley, Susie. E-mail interview, March 5, 2004.

Stock, Sunny. Telephone interview, July 16, 2004.

Stuart, Sally E. E-mail interview, February 19, 2003.

Susek, Diane King. E-mail interview, March 26, 2004.

Thomas, Donna S. E-mail interview, March 2, 2004.

Wallace, Georgia. E-mail interview regarding her late mother, Leona Audrey James Rundall, March 13, 2004.

Wells, Thelma. Correspondence, July 30, 2004.

Whitman, Judy Cave. Telephone interview, March 2, 2004.

Williams, Joyce. E-mail interview, April 7, 2004.

Wilson, Wendy L. E-mail interview, April 21, 2004.

Witmer, Jean. Telephone interview, April 11, 2003.

Wray, Mable Ruth. Correspondence, February 26, 2004.

Miscellaneous Sources

Women of Faith Conference. The Great Adventure Tour, Philadelphia, 2003. Relating to Sheila Walsh, Thelma Wells, Patsy Clairmont, Luci Swindoll, and CeCe Winans.